MAYBERRY
HUMOR
ACROSS THE USA

MAYBERRY
HUMOR
ACROSS THE USA

Jeanne Robertson

First Edition hardback published 1995 by the Rich Publishing Co., Houston, TX.

Second Edition paperback published October, 2022 by JSR Inc.

Edited by Peg McCree

ISBN 979-8-9861400-2-5

eISBN 979-8-9861400-3-2

Printed in the United States of America

First eBook edition, October, 2022

Previous Works

Books by Jeanne Robertson
Don't Let the Funny Stuff Get Away
Humor The Magic of Jeanne
Don't Bungee Jump Naked and Other Important Stuff

Audio and video recording by Jeanne
Here She Is
Not Just For Laughs
Talkin' Funny
Southern Style
Flat Out Funny
Just For Fun!
Looking For Humor
Fabulously Funny
Rocking Humor
Don't Bungee Jump Naked and Other Important Stuff
(Audiobook)

To learn more about her products
go to JeanneRobertson.com
To purchase Original Jeanne Stuff apparel,
visit OriginalJeanneStuff.com

To Toni Meredith,
who has run my office since 1979 with
the enthusiasm of Barney Fife and the "smarts" of
Andy Taylor. To paraphrase Sheriff Taylor's words
about his deputy, Toni doesn't just work for me.
We're pretty close friends.

CONTENTS

Foreword

Jeanne began her speaking career in 1963. She had an enormously successful career as a professional speaker that took her to 49 states and numerous countries. Ten years ago, she teamed up with Al McCree and The Nashville People, to bring her humor to theater stages. When she passed unexpectedly in 2021, she had 55 bookings on her calendar as well as numerous convention speeches.

The goal of Jeanne's family and friends and "Thuh Nashville People" - as she called us, is to continue to protect her legacy and promote her life's work. We have already published a revised edition of her earlier book – *Humor: The Magic of Jeanne.* Its addition to the current genre of Humor books has clearly demonstrated that her humor is timeless.

Jeanne was a HUGE fan of everything Mayberry. She wrote *Mayberry Humor Across the USA* in part, to pay tribute to *The Andy Griffith Show*, to its characters, its actors and to the writers. But, as she makes clear in her introduction, she also wrote this book to demonstrate that Mayberry humor is not confined to a television show, it exists everywhere – you just have to look for it. And look for it - she did! Where and what she found is contained in these pages.

Mayberry Humor Across the USA is the closest we will come to Jeanne's own autobiography of her years on the road as a professional speaker.

In this new edition, we have corrected a few minor errors, added several footnotes, and removed a few commas. Otherwise, *Mayberry Humor Across the USA* is just as Jeanne wrote it in 1995. We hope that while you enjoy the stories within these pages, you will also look for Mayberry Humor in your hometown and around the USA.

Acknowledgments

This book is not associated with *The Andy Griffith Show*, nor has it been endorsed, created, licensed, or authorized by either Mayberry Enterprises, Danny Thomas Enterprises, Andy Griffith, Viacom, Inc., CBS, Inc., or their successors in interest. However, it is to these people that I and all fans of Mayberry owe a big THANK YOU for providing quality entertainment that stands the test of time.

It is not my intention to in any way take credit for the superb writing, acting, producing, or directing connected with my all-time favorite television series, *The Andy Griffith Show*. I will be the first to praise those responsible for it, and to acknowledge that their talents certainly surpass mine. In doing research for this project, my admiration grew daily for what was accomplished by North Carolinian Andy Griffith, Executive Producer Sheldon Leonard, and the entire creative team.

Without examples from the series, it would have been impossible to lay out my theory of the current prevalence of Mayberry-type humor across the USA. Therefore, it was necessary to quote from scenes and discuss situations from the episodes. Although I had no scripts, I worked diligently to make sure the direct quotes used in this book were correct. Often, I had to guess at the spelling and used several of the excellent books about the show as resources. When in doubt, I had to guess how we would have spelled it in Graham, North Carolina.

All episodes are listed in the back of this book in numerical order according to when they were filmed, which is also the order in which they are most often aired in syndication. The writers, directors, and episode titles are also listed. Direct quotes setting the stage for current humor examples are credited by episode number and title. For smoother reading in the body of the work, direct quotes are credited by episode title only. In order to expedite the reader's location of the creative source of specific lines from the series, the shows are also listed in the back of the book in alphabetical order. Repeated phrases and colloquialisms unique to the series are put in quotes to indicate . . . it's Mayberry. Common, everyday southern colloquialisms and phrases that show up in the series but which have always been used regularly where I live, slide right through on their own.

The emphasis of this book is placed on a type of humor that evolved from the characters who lived in or occasionally passed through this small "pretend" North Carolina town of Mayberry. Therefore, there will be little naming of the actors and actresses who brought Mayberry characters to life. It is my hope they will take this as a compliment. They were so good at what they did that we know their characters as "real" people. Books written about the series provide an abundance of information about all individuals connected with the project. While that is not my purpose, let me take this opportunity to acknowledge the actors and actresses who played the most frequent and remembered roles. I have a genuine admiration for these individuals.

CHARACTER	ACTOR OR ACTRESS
Andy Taylor	Andy Griffith
Barney Fife	Don Knotts
Aunt Bee Taylor	Frances Bavier
Opie Taylor	Ronny Howard
Floyd Lawson	Howard McNear
Otis Campbell	Hal Smith
Ellie Walker	Elinor Donahue
Thelma Lou	Betty Lynn
Helen Crump	Aneta Corsaut

CHARACTER	ACTOR OR ACTRESS
Gomer Pyle	Jim Nabors
Goober Pyle	George Lindsey
Howard Sprague	Jack Dodson
Emmett Clark	Paul Hartman
Clara Edwards Johnson	Hope Summers
Warren Ferguson	Jack Burns
Ernest T. Bass	Howard Morris
Briscoe Darling	Denver Pyle
Charlene Darling Wash	Maggie Peterson

Five books were of tremendous help to me in this project and they are listed below. I eagerly recommend them if reading this book whets the appetite to know more about the series.

- Kelly, Richard. *The Andy Griffith Show*. Winston-Salem, J.F. Blair, 1981.
- Beck, Ken, and Jim Clark. *The Andy Griffith Show Book*. St. Martin's, 1995. (Make sure to get this 35th Anniversary edition.)
- Spignesi, Stephen J. *Mayberry My Hometown: The Ultimate Guidebook to America's Favorite T.V. Small Town*. Ann Arbor, Pierian, 1987.
- Pfeiffer, Lee. *The Official Andy Griffith Show Scrapbook*. Citadel, 1994.
- Harrison, Dan, and Bill Habeeb. *Inside Mayberry*. HarperCollins, 1994.
- *The Bullet*, the official publication of *The Andy Griffith Show* Rerun Watchers Club, was another excellent written source of information. Written by Jim Clark, co-founder of the club and Presiding Goober of TAGSRWC, it is a quarterly, sixteen-page newsletter containing up-to-date information about everything and everybody connected with the show. In addition to writing and publishing *The Bullet*, Jim Clark is to be commended for his

devotion to keeping Mayberry alive and serving as headquarters for the over 850 fan clubs spread throughout the world.

Editor's note: "The Bullet" and the TAGSRWC are now available on the website: https://www.imayberry.com. TAGSRWC also has a Facebook page: https://www.facebook.com/tagsrwc.

A special thanks goes to Neal Brower, known as "The Professor" by ardent fans because of his continuing education course, "*The Andy Griffith Show*: An In-depth Study." This ten-week course was extremely valuable in my work, and Neal's friendship and his encouragement with this project have been particularly appreciated. Mayberry fans appreciate his dedication in planning the 30th and 35th Anniversary Cast Reunions.

Editor's note: Information about Prof. Brower's lectures are located on the Andy Griffith Museum homepage: https://www.surryarts.org/agmuseum/index.html

My gratitude extends to the members of the Barney Chapter of *TAGSRWC* for their friendship and interest in this project and just for being good representatives of the Mayberry Attitude.

And also, my tremendous indebtedness to Jim Ballance, friend, and editor of the Barney Chapter (Greensboro, NC) newsletter, for proofing this book and for sharing his extensive knowledge of the show. Jim is a living example of the best Mayberry citizen.

Warmest thanks to Olivia Miller, Miller Information Services, Tricia Ann Allen, Linda Pulliam, Angie Odom, Bill Habeeb, and Norma White for their assistance and encouragement on the project.

Special recognition and appreciation to two loyal supporters, Dobby Dobson and Sherry Roeser with Rich Publishing, for the task of editing, designing, compiling, and publishing.

My deepest thanks to my husband Jerry who taped episodes, attended classes, read stories, and never complained when I spent time in Mayberry.[1]

With all this thanking and acknowledging and recommending, one might think the heroes and heroines of this book are characters from *The Andy Griffith Show*, or that it is another book about the series. Nothing could be further from the truth. In this instance, these characters play important but supporting roles. Many of the prime players in this written work include my family members and friends who granted me permission to share humorous incidents about them. Their names are given in their stories.

Although there are many references to *The Andy Griffith* Show included in this book, I do hope the strength of this book is the collection of stories that offer proof of the existence of this special kind of humor. So, finally, thanks to the real "stars" of my project—the thousands of regular, A-OK people whom I have observed in my travels and in my audiences while looking for examples of *Mayberry Humor Across the USA*.

---

1   aka "Left Brain."

Preface

Television of the nineties rolls like a high-tech avalanche, pouring down on viewers tons of suggestive humor and off-color, put-down comedy laced with four-letter words. The clean, kind, slow-paced humor from the fifties and sixties seems buried forever, smothered underneath the heap.

But wait! Shssh. What is this? Off in the distance are the sounds of small shovels, fueled by clicks of remote controls, steadfastly digging through the mass. Click, click, clicks on a quest for the wonderful humor of a fictitious town called Mayberry. Laughter erupts from rescue teams of fans of all ages and backgrounds who choose to search for reruns of a television series that aired its last episode over twenty-five years ago. Listen again. Is that a nervous deputy shouting instructions at them through a bullhorn?

Shazam! Tuscarora! Geronimo! *The Andy Griffith Show* is pushing through the pile as millions tune in to Mayberry humor. I am one of these longtime fans with a shovel and remote control in hand. Because of my profession, I also have my own bullhorn.

As a North Carolinian who has traveled this country for over thirty years as a professional speaker, I have made it a habit to look for the type of humor found in Mayberry. Sharing my findings has served me well in speeches, and now I offer a collection of these stories as evidence that Mayberry humor is alive, well, and far beyond our television screens. The accounts presented here are not fabrications. No siree, these are flesh and blood, real-life examples. I will lay them out. You read them, and then be the judge.

DO READERS HAVE TO BE AVID MAYBERRY FANS? That is a natural question. Do readers have to be caught up in *The Andy Griffith Show* to enjoy this book? Absolutely not! I realize there are people out there who are not avid fans of the series. Naturally, I am hoping to entice them to take another look at it through Mayberry eyes, but new recruits are not the main objective. This book is not about the production, history, or trivia of the show, nor is it a study of the characters, episodes, or the series in general. This is a book on a special type of humor that I call "Mayberry humor." Because it is not about *The Andy Griffith Show*, one does not have to be a big fan of the series or to have ever seen it to enjoy these pages. (Can there REALLY be someone who has never seen it?) If you are not an avid fan but like humor from everyday experiences, ignore all the Mayberry references. Just shake your head when the words or the grammar are deliberately "Mayberryized." You do not have to understand that part of it. Simply curl up in your reading place and enjoy stories from the life of a humorist who has more than likely been in your area of the country or maybe even on the program at your last convention.

AND FOR THE MAYBERRYHOLIC, this is a book within a book! There is a fun subplot that Barney might call subtle. Because I am explaining it now, Andy would say it is, "as subtle as a pig squealing for his supper." As I lay out my evidence of the existence of Mayberry humor and urge readers to look for it, I will also present a fun challenge to trivia buffs. The challenge is to enjoy the book, laugh at what I have seen in my travels, but be on the lookout for similarities from the television series that have been woven into each of my stories—not the direct quotes that will be credited, but the fun similarities. When all is said and done, each of the 249 episodes will be represented. Some stories may have only one hidden Mayberry moment while others are filled to the brim. That ought to keep the trivia buffs licking their chops for a while. If you do not see all the references, you're no good. NO GOOD! (Did you get that?) I hope you trivia junkies have one-tenth the fun in searching that I had in putting it all together. As Gomer would say, "Lotsa luck to you and yours."

PART I.

INTRODUCING MAYBERRY HUMOR

It's Me! It's Me! It's Jean . . . ne!

Ernest T. Bass, the curious-acting visitor to Mayberry: Hidee do to
you and you. It's me. It's me. It's Ernest T!
- **Episode #133, "The Education of Ernest T. Bass"**

Mayberry Humor Across the USA is written by a person who
grew up and lived most of her life in a small town in North
Carolina. She even had the privilege of representing her state in the
Miss America Pageant—an experience that gave her the opportunity
to visit almost every village, hamlet, and crossroads in the state. Since
that time, she has traveled as a professional speaker, visiting thousands of other small towns as well as big-city places where people
are accustomed to a faster pace. It is little wonder then that through
the years she has loved watching a television show that takes place
in a mythical North Carolina town called Mayberry. The show, of
course, is *The Andy Griffith Show*, often labeled *TAGS*. And the ardent
Mayberry fan? She can best be introduced by paraphrasing the unforgettable words of Ernest T. Bass, the strange Mayberry visitor who
comes down out of the mountains toting a burlap sack of rocks bound
for windows, "If you wonder who I be. It's me! It's me! It's Jean . . . ne!"

Those familiar with *TAGS* will also remember another phrase used
by Mr. Bass, "I don't chew my cabbage twice." I might have to do that
about now. By this point, you might be thoroughly confused. The
author is a what?

3

I am a professional speaker. Not everybody knows about us, but we go from convention to convention, meeting to meeting, luncheon to banquet, giving speeches. In general, we are invited places because of our topics and speaking ability, not for our celebrity status. No folks are running along after us for autographs. We are on the road much of the time, but we are in the service industry rather than any jet-set world. Jet-setters do not go to places like Eudora, Arkansas, and Baxley, Georgia. I love to. My buddies in this business come from diverse backgrounds and speak on topics such as the information highway, total quality management, and assertiveness—serious, there-will-be-a-test stuff. I speak on none of the above. I am a humorist; we eat tests.

USA Today has labeled people like me "road warriors." During an average year, I spend almost two hundred nights in hotels and rarely stay in the same place two days in a row. As of the fall of 1995, I reached four million miles with Delta Air Lines and a million with USAir, and have flown numerous miles with the other carriers.[2] These airline miles have been accumulated from going state to state because I am not an intercontinental flyer.

This is NOT putting on airs. This much traveling often makes me feel like a woman in a hurry, but it goes with the territory because meetings do not come to me in Burlington, North Carolina. I go to the meetings. My gypsy lifestyle is certainly not wild and carefree; it is tough. Even though I am usually surrounded by people, sometimes I feel as though I am looking down a long lonesome road. Even so, I love speaking so much that I do what is necessary in order to speak professionally.

My speaking career has given me the best of two worlds. I travel all over the United States, but I live just a couple of miles from my hometown of Graham, North Carolina, and a few interstate exits away from most of the locations mentioned on *The Andy Griffith Show*—places like Siler City, Raleigh, Greensboro, Charlotte, Asheville, Morehead

---

2 US Airways was a major airline that was in business from 1937 until it merged with American Airlines in 2015.

City, Wilmington, Elm City and, of course, Mt. Pilot, which sounds suspiciously like Pilot Mountain if you are from the area. When I was growing up, and up, and up (I am 6'2" tall), I spent a lot of time with relatives in Auburn and Luverne, Alabama—small towns where a high priority is placed on manners, doing right, living by rules . . . and humorous storytelling.

In traveling over thirty years, I have met a wide assortment of people and have been in thousands of situations that reminded me of Mayberry and *The Andy Griffith Show*. My small-town, southern roots and experiences as Miss North Carolina may have initially attracted me to this television series, but my lifestyle as a professional speaker is what led me to develop a "compelshion" complex.

The "Compelshion" Complex

Barney: Didn't you ever hear of a person with a compelshion complex?

Andy: A what?

Barney: A compelshion complex. You know, like when folks gotta be washing their hands all day long. That's a hand washing compelshion. . . . Listen, you find compelshion nuts all over.

- Episode #60, "The Bookie Barber"

B arney Fife's pronunciation might be a little askew, as it often is, but his idea is correct. "Compelshion nuts" are indeed, all over. If you look for one, you might find me. My "compelshion" is with *The Andy Griffith Show*. This delightful thirty-minute television series from the sixties snuck up on me over thirty years after it first aired; and before I realized it, I was looking for Mayberry humor every day, and finding it. At this point Sheriff Andy Taylor might say, "You want to run that by me again?" Sure. No use in giving it to you in dribs and drabs. It started as a result of my travels as a professional speaker. The following experience will help explain my "compelshion," because as Barney also knows, life can be an asphalt jungle out there.

What a day. WHAT A DAY! I had been traveling for eleven long hours. A trip of this duration could have landed me in warm, sunny Hawaii; instead, I had reached my speaking destination in Fargo, North Dakota. I was tired but proud. On this cold winter day, I had once again prevailed over poor service, screaming babies, and talkative seatmates. Once again, I had arrived at my destination on schedule to check into a hotel room with a freeway view. And once again, the first thing I did when I got to that room was pick up the remote control and start mashing the tiny buttons as I sat down on the bed.

(click)

TALK SHOW. Topic: The third sex change was the toughest.

(click)

TALK SHOW. Topic: Triplets proclaim, "You can trust us even though we slept with your twin brothers."

(click)

(click)

EXERCISE. Suck in that gut!

(click)

(reverse click) How can they jump around in those outfits?

(click)

CNN HEADLINE NEWS. Same as in airports all day.

(click)

ESPN. Weight lifting. Mighty oily bodies. I guess Andy is right. What is wrestling to some SURE IS dancing to others.

(click)

(click)

HOME SHOPPING NETWORK. "Only thirty more seconds to call for the Blue Moonlight cologne. Four ounces for only sixty-four dollars!"

(click)

POLITICIANS ARGUING.

(click)

NEWSPEOPLE ARGUING.

(click)

For Pete's sake, it's time. Where IS it?

(click)

(click)

(click)

Whew. FINALLY. Yeahhhh boy.

Dada da . . . dah, dada da . . . dah. Dada da, da da da . . . dada. Dada da . . . dah, dada da . . . dah, dada da da da da (dada da da) . . .

The familiar whistling of "The Fishin' Hole" (the theme song from The Andy Griffith Show) filled my hotel room, and I eased back onto the pillow. Andy Taylor and his son Opie, fishing poles in hand, were ambling down the dirt road I knew so well. Seconds later, Opie threw a pebble into the lake, and hours of accumulated travel tension began to slip from my shoulders. ONCE AGAIN, harmony was about to be restored to my chaotic world.

Pretty dramatic, huh? I know, and it gets more peculiar all the time. Let me keep explaining. There are multitudes of polite, friendly, abide-by-the-rules-of-life people out there. People who, just like the citizens of Mayberry, act like somebody. Their counterparts, however, lurk conspicuously rude, unfriendly, sometimes aggressive people who like Ernest T. Bass carry their own sack full of rocks to throw at others. When people live and work in one place most of the time, they can try to avoid these non-courteous types or learn when to duck. Unfortunately, when you make your living on the road, you do not know when they are going to jump out at you . . . and some days, they jump quite often. Paraphrasing Barney, it is enough to make a quiet, sweet, "demore" woman suddenly go ape.

My road-warrior's schedule varies daily so I spend much time in airports, cabs, restaurants, and hotel rooms channel surfing with the remote. Observing folks, I find that the world can be right-odd. I try to practice what I preach by seeing the humor in all of it and by taking even the strangest things in stride. In addition to keeping my sense of humor, I have discovered that an important tool for survival on the road is to establish some consistency to my routine: a few patterns that remain the same, day after day, no matter where I am. Some speakers take their favorite goose-down pillow or special coffee mug with them. Others want to be on the same floor in every hotel. Me? I watch *The Andy Griffith Show*. Like Barney said, it is a "compelshion."

Let this be a warning! "Compelshion" complexes do not occur overnight. They sneak up on you. I did not even realize it was happening until it had a hold on me. Like millions of Americans, I have always enjoyed the series. It premiered during my senior year in high school and hit its stride when I was traveling as Miss North Carolina. (That was a while back. I can still get in the gown, but cannot breathe.) *TAGS* has been a part of my life since then, most prominently playing in the background during supper time when my son was growing up. It was a safe, wholesome, funny TV show to watch as a family, but now our son is grown and gone. By special request from my husband, I no longer cook because my biscuits lay awful heavy and I put too much allspice in everything. Room service is my new best friend. So why do I watch *The Andy Griffith Show* now? Why choose it over others on cable's crowded menu?

I understand the questions. Other than the occasional stumbling onto a favorite episode, what would entice someone to make a television series filmed several decades earlier a part of her travel routine today? Well, I crave whatever brings a little world order into my schedule. Not the big "world order" that politicians talk about, but just a semblance of sanity in my little bitty part of everything. Somewhere along the way, I discovered this could be achieved if I could find *The Andy Griffith Show* on TV. It would be "therapetic," as Barney calls it if I could just get to Mayberry, the "Friendly City" where people usually act right. Personal service is not dead in Mayberry. Its citizens are courteous and polite. They accept responsibility and do not blame others for their problems. Best of all—BEST OF ALL—they have a good time. "Extry" good. So, when I go to Mayberry, I have a good time too, and I laugh and laugh.

Slowly, Mayberry became my favorite place to visit regardless of the location of my speaking engagement. It became a little home away from home that was available any day, every day, and mine for the choosing.

Fortunately, *The Andy Griffith Show* is in syndication through Viacom, Inc., and plays nationwide several times daily on TBS and WGN, and usually, I can find it on a local channel.[3] In the late eighties, I started setting my alarm clock to stop what I was doing when it came on. If I walked, I began to pick up my pace to hurry back to the hotel when it was time to see my Mayberry buddies. I looked forward to hearing my favorite lines and went from being surprised by certain bits to anticipating them. Sometimes I would laugh out loud and shout lines before the TV character did. It is a wonder someone did not report me to the hotel detectives. They would have thought I needed some of Barney's "psychological therapy."

Soon I started mentally comparing the way I—and others—acted to the way people in Mayberry behave. If a flight attendant or hotel clerk extended an exceptional courtesy to me, I would think, "Now, you have a Mayberry attitude." When a convenience store clerk did not charge me for popcorn because it had been popped so much earlier in the day, I would smile and think, "Well, aren't you extending the courtesy of Mayberry?" It worked in reverse too. If service people or my fellow passengers were rude, I found myself thinking, "Boy hi dee, you would not be in business a week in Mayberry." When I, too, forgot my southern manners and snapped at a gate agent or hotel clerk, I would think, "Come on, Jeanne, act like somebody!"

---

3   As of this printing, all 249 episodes are available on IMDb https://www.imdb.com/title/tt0053479/ as well as through a variety of streaming services. They are also for sale through Amazon, Apple TV, etc.

People I met began to remind me of certain characters in the series. I would fill up a rental car and meet a Gomer-type guy and secretly want him to say as the real McCoy does in "Citizen's Arrest," "Help yourself. Water and air is free. We do have to charge you for the gas though." At Chamber of Commerce banquets, politicians worked their way into all the photographs, and I would think of Mayberry's Mayor Pike in "A Plaque for Mayberry," when he says, "As long as we're waiting, why not get another picture of me?" To women with upswept, bouffant hairdos, I would almost say, "You look real nice, Miss Edwards."

When I stopped thinking lines like these and started voicing them, it got scary. Right out of the blue, I would twang in my best Gomer impersonation to impolite strangers, "Well, gol-ah-ah-lee, that's not a very friendly thing to do." People looked at me strange. After a few times of chiming in with stuff like, "He's ugly, but he ain't stupid," I realized I might have a problem. One night in an airline club room, I was watching television, and a man came in and without asking, switched the channel. I was polite. I was nice, but I made my eyes smaller and said, "Mister, TURN LEONARD BLUSH BACK ON!" He had no idea what I was talking about, and I did not bother to explain. However, he turned the channel back.

Soon my "compelshion" infiltrated my work. One night at a banquet where I was to be the after-dinner speaker, potatoes were served. Not unusual, potatoes and chicken were put on earth for banquet speakers. During the meal I saw a gentleman across the other side of the table attempt to cut a small potato in half, only to have it scoot through the green beans, off the plate, and into his sleeve. No one saw it but me. He looked in his lap and on the table and twisted around in his chair to check the floor. I could see the tiny spud still lodged between his shirt cuff and the jacket lining, but rather than indicate quietly its location, I leaned across the table, pointed to his arm, and shouted a la Briscoe Darling, "TATERS!" Heads turned. It was kind of embarrassing to me.

I had watched the show so often that favorite phrases did more than sneak out occasionally, they rolled in my head constantly. After the tater incident, I found myself fighting not to throw Mayberry phrases into speeches in front of thousands of people, all of whom clearly could not be as familiar with Mayberry as I. After all, I was invited to places to make people laugh, and the audience had to be able to identify for something to be funny.

Didn't I tell you? Peculiar. What was happening to me? I was not losing my mind, or at least I did not think so. I continued to function in my world as a wife, friend, and professional speaker, but I was turning into a Mayberryholic. I began to think about why I was so attracted to this mythical place. I was forming strong opinions about the salt-of-the-earth people of Mayberry and the rules by which they lived, opinions that would soon surface unexpectedly . . . when I least expected them.

How Looking for Mayberry Humor Evolved

Thelma Lou: Will you stop being so dramatic and just tell me what's
              on your mind?

- Episode #125, "The Rumor"

O K, so far you know that my "compelshion" complex is watching
The Andy Griffith Show so much that I think the lines from the
episodes and shout them out loud when least expected by listeners
and me. All this, however, does not answer another question. How
does a simple, ordinary, run-of-the-mill "compelshion" complex
become a determined effort to look for Mayberry humor and an even
more determined effort to prove that it exists? Watching the shows
and repeating lines is not enough?

I'm getting there.

Although the man in the airline club room showed no inkling of
recognition at "TURN LEONARD BLUSH BACK ON," I began to
realize that many people did indeed know familiar *TAGS* phrases.
For example, leaving an airplane I once sang out to a flight attendant,
"Best of luck to you and yours," only to have her quickly respond,
"Gomer says bye." Hmm . . . She pulled a variation of a Gomer expression out of thin air to respond to one from me. Checking into a hotel,
I overheard two clerks discussing an irate guest, and one said, "Don't
mollycoddle him." The second one quipped, "I won't, but can I nip
him in the bud?"

My confidence level rose. It was only a matter of time before I brought up *TAGS* for discussion, and the time came at a banquet in Orlando. The event began with the usual chicken and potatoes, and before long, someone asked a question I have heard many times, "What do you do to kill time while you are traveling?" In the past, I had always truthfully answered that I worked on my speeches, read, or walked around each city. So, my quick response surprised even me.

"Well, quite frankly," I heard myself say, "when I can find it, I watch *The Andy Griffith Show*." The table conversation ceased. Other speakers surely had not answered that way in the past, had they? Heads turned in my direction, but no one spoke. Like Gomer in "Citizen's Arrest," it was "my turn to talk" and I had not even been introduced.

"*The Andy Griffith Show* is the greatest television series ever produced," I heard myself proclaim. There were no comments, so I rambled on. "There is a little moral lesson in every show that makes me feel good. Nobody gets murdered. They treat one another with respect and care about their neighbors. It takes me back to a simpler, safer time." More blank stares, but I persevered. "You see, I'm on the road over twenty days a month, and I watch a lot of TV. Sometimes I think the world has gone nuts, and spending time in Mayberry is like getting a little booster shot of common sense."

The reaction of the others at the table would not surprise me now, but I must admit it did that night. Suddenly, this group of people from around the country chimed in with what they liked—LOVED—about *The Andy Griffith Show*. They gushed affection and their comments flowed freely. "It is a show we can watch with our children . . . People do not climb in the bed with each other . . . Barney is the funniest person ever to be on TV," echoed the Mayberry admirers. The Mayberry characters and their lifestyle simply reminded them of the way things were when they were growing up! The quip exchange went on and on and on as each person shared a favorite Mayberry memory. Everyone was happy and everyone was smiling. Their eyes lit up as they talked, and though they mentioned a variety of serious reasons they enjoyed *TAGS*, there was one thing they always came back to—the funny stuff . . . the humor! They laughed uproariously in unison at the mention of any humorous segment.

"How 'bout the time Barney takes karate lessons?" "Pass some of Aunt Bee's kerosene pickles, please!" "Citizen's Arrest!" The conversation rose to such a fevered pitch that within minutes someone had to shout a Barney phrase that occurred throughout the series. "Nip it! Nip it! Nip it in the bud!" Amazingly, the mere mention of one of the episodes brought affirmative head nodding from the entire group, and, "Oh, yeah, that is a good one, but my favorite is . . ." And so it went, more laughter with each ensuing recollection.

Let me make sure you understand. I was not at a pig pickin' outside Siler City.[4] The majority of these people were not North Carolinians or even southerners. A few of them lived in small towns, but the majority came from big cities. No, the people who told me that night how much they love *TAGS* came from all over the country and from towns of all sizes. They were white and black, old and young, male and female. It was a politically correct group. One was even from New York City. New York City!

Then, an interesting thing happened that set the stage for me to write this book. Someone made a comment, and his exact words might as well have been etched in my mind with Opie's wood-burning set. I will never forget them. This person said, "Well, of course, those people are unrealistic and are taken to the extreme. They are not like REAL people. Real people today do not act like they do on that show, and they probably never did."

"REAL" PEOPLE TODAY DON'T ACT LIKE THEY DO ON THAT SHOW? THEY PROBABLY NEVER DID? What was this guy, a Grade A nut?

A familiar voice spoke up. "Oh, yes, they do!" The voice belonged to me, and it started saying things that my mind had not actually thought about. "Sometimes I am like Goober in 'Andy's Old Girlfriend,'

---

4 Siler City N.C.

when Andy asks if anybody has ever told him that he has a big mouth. Goober says, 'Yeah, but I don't pay no attention to 'em.'"

"The more I travel, the more I see people who act just like Mayberry characters. There are Floyds and Gomers and Barneys everywhere . . . and Andys . . . and Aunt Bees! We are all like them and they are like us. That is why we enjoy the show so much, and why everybody here tonight remembers it. The characters remind us of ourselves, our friends, and our families—even strangers we meet. I see Mayberry-type folks every day." I was wound up.

A skeptic murmured, "In a few small towns in the South maybe." Another one said, "Well, I wouldn't say REAL people would get themselves into situations like the ones on the television show." I jumped in again. "No. No. Trust me. I see people everywhere in situations very similar to the ones on *The Andy Griffith Show*, and they react about the same way. This type of humor is still out there. ALL WE HAVE TO DO IS LOOK FOR IT."

By this point, the meeting planner's eyes looked troubled. Very shortly the speaker for the evening was to be introduced and expected to be funny for forty-five minutes, and that speaker was now rambling on about humor in a place that did not even exist. "It is time for your speech," she pronounced in my direction. She was getting a little high-strung.

I snapped back to reality, my "compelshion" under control. The situation was frustrating, however, because I wanted to prove RIGHT THEN that Mayberry humor is still abundant. From the stage came the introducer's words, "Our speaker tonight is Jeanne . . ." There was nothing to do but put Mayberry on hold. I leaned in toward the center of the table and whispered, "Y'all give me a chance later to prove my point about Mayberry humor. I can do it." We all laughed, and I stepped to the microphone.

My topic that evening dealt with keeping a sense of humor, a subject on which I have spoken and written for years. As usual, it consisted of stories from my experiences of growing up large-sized in a small southern town, competing in the Miss America Pageant, and traveling as a humorous speaker. I was far away from Mayberry, or was I?

Forty-five minutes later I sat down and nine people leaned in my direction to say almost in unison, "We see what you mean about Mayberry humor."

Huh?

"If the stories you just told are true, Mayberry humor is alive and well," someone said with a laugh.

As they mentioned to me the accounts that I had just told from the platform, it sank in as if they had dropped Aunt Bee's mighty cumbersome sack of sugar slowly on my head. Thud! I had been telling examples of Mayberry humor for years because Mayberry humor is representative of true life. I should have sat a little straighter as Barney would have done, and said, "Well, sure, that was what I was trying to tell you, but you wouldn't listen."

As others crowded around, my attention was diverted and my dinner friends disappeared. When everything was all wrapped up, I boarded the elevator to head back to my room. A voice sang out from across the lobby, "Thank you, Jeanne. Keep looking for that Mayberry humor!"

I stood there grinning like a mule eating briers as the doors closed in front of me. "I will, and I will find it!"

So, I began to study *The Andy Griffith Show.* I watched it at every opportunity on the road and got my husband to record it for me at home. It took a year of relentless taping for us to get all the episodes because each station in our area cuts different segments—including the important epilogues—in order to sell more commercial time. (Special thanks to Channel 2, WFMY in Greensboro for always including these closing segments.) We had to record all four versions coming into our home to see episodes in their entirety. To this day, I occasionally see a new segment. More and more of the 249 shows are now available for purchase, but that was not the case when I began my quest.

I read everything I could find about the show to become familiar with the history of the telecasts and the lives of the cast members. I even read the trivia, and I do not like trivia because I cannot remember "trivial trivialities" an hour after I have heard them. I joined *TAGSRWC* (*The Andy Griffith Show* Rerun Watchers Club) with headquarters in Nashville, Tennessee, and eagerly awaited each issue of the newsletter, *The Bullet*, from co-founder and Presiding Goober, Jim Clark.

One spring I turned down speeches on Mondays, and my husband Jerry and I made the seven-hour trip to take Professor Neal Brower's famous continuing education class on the show. The few times I could not get back to North Carolina, Jerry made the trip and took notes for me. We joined the Barney Chapter of *TAGSRWC* and met people who shared our interest in the show. We went to Mayberry Days and met a white pearl cockatiel that could whistle the theme song from the series. I purchased Mayberry T-shirts, hats, and trading cards. I even got the limited-edition Bobbin' Head figures of Andy and Barney. Two sets. I was—and still am—caught up in Mayberry.

This was all fun, and I enjoyed meeting others who also love the show, but it had little to do with looking for examples of the Mayberry humor that so appealed to me. Studying the show is for the most ardent fan, and it takes time and energy. ANYONE can look for and find Mayberry humor with no time expenditure and minimal effort. It is not necessary to read the books, attend classes, or join chapters, although that is all exciting. (You do not even need the Bobbin' Head figures, but I will make you a real good deal on my spare set if you want them.) Most of us just need to be reminded what we are looking for and where to find it.

And THAT explains how a simple, ordinary, run-of-the-mill "compelshion" complex became a determined effort to look for Mayberry humor.

So, What is . . . Mayberry Humor

Opie: I never heard Mr. Sprague say anything funny.

Andy: Well, you would if you had been at the Lodge banquet the other night. He had 'em rollin' in the aisle. [5]

Aunt Bee: OUR Howard Sprague?

Andy: Yeah, he told one about this farmer and his . . .

Aunt Bee: Andy!

Andy: . . . his cow.

- Episode #216, "Howard, the Comedian"

What is this thing I keep referring to . . . Mayberry humor? What exactly are we looking for? Jokes about farmers? One-liners? Funniest characters? Favorite sketches from episodes? The answer is - none of the above.

The Andy Griffith Show ranked in the top ten television shows in the nation all eight years that it ran, and was number one when Andy Griffith left the series in 1968. Reruns of the show have been aired constantly since that time, playing as many as four times a day in some markets. Generations seem pulled to Mayberry by the clean, wholesome, gentle humor that is constant among the citizens—humor that is funny but does not stem from jokes. Other than county clerk Howard

---

5 The Lodge or the "Regal Order of the Golden Door to Good Fellowship" was similar to a Masonic Lodge

Sprague's brief stint at stand-up comedy, the people in Mayberry are not comedians. True, they swap jokes down at Floyd's barbershop or on the courthouse bench, but the viewers rarely hear them. When we do, they are usually not that funny, which is the way it often is with planned jokes. In these situations, the humor for us comes from the way the characters react to someone's attempt to be funny.

For the viewer, the true humor on *TAGS* comes in watching the characters go about the business of acting human. It flows from their personalities. With amazing coincidence—and superb actors, writers, directors, and producers—they act as we act. Their daily routines ring familiar, even to fans from large cities away from the South. Of course, there are the occasional bizarre incidents around which episodes revolve, but even these events are not farfetched compared to what I see in the "real" world across the USA.

This is one of the reasons Mayberry humor continues its appeal. Other than the rare absolute absurdity, it springs not from one-liners, slapstick, or quick punch lines, but rather from the believable, daily mingling of human beings who could be put into any decade or any size town located anywhere in the country.

Mayberry humor reflects the way the citizens of the town treat one another. They live by what I call the Mayberry Attitude, which is best summed up in a rambling statement by Aunt Bee in "Aunt Bee the Crusader."

"You seem to forget there are some things in this world more important than money! Things like home, and people's feelings and where they grew up, and things like . . . DO UNTO OTHERS!"

The good citizens of Mayberry do indeed strive to live by the Golden Rule. Along with religion, it is the foundation of their approach to living. In Mayberry, people respect all human beings regardless of their station in life. They truly love and care about one another and are accepting of shortcomings and personality traits. Mayberryites are friendly, courteous, good-natured folks with a wide range of feelings. They live by a moral code that includes honesty, fairness, and doing the right thing. The entire adult community is involved in bringing up its young people and passes this code to them mainly through example. The type of humor found in Mayberry reflects these truly admirable qualities.

They laugh. Oh, the citizens of Mayberry love to laugh. Like everyone else, they kid and poke fun and swap stories. They even pull harmless practical jokes, like tucking blankets under someone who is asleep, or hiding shoes in a desk drawer. But all this good-natured humor is done because they like one another, not to intentionally hurt feelings. Their humor is part of their positive approach to life—their Mayberry Attitude. Because the people in Mayberry live by "do unto others," their humor is not an avenue for getting even or putting people down. When they occasionally step over the line, that Mayberry Attitude takes a bigger step and leads them to correct the situation. In the long run, it is inexcusable to be funny at a friend's expense.

Because the humor on *TAGS* comes from the Mayberry Attitude of the characters and not from jokes, the series continues to be funny today. When we return to our favorite small town through reruns, we watch through Mayberry eyes and listen with Mayberry ears. We want to be entertained, so we are. We want to see ourselves, thus we do. If we want to see Mayberry humor at other times, we just have to make sure we view the world in the same manner.

I try to make that choice daily. Sure, I can mash the remote control and see comedy for hours, but I do not like off-color, offensive comedy. I am tolerant of four-letter words, but I just do not want to hear strings of them. I am not a prude, but I am turned off by all the sexual comments and intimations in most of today's comedy.

The Mayberry humor I am seeking usually is not found in comedy clubs or on most television shows. It is out there amongst the authentic people who live by the Golden Rule—people very much like the fictional citizens of Mayberry.

So . . . the definition of Mayberry humor? MAYBERRY HUMOR IS THE CLEAN, KIND, YET HILARIOUS HUMOR THAT EVOLVES WHEN HUMAN BEINGS GO ABOUT THEIR DAILY LIVING INTERACTING WITH ONE ANOTHER.

This humor can be found in simple, seemingly insignificant remarks or the most bizarre situations. Mostly it is unintentional, like when Barney pronounces "naive" as "nave." However, it may also be planned like in "The Merchant of Mayberry," when Andy says, "Hey, Barn, we ain't got much to do right here in the middle of the week, have we? Wanna have some fun?" Mayberry humor springs from everyday experiences, so it is usually around when we are with others, bringing smiles, chuckles, or loud guffaws. Sadly, it often goes unnoticed. This does not mean it is not out there. It means we are not looking for it. It is time to lighten up and start looking.

I know you are wondering—Figured all this out by herself, did she? And just now?—Nooooo, it has been creeping up on me for years. If Emmett Clark were reading this, he might remind me about now that this had better be good—the way I am dragging it out.[6] I know, but STICK WITH ME ON THIS. IT IS THE FRAME FOR THE BIG PICTURE.

How I got into professional speaking offers a further explanation of why I am attracted so strongly to humor on *TAGS*. When I won the pageant title of Miss North Carolina, I dropped out of college for a year and traveled around the state appearing at scores of Apricot Blossom Festivals, Miss Mayberry Pageants, and Founders' Day parades. I attended countless banquets in Kiwanis Club meeting halls, Moravian Church basements, and banquet rooms of Bluevue Motels. I never met a chicken or potato I did not recognize no matter how they were disguised. At each event, I was expected to say a few words. I was only nineteen years old, but it did not take me long to figure out that audiences liked it when I was funny. Honestly, I am not so sure they liked the fact that I was funny or respected that a Miss North Carolina TRIED to be funny. Whichever the case, they laughed, and I was hooked.

In those ground-laying days of my speaking career, I told pat, clean, well-worn jokes out of a book similar to *JOKES FOR ALL OCCASIONS*.

---

6 Emmett Clark is Mayberry's handyman who runs Emmett's Fix-It Shop.

My pride tells me they were better than Floyd's joke about a zebra falling in love with a pair of striped pajamas, but I would not swear to it. Over twelve months I perfected about seven of these jewels, and I told them well because I told them so often. Sometimes, I reeled them off two and three times a day. It has been years since I have repeated any of those jokes, but I believe I could bolt straight up in the middle of the night and deliver them verbatim if I had to.

As that year progressed, I begin sharing with audiences the amusing incidents that naturally occurred for a 6'2" basketball player, with a crown on her head. This was during the radical, hippie years of the sixties when many of us thought that Woodstock was a place to keep fire logs and "tripping" was stumbling over your feet. The response was positive when I told true stories about kids shooting me with peas in a parade in Mt. Olive or eating from my finger bowl with a spoon at a banquet in Greensboro, NC. Truthfully announcing that I was the tallest contestant to ever compete in the Miss America Pageant was just a setup. Seconds later, it let me deadpan, "That also makes me THE TALLEST CONTESTANT to ever LOSE in the Miss America Pageant."

In Atlantic City, the other contestants named me Miss Congeniality, something I have always cherished. To the folks at home, I got more mileage out of saying, "That's the contestant the others thought had the LEAST CHANCE of winning the title of Miss America." Audiences enjoyed hearing the true tales, and I was careful to make sure that the stories were not negative toward the pageant experience because it was certainly a positive experience for me.

The more audiences laughed, the harder I looked for true, humorous incidents to add to my remarks. Word spread quickly through the state that the 6'2" Miss North Carolina could do more than smile and wave equally to both sides of the street during parades. Cutting ribbons was only one of her talents; she could do fifteen minutes of "talkin' funny" if needed, but you might have trouble getting her off the stage.

Toward the end of the year, the state Jaycees gave me two opportunities that further explain why the humor in Mayberry so strongly appeals to me.[7] The annual week-long state pageant was kicked off with a big banquet for the eighty-four contestants, chaperons, judges, and numerous dignitaries. Traditionally, this was a staid, formal affair. To make it worse, they usually served something like Cornish Hens— small, snobbish-looking chickens—and the potatoes were "au gratin." The Jaycees asked me to speak at the banquet and do what I had done all year, be funny. They wanted me to tell the true stories about what I had seen while visiting the Mayberries in our state. Knowing months in advance that I would be speaking for thirty minutes only height- ened my resolve to find material.

Ours was the largest state pageant in the nation in those days. It was a four-night event with three evenings of preliminary com- petition and a big final night on statewide television. The era was pre-computer and quite possibly pre-adding machine. Toward the end of each evening of competition, there was a lull in the show while all the points were tabulated. Sometimes, the judges even left the hall while everyone waited and waited for the results. Typically, musical acts were inserted during the balloting, but in my year, the state Jaycees asked me to "fill" during that slot each night. My instructions were to just walk out on the stage and be funny until the scores were tabulated. No singers. No dancers. Just me and my stories. Nobody knew in advance how long I would have to "kill time." Fifteen minutes each night? Twenty-five? I was to just keep talking until SOMEBODY gave me the signal to stop. (Oh, what my husband would pay today to know that signal.) I was THRILLED.

Again, my well-worn jokes were out. Everyone in the statewide pageant community had heard them, and I certainly could not tell identical jokes four nights in a row. . . my own mother would have left. I spent the last months of my year working new vignettes into my "acts." When a story clicked, I would put it aside for pageant week and work on something else.

---

7 U.S. Junior Chamber of Commerce is a not-for-profit organization of active cit- izens ages 18-40.

That one state pageant week of "filling" with original humorous stories every night, plus the thirty-minute after-dinner speech I had to present, moved me from being a pageant winner to a young speaker.

On the final night of the state pageant, I crowned my successor and turned over the keys to the slick convertible—the one with my name on the side that I had wrecked on the outskirts of Siler City. (I had been looking at all the nice scenery between home and there.) Three days later I pulled out of Graham in my daddy's old, tuned-up 1954 Valiant, and headed for Wrightsville Beach to make my first speech "crownless." It was for the North Carolina Alcoholic Beverage Control Board. I have been speaking since, and I believe they are still selling spirits.

My stock in trade has been to tell what I saw. Sure, sometimes I embellish it, but mostly I tell true stories. I cannot make it up funnier than it actually happens.

THAT is what we are looking for in this book. The positive proof that Mayberry humor—the clean, kind, yet hilarious humor that evolves when human beings go about interacting with one another in their daily living—can still be found across the USA.

An Invitation Spread with a Little Jam

Andy: You aren't using your truck, are you?
Goober: Go right ahead. I always say my truck is your truck.

- Episode #169, "A Warning from Warren"

Well, it is finally time to go, and in true Mayberry form, we are going to start out on a truck. I do hope you will join me as I present my evidence of Mayberry humor. Pack a satchel and don't forget nary a thing. I have the traditional brown sack full of sandwiches. Whether by truck, foot, bus, car, or plane, somehow, we will get everywhere I want to take you to introduce you to folks I have met and situations I have encountered or heard about. You might occasionally see a slight comparison to scenes watched for years on *The Andy Griffith Show* or Mayberry characters we have grown to love. THAT'S THE POINT! Nod your head when someone acts in the sixties Mayberry style right here in the nineties. When it is all said and done, I believe you will agree that there is plenty of the good ol' Mayberry humor out there in the USA. Thank goodness.

Oh, one more thing . . . the jam. We are going to need a little for the sandwiches. In "Andy Discovers America," how does Andy put it to Miss Crump? "I didn't know what to say to them. I just, uh, kinda told 'em a little tale . . . well, you know, put a little extra jam on the bread."

Humorists have a tendency to exaggerate. (Surprise! Surprise!) Story embellishing is as much a part of my business as a cord is to a bungee jumper. Officially, we call it "creative license." If you read my first book, *The Magic of Jeanne*, you surely questioned a few things. Did I really finish 49th out of 50 in the Miss America Pageant, edging out that pitiful contestant who played the comb for her talent? Well of course not. After they named the Top Ten, the rest of us went back to the dressing room for further discussion. At 6'2" tall and weighing in at 160 pounds, who do you think came in strong for eleventh place?

OK, I am not above spreading a little extra jam on the bread for a chuckle. But it will not work well in this case. Remember, I am trying my best to illustrate that Mayberry humor is still prevalent.

Therefore, it is imperative that the stories I relate actually happened . . . or ALMOST did. When appropriate, I will furnish the name and place involved unless I cannot remember for sure or think someone might get their feelings hurt. (I have this one sensitive cousin. Thank goodness not everybody in the family is sensitive.) And I do not want to ruffle any hen feathers. If I do not know for sure it happened, I will "fess up." Still, the majority of the incidents are described as I saw them or as told to me by friends. And I will go light on the extra jam . . . most of the time.

Everybody up on the truck!

PART II.
LOOKING NEARBY FOR
MAYBERRY HUMOR

In the Mirror

Floyd, looking in his barbershop mirror: Floyd Lawson, you're nothing but a liar and a cheat and a scoundrel. I hate you!
- **Episode #71, "Floyd, the Gay Deceiver"**

It is little wonder that Floyd Lawson, Mayberry's lovable barber, is
disgusted with himself in "Floyd, the Gay Deceiver." After all, he
led his Lonely-hearts Club pen pal to believe he is a rich widower
and the head of Floyd Lawson Enterprises. Who would have thought
that she would ever come to Mayberry? Of course, the viewers know
Andy will solve the problem within the allotted thirty minutes of television time, so that lets us gleefully watch Floyd's agony and repeated
personal beratement, "Oh, the deception of it all . . . . The vanity of it
all . . . . Wretch, wretch, deceitful wretch!" Contributing to the hilarity
is the fact that Floyd returns to his barbershop mirror to confront
himself with several admonishments. "Floyd Lawson, I am ashamed
of you," he says to himself in the looking glass. "Floyd Lawson, you're
a miserable, deceitful wretch." And television audiences double over
with laughter.

I am a firm believer in occasionally taking a long look (pun
intended) at myself in the mirror. "Uh-huh," one might think, "it's that
Miss America Pageant thing. You and the Potato Queen . . . ." Nah,
that is not it at all. At this stage of my life, I just need a quick glance
to see if everything is tucked in, such as my stomach. I am referring

to the little bit of introspective mirror-examining we all need every so often to make sure our humor is still looking good.

Let's go back to the banquet in Orlando where all this surfaced. (As Barney explains in "Opie's Ill-Gotten Gain," "It's amazing how that stuff stays with you. Once you learn something, it never leaves you. Just stays locked up tight right in the old noodle.") Someone at the table that night remarked he enjoyed watching *TAGS*, but that the people in Mayberry are unrealistic and taken to extremes. His exact words were "not like REAL people." That seemed to be fine with him because he looked at my Mayberry pals only as characters on a television show. I look at them as examples of real folks.

I will agree that in a few rare segments, the personalities in Mayberry are taken to extremes. Sure, they have some pretty funny traits and do eccentric things at times, but unrealistic? Not like real people? I beg to differ.

The Andy Griffith Show was not produced to generate fan clubs and weekend events for devoted viewers years later. True, the writers worked in little messages without being preachy, but the primary purpose was to entertain. The show does so very well because the writers, directors, actors, and producers who brought Mayberry to life for the rest of us were masters at seeing human beings as we truly are. The creative team working on the show knew that certain human traits never change, not with technology, self-help books, or talk shows. Not even with articles in the magazine section of the Sunday paper, and we all know the magazine section of the Sunday paper would not lie. The series is placed in the sixties, but it could have been set in the forties, or the thirties, or even today. Believable characters transcend time.

The citizens of Mayberry are believable. We love them because they are honest, dependable, caring, and basically good people, as we would all like to be. But we also love them because they act as we do when we are not at our best. Sometimes they jump to conclusions, overreact and let their tempers guide their thinking. The green-eyed monster bites all of them now and then, even Andy. The Fifes are not the only ones who are sensitive; most people in Mayberry get their feelings hurt once in a while. Fortunately, they are not the kind of folks who hold grudges. They know that they ought not to stick their noses in other people's business, but they are naturally nosy and cannot help but interfere occasionally. They gossip. They love flattery, like to win, and can be generous as well as cheap. Sometimes they say and do things they regret, and every so often, their egos and pride wedge in the way of good common sense. The comparisons could go on and on. The point is that all of this is humorous to those of us who are watching because we act the same. When we watch our friends in Mayberry, it is as though we see ourselves reflected in Floyd's mirror.

When we want to see Mayberry humor, step back and look for it. But before we observe others, it is always best to glance in the mirror and take a good look at ourselves. After all, in "Stranger in Town," it is Andy who says, "Aw, Barney, if I was to run everybody out of town that acted a little bit strange, I'd wind up emptying the whole town. I might have to reach around and get a good holt on the seat of my own britches." So, before I share humor I have seen in others, permit me to reach around and get a good hold on the seat of my own britches. You just sit back and have a few laughs on me before we move to the rest of the world.

Most Likely to Become Charming

Barney: Can't hardly call 'em babies anymore. Course, you can't call
            'em full growed either.

- Episode #101, "Opie the Birdman"

My speech was scheduled for high school students in Port St. Joe,
Florida. The school superintendent and I were standing in the "gym-
natorium" waiting for the students to arrive when he said, "We got
so excited about having a speaker from out of the county, that we
decided to bring in ALL the students, kindergarten through grade
twelve." KINDERGARTEN! It was like having that iron door clang
shut in my face, and everyone knows it is definitely no fun when that
iron door clangs shut! Four and five-year-olds? The kind that walks
around with peanut butter and jelly sandwiches in their hands? Quite
frankly, I am not suited for them psychologically. They are not even
people yet! Well, that is not fair. Of course, they are people. They are
just not "full growed."

"What do you want me to talk to kindergarten students about?" I
finally managed to utter. "Assertiveness? Leadership? Tying shoes?"
(My hat goes off to those who teach this age group, but the best
thing I say to five-year-olds is, "I will give you some money if you
will go away.")

The superintendent said, "We knew this would be a challenge. So,
with the little ones, we played up the Miss North Carolina angle. We
showed them dozens of pictures of young women holding roses,
wearing crowns in long flowing gowns."

I was about to hyperventilate, but as the morning would prove,
five-year-olds can be made to understand the words "Miss North
Carolina" if shown enough pictures. Unfortunately, there is no picture
for the word "former."

They came off the buses looking for her, teachers herding them
along like city slickers on a cattle drive. They filled the front bleach-
ers, but before long one of the tykes broke loose and was at my

knees. She gazed all the way up to my face and said, "Where is Miss North Carolina?"

Speakers certainly know the importance of truth and honesty at all times, but especially when dealing with young, impressionable children. I looked straight down at her little cherubic face and said, "She's sick."

She stared up at me and asked, "Are you her mother?"

Cheap Thread

Andy: It must get tiresome, just doing all that sewing.

- **Episode #138, "The Pageant"**

All the women in Mayberry seem to enjoy sewing, especially Aunt Bee. She does the repair work on the costumes for the Centennial Pageant. They count on her. Another time she feels it an honor to be invited over to a friend's house to start on a quilt. In show after show Aunt Bee mends while on the porch or on the living room sofa. One Sunday afternoon she and Clara try to whip the old band uniforms into shape, but meet an unforeseen opponent—cheap thread. I have trouble identifying.

For high school home economics class, I spent sleepless nights at Mother's heavy black Singer sewing machine toiling over my six-week project, an apron. (Maybe if I had known what an apron was for?) Quite frankly, I was lucky that I did not sew up my fingers because I did not know which end of a thimble was up. Only in college did I learn that it was actually a little liqueur glass for southern ladies.

Fortunately, Mother could sew.

My older sister Katherine and I grew up in the fifties. When she was fifteen, she stopped growing at 5'5", the same height as our mother. I was two years younger and already 6'2". The third sister was still a baby in the crib, so we did not know about her yet. Sewing was the accepted practice of the era, so Mother made most of our clothes and worked hard to keep up with the latest trends. We did not look too

"Ivory League," more like "a league by ourselves." While the main goal was to look "store-bought," not homemade, multiple outfits out of the same material gave us away.

One day Mama read in a fashion magazine that she could change our size by the way she dressed us. This was exciting news for a woman with daughters at each end of the size spectrum. For example, according to one article, wearing a black belt would cut a person's height. After that, I would be walking out of the house in a swimsuit, and Mother would say, "I think a black belt would look good with that."

Then it was as if the heavens opened up and sent a message, and the magic word that came down was "Stripes." According to fashion experts, if a person wore stripes going up and down, it made her look taller. If she wore stripes going around, it made her look shorter.

But Mama was a real smart shopper, and never could pass up a good buy. Soon after reading this fashion information, she came upon a bolt of red and white striped material that was ON SALE. She bought the whole thing. Back home, she laid out that material with the stripes going north to south on the kitchen table. Then she got out her good size pair of clunker pinking shears that would have broken her foot if she had dropped them and cut out dresses for herself and my sister Katherine with the stripes going up and down. They put them on and in front of my very eyes—Alakazam!—appeared to shoot up to over six feet. I remember thinking that if Mama kept cutting in that direction, I was going to look over nine feet tall.

Then she turned that material east to west, and cut out a dress for me with the stripes going around. From below my neck to below my knees, I looked like a gigantic version of one of those spinning tops. If someone could have placed a flat hand on the top of my head and pumped up and down, I would have spun up the street.

The next Sunday, the three of us put on those striped dresses and headed as usual to the Graham Presbyterian Church to hear about one of the deadly sins. When we walked toward the smokers hanging around outside the vestibule, they got dizzy and groped for the sides of the building. Inside, the woman who always sat in the pew behind us felt seasick and pumped her Popsicle-stick, cardboard, funeral-home fan even faster than usual. I could feel the breeze on the back of my neck. Tears welled up in Reverend Kryder's eyes every time he looked in our direction. None of this bothered us, however. We sat there like peppermints, singing "Bringing In The Sheaves" at the top of our lungs. "Bringing in the sheaves. BRING-ing IN THE SHEAVES."

I heard that an elderly parishioner with failing eyesight went downtown the next day. When she passed the local barbershop, rumor was that she looked up at the striped pole, nodded, and said, "Good morning, Jeanne."

This is Big! Really Big!

Barney: Listen, Ange, I can't talk now, I'm right in the middle of a big meeting here at headquarters. But I can tell you this much. I'm working on something big, for you and the whole town. And Andy, I mean this is something really big. It's big!

- Episode #240, "Barney Hosts a Summit Meeting"

Helen Crump was a state spelling champion in the eighth grade.[8] Goober won the pancake eating contest at the county fair by whiffing down fifty-seven. Andy caught the winning touchdown pass against Mt. Pilot High in the fourth quarter with only four seconds to go. Howard recalls moving to the Caribbean for a while. It is not surprising that Aunt Bee feels a little left out during all the reminiscing in "Aunt Bee's Big Moment." Eventually, though, America's favorite aunt learns to fly because everyone needs something to look back on—kinda high points.

"I remember when you were Miss North Carolina," said a stranger in the restaurant line in Greensboro. When the woman moved on, my

---

8 Helen was a schoolteacher and became Sheriff Andy Taylor's girlfriend.

friend Norma Rose rolled her eyes and slowly shook her head. "If I hadn't heard it with my own two ears . . .."

Suddenly, she was suspicious. "You set her up, didn't you, Jeanne?"

"Set her up?"

"Yes. Do not get offended. You look fairly well-preserved for your age, but I can't believe a stranger would recognize you as a former Miss North Carolina. Not at this stage of the game. Who's the friend in on the joke?"

It was not a joke. What Norma Rose did not know was the REASON people look at me thirty years after the fact, search their memories, and put the pieces together. "Weren't you THAT Miss North Carolina?" they ask. I know the reason.

Barefooted with my hair mashed down, I am 6'2" tall, and I was that height when I was in the Miss America Pageant. In two-inch high heels, which I usually wore, I hit 6'4".

I was Miss North Carolina when hair was at its height from unmerciful teasing. The style was bouffant, and I "bouffed" with the best of them. Clara Edwards may have worn a look that was "upswept," but I outdid even her.[9] I pulled my hair straight up toward the ceiling, brushed it backward towards my scalp, and then smoothed the top layer over the underlying mess, ever careful not to disturb any tiny birds that may have nested. Teasing my hair added another four inches. That made me 6'8".

On top of that 6'8" figure, I placed the official, three-inch, Miss North Carolina crown, and bobby pinned it into the ratted disorder beneath. The bobby pins could go straight down and never touch my head. (This much metal should have made me nervous because lightning will strike tall things, or so I have heard.) Combining my height, heels, teasing, and crown, I measured out at 6'11". For one year, I traveled around the state at that 6'11" towering size, attracting large crowds and scaring dogs and small children.

---

9 Another Mayberry character.

A particularly vivid recollection was the time a mother brought her young daughter to meet Miss North Carolina. The mother encouraged the little darling to walk up to me. Clearly hesitant with a 6'11" figure looming in front of her, the child backed away. Suddenly, she turned and buried her face in her mother's skirt, grabbed her thighs, and entwined her legs around one of her mother's ankles like an Australian koala bear hanging by all fours on a tree limb. It was the first time I saw a human move forward and back up at the same time. The child thought she was going away from me, but the mother masterfully carried her in my direction. Her daughter was GOING TO MEET Miss North Carolina!

The woman plodded steadily forward. The koala clung to her mother's thighs for dear life. Step, drag. Step, draggggg. When they were within several feet of where I stood at 6'11", the child suddenly arched her back and screamed upward, "I DON'T WANT TO MEET THE BIG QUEEN!"

Every Head a Walking Testimony

Barney: The next time I want a haircut, I'm gonna stick my head in a pencil sharpener!

- Episode #10, "Stranger in Town"

Maybe the young man who knocked on my door promptly at 6:00 a.m. with coffee thought I had been to a poodle trimmer over in Mt. Pilot. From a sound sleep, I fumbled in the dark for a T-shirt and my warm-up suit, all the time shouting, "Just a minute." I certainly did not look in the mirror, or I would have seen that my hair was mashed flat to the sides of my head and sticking straight up in matted chunks on the top. It was not a cowlick situation. It was as though I had been run over by a team of hogs.

After bumping into a few chairs, I made it to the door and was greeted by a cheery young fellow whose entrance spread a little sunshine into the room. The breakfast tray even had flowers on it.

Well, only a rose. He was so personable that before he left, I asked my question about the funniest thing he had seen while working at the hotel, the Marriott River Center in San Antonio. He chuckled as he poured the coffee, and I signed the check. "There are so many things," he mumbled.

I pressed ahead. "Does one incident stand out in your mind?" Another big smile. "Can't think of anything." He walked to the door, then suddenly turned and said, "Well, there is ONE funny thing. Ma'am, you ought to look in the mirror at your hair!"

Only in America

Andy: Now, uh, as judge of this here contest, I wish that I could present the title to each and every one of you. But as you know, in a beauty contest, there can only be one winner.

- **Episode #20, "The Beauty Contest"**

If farmers grow it, the South has a pageant for it. From strawberries to squash, there is a queen perched on a red convertible leading a parade through small towns during annual celebrations. In Mayberry, the heralded crop is the potato. One of the thousands of quick facial expressions that say so much on *TAGS* comes when the Potato Queen, in a bathing suit—much to Aunt Bee's displeasure—presents the Governor with a big spud in the episode, "The Cannon." He later puts it in his pocket. The crowd cheers.

Mayberry has its share of other queens and pageants. Years after the fact, Barney still gets angry when he recalls the time the Apricot Queen came through town and Andy escorted her around. After all, HE ate all the apricots. In "The Beauty Contest," Andy gets pressured into judging the Miss Mayberry Pageant even though he swears he is not qualified. It does not take long for him to realize he must have been out of his ever-loving mind. I understand.

Through all the years of emceeing local and state pageants, I never went back to the Miss America Pageant until 1990. This was not because I do not support the program. I do! It is just that I am not a pageant fanatic, and I was always busy.

When my first book came out a feature story appeared in the newspaper in Atlantic City. Pageant officials must have slapped their foreheads with the heel of their hands and said, "Hey, she's smarter than we thought! Let's get her up here to be a judge." It is amazing, but that is the way it is in America. One day you cannot butter bread right, and the next day, you are a genius.

Thus, twenty-seven years after I competed, I headed back to the BIG SHOW to be a preliminary judge. This meant staying in Atlantic City for nine days to interview the contestants, judge talent and evening gowns, etc. ("etc." meaning the always controversial swimsuit competition). Eventually, we selected the Top Ten for the televised program on Saturday night. Celebrities came in on the last day and named the winner.

Women will be interested to know that I needed three outfits each day, one of which needed to be "dressy." Twenty-seven outfits! I sure was not going on a spree and buy all new clothes, although I did fork over for a few accessories. For months before the pageant, I stopped tall women in airports and asked, "Do you have a good-looking outfit I could borrow the second week in September?" Statuesque women have a common bond about this, so they usually just looked at me for a few seconds and without further explanation, responded, "Will you be needing the shoes and jewelry?"

When I was packing all my accumulated outfits, son Beaver came through and saw the suitcases piled high. "Where are you going with all these clothes?"

I was frantically folding, packing, and stuffing. Barely looking up, I answered proudly, "I am going back up to the Miss America Pageant!"

Beaver's retort was quick and sincere. "Mama, don't go! I do not know how to tell you this, but . . . you are NOT going to win." Pageant images flashed before his eyes producing a second thought. "You're not going to put on a swimsuit in front of anybody who KNOWS ME, are you!" He left the room mumbling something about "dimples on the sides of your thighs." I believe I mumbled, "But Beaver, I'm your mother."

So back to Atlantic City I went . . . without my swimsuit. During the judges' briefing, we were told there would be a press conference for the preliminary judges on Friday morning after we had selected the ten semi-finalists, but before they were announced. We could expect tough questions, and the composition of the press corps would be interesting.

A third of the reporters would be first-timers. They were in Atlantic City to cover a young woman from their area who had made it to the Miss America Pageant. Those reporters would be just as star-struck with the events of the week as many of the contestants. History showed that they would ask few questions.

A second third of the reporters would be the ones who loved the Miss America Pageant. They were very much in support of the entire program and always touted the opportunities it presents. They would also ask very few questions for they already knew most of the answers.

Then there would be the remaining third. The last group disliked pageants in general and viewed the entire event as exploitation of women. These reporters would be chomping at the bit to ask any question that might possibly put the Pageant in an unfavorable light. They wanted a tabloid twist to their stories. Miss so-and-so was a blonde out of a bottle. Miss here-and-there was kicked out of the Philomathian Literary Society in high school.[10] Miss girl-next-door joined one of those "travelin' religions."

And which third could we expect to ask most of the questions? Sure, the last third. We could count on them to be sitting in the front rows, salivating at the thought of any slip-up that could be the next day's headline.

---

10 Philomathian Literary Society was founded at the University of Pennsylvania in 1813 for the advancement of learning. See https://archives.upenn.edu/exhibits/penn-history/philomathean/

Hearing all this brought to mind the physical education teacher in me. It certainly had been easier to be a finish-line judge or call balls and strikes.

All three groups were ready and waiting when we came into the room that Friday. We could put them into categories by body demeanor. They sat eagerly or semi-patiently, depending on their viewpoints, while the preliminary judges were introduced.

The floor was opened for questions and hands shot up, but the prevailing reporter did not wait to be recognized. She launched into her first question, raising her voice three decibels louder than her associates. Her words leaped in our direction. "What is the opinion of the panel concerning contestants having plastic surgery to compete in the Miss America Pageant?"

Plastic surgery? A bomb dropped over the room and brought silence with it. Did she say plastic surgery? The first question was about PLASTIC SURGERY? One of Andy's southern phrases during his judging experience rang in my ears. "Law, what'd I get into."

I glanced right and left at the other six judges on the panel. They just sat there, their minds reeling and knowing as I did that someone needed to say something fast.

The official, enforced policy of the Miss America Pageant is well-known. Any franchise suggesting to a contestant that she have plastic surgery to compete will have its franchise pulled. But that information was in their printed materials. They wanted a personal opinion. That slip of the tongue. That possible shocking headline.

The hush over the room was broken only by a slight murmur among the reporters which grew louder with each second of delay. The last time I saw anything like it was when I came upon buzzards on the highway, circling the carcass of a long-dead animal. The dead animal probably wore a badge that proclaimed "Judge."

I too wore a badge that proclaimed "Judge."-Might as well speak up. "My name is Jeanne Robertson. I will take this one," I managed to say. Like spectators at Wimbledon, heads turned in unison in my direction. No one wrote down a word. I forged ahead.

"I was Miss North Carolina in 1963." Pencils stood still. Reporters looked at me like monkeys waiting for peanuts.

Loving the situation, I took a deep breath and continued, "And I had plastic surgery to compete in the Miss America Pageant."

What did she say her name is?

When was she in the Pageant?

Who is she?

Pencils flew. There was so much commotion in the room that it was difficult to wait for the attention to return to me, but I managed. My fellow judges arched their eyebrows in my direction. We had just worked together for nine days. This was news to them.

"I always wanted to be in the pageant," I continued, staring earnestly at the flock hovering in front of me. "But I understood that most of the contestants were tall. I was only 5'7", so I opted for plastic surgery." At that point, I slowly stood up, stretching all the way to my 6'2" height. "As you can see, the doctor got carried away."

The stunned silence lasted only seconds and then the room filled with laughter. I smiled and sat down.

A reporter launched a second guided missile from the other side of the room. "One of the contestants said she lost seventy pounds in order to compete in the Pageant. What are your feelings about that?" From my left, Flo Anthony, fellow panelist, and gossip columnist announced, "I will take that one." [11] The ball bounced to her court, where she said, "I do not know about a contestant losing seventy pounds to compete, but I lost thirty just to judge."

There were no more tough questions.

---

11 Flo Anthony is a gossip columnist for the *Philadelphia Sun*. She is a radio show host, reporter for the *New York Daily News*, publisher and editor-in-chief of *Black Noir Magazine*, and blogger. A graduate of Howard University, she resides in the East Harlem section of New York City.

Before My Time

Opie and Andy, discussing Aunt Bee's age -

Opie: She don't know how old she is?

Andy: Nothing too surprising about that. It's easy for her to forget.

Opie: Don't she even know the day she was born on?

Andy: She knows the day all right. It's the year she's a little fuzzy on.

- Episode #75, "The Bed Jacket"

Aunt Bee tries to tell Opie she is twenty-one years old in "The Bed Jacket," but the youngster remembers she was that age the year before. Andy jumps in to explain that the year worked out so well that Aunt Bee is going around again. His explanation is unnecessary. Aunt Bee suddenly remembers she is going on twenty-two. Maybe she has some sort of miracle salve.

My secretary Toni arranged for me to speak at a statewide meeting of her sorority held on the campus of the University of North Carolina at Chapel Hill. She went with me that afternoon, as did a carload of women from Burlington who were alumnae of that group. Toni and I went to Auburn University, but our friends attended UNC. They were proudly showing us around their old sorority house when we came to a hall lined with "composites"—large frames which contain individual pictures of the sisters of a sorority who were in school during each particular year.

We began to look for a photo of a friend who could not come that day, but had graduated from Carolina and was a member of that sorority. As we peered from picture to picture, an undergraduate came bouncing down the hall and asked if she could help. We explained what we were doing and told her our friend's maiden name. She glanced at the numerous pictures and asked, "Do you know when she graduated?"

"Not exactly," I replied, "but she's my age."

I admit I am a little gray for my age, but the coed's response was still a little quick for me. She said, "She'd be in the attic."

It was tragic. Just tragic.

The Big Philanderer

Gomer: Do you want me to drive you? You can sit in the back and
          put your feet up.

                              - Episode #119, "Andy Saves Gomer"

Barney does not hide his concern in "Ernest T. Bass Joins the Army"
when he discovers both he and Andy have left a quarter tip at the
diner. It is throwing money away! Maybe he should run back over
there and put his hat down on one of them and get it back? Andy
reminds him that the waitress, Olive, is a widow with four children.
She can use it. Bless her heart.

My husband thinks a lot like Barney and is convinced that I over
tip. He swears I not only leave more money than necessary but that I
tip when I do not have to and for service that should be automatic. He
thinks my picture is posted on bulletin boards in hotel kitchens and
taxi headquarters with the words "easy target" printed in large letters
over it. (It is probably right there next to thieves and smugglers, not
to mention foreign spies.)

He does not understand the world as I see it. I do not tip just for
service. I tip for creativity.

My client in Florida sent half an acre of a car to meet me at the airport. The driver was a nice young man, and during the trip, we talked
about the weather, the resort, and his job . . . typical limo chitchat.
Somewhere in our comments, I mentioned sports and that I was an
Auburn University fan. He did not react, and the conversation turned
toward the fact that Florida is a pretty state. There was no other mention of the Auburn War Eagles. No problem. I can discuss pretty states
with the best of them.

I had been told that my client would pay for the limo and the gra-
tuity, but the young man was so nice that I got out a five-dollar bill as
we neared the resort. It was a thirty-minute trip, for heaven's sake! He
was a good guy and was working his way through school. Probably
getting a master's in psychology.

When we arrived, the driver maneuvered the long black car up to the guard at the gatehouse and leaned out. "Jim," he announced, just loud enough for me to hear way back there in the back seat. "I am PROUD to say that I have Jeanne WAR EAGLE Robertson in this limousine."

Discreetly, I pulled ten more dollars out of my billfold and dug twenty-seven cents out of my pocket.

I hope they are using a recent photo in their kitchen.

Be Nice

Andy: I don't like for the boy to raise his voice at the table.
Briscoe Darling: Hear that boys? No yelling at the table. It'll take a while, but I'll learn 'em.

- Episode #96, "Briscoe Declares for Aunt Bee"

Many things our mothers told us—like writing Thank You notes—are in our heads. We who grew up in the South got a triple dose of sayings and adages, as did Sheriff Andrew Taylor. For example, when a family friend comes from Siler City in "Guest in the House," Aunt Bee commands, "I want you to be nice to her and that is that!"

I admit that some of my mother's strangest little tenets—like her standard reminder to "talk to the people no one is talking to"—have eventually proven beneficial. Mother always reminded me to do this when I left for social occasions. During my pageant year, I would return home from speaking appearances, and in the middle of telling something exciting she would interrupt and ask, "Did you talk to the people no one was talking to?" Evidently, no one had talked to Mother at some big event in her early life.

Stuff like that sticks with you. It sprang to mind when I visited fellow speaker Doc Blakely and his wife Pat in Wharton, Texas.[12] We went out to eat with a crowd of friends, and one person brought along

---

12 Doc Blakely is the author of seven books, a musician, a popular humorist, and winner of the National Speaker's Association's highest award, The Cavett Award.

her mother, Mrs. Della Mae Farris. "Mother was born on July 4, 1900, and is a little hard of hearing," the daughter whispered. Her hushed tone was unnecessary. The older woman could not have heard the four o'clock train blasting into the restaurant. After initial courtesy remarks, she just sat as the rest of us became involved in conversations.

It did not take long for my upbringing to take over. I felt as though Mother were tapping me on the shoulder and admonishing, "Psst, Jeanne. No one is talking to Mrs. Farris." I ignored my conscience at first because the woman sat exactly opposite me at our round table. It was not my responsibility. If I had been closer, certainly I would engage her in conversation. Finally, though, I realized I was not going to enjoy my meal until I chatted with "the one no one was talking to."

Leaning over the table, I raised my voice and said, "MRS. FARRIS." She did not flinch. The others glanced in my direction, and her daughter nudged her. When she looked in my eyes, I tried again, this time shouting. "MRS. FARRIS, WHAT DO YOU DO IN YOUR SPARE TIME?" Everyone at the table stopped talking. Who am I kidding? Everyone in the restaurant stopped talking.

Mrs. Farris turned to her daughter and yelled, "WHAT DID SHE SAY?" The daughter looked back at me, and I repeated my question a little slower and even louder. "WHAT—DO—YOU—DO—IN—YOUR—SPARE—TIME?"

Mrs. Farris turned back to stare at me blankly for a few seconds and then jolted all of us when she shouted, "READ!"

I did not give up. "WHAT—DO—YOU—READ?" I continued.

All eyes focused on the elderly woman who at the next moment proved that a hearing loss did not necessarily mean the loss of one's humor. She looked me in the eyes and screeched at the top of her lungs, "BOOKS!"

My mother could have heard her . . . and Mother is dead.

"Lergics!"

Couple leaving Aunt Bee's Chinese restaurant -
Husband: I don't get Moo Goo Gai Pan like that at home.
Wife: Oh, you didn't even know what it was until tonight.

- Episode #209, "Aunt Bee's Restaurant"

Opie does not understand why Aunt Bee is crying during dinner in "The Rumor." After all, his face and hands are clean, and there is no dirt in his pant cuffs. His lizard is even outside in his lizard house. Andy uses the opportunity to explain sensitivity. "She could have heard a song on the radio today that reminded her of, oh, a rowboat ride or a dance where she met somebody nice, things like that."

Before Andy's explanation, Opie figures it another way. He thinks Aunt Bee might have "one of them 'lergics" like his buddy, Johnny Paul Jason. During April and May, Johnny Paul is not even allowed to breathe. Somehow, he gets by. The official word may be slightly abbreviated, but the thought is the same. "Lergics" can get to a person.

Lola Gillebaard, a California speaker, was coming to North Carolina. She told my secretary that she and her husband wanted to take Jerry and me out to dinner any night during the first week in July. The third was best for them.

I knew Lola—barely. She seemed nice and was a funny speaker, but after days on the road, I did not want to spend a precious vacation evening "talking speaking."

"You can't tell her you are not available ANY night out of seven," my secretary admonished. "Select a night, go out, eat an early dinner, and come home." She was right. I decided to let Jerry choose the evening and assured him it would not take all night. July third was not best for him. It was in the middle of the local Huck Finn - Tom Sawyer Tennis Tournament. He needed sleep. That settled it as far as I was concerned. It was not convenient. We just were not available.

However, Jerry stopped me on the way to the telephone. "Lola and Hank Gillebaard," he mused, saying their names over and over. "Lola and Hank. Lola . . . and Hank." It turned out, he knew the couple. "I do not know many people on the West Coast, but I believe I have talked to Lola and Hank several times at the speakers' convention," he added. "We should go out with them. If the third is their best night, I will survive the tournament the next day."

He gave it more thought and returned to my office. Lola and Hank had been VERY NICE to him. They were coming all the way from California. We should have them in our home, southern hospitality being what it is boasted to be. I protested that I barely knew the people, but Jerry insisted. "I really do talk to them at every convention. Let's have them over. Fix your Chinese."

It made sense to me. I sure was not going to serve wieners and beans. The only dish I prepare well is spaghetti, and even though I load it up with oregano, sometimes I just get up to my eyeballs in spaghetti. Fixing my Chinese - and I do it often - means putting all the woks, wooden sticks, and oriental spices around the kitchen, and at five o'clock, picking up a number of exotic Chinese dishes like Moo Goo Gai Pan (chicken and Chinese vegetables) from the local restaurant. We get stuff like Aunt Bee served in her restaurant. There are no little parasols in the food, but the owner of our local place does a great job. The recipes are not from the newspaper. More than likely, he learned to cook Chinese somewhere like Pittsburgh. Right before the company arrives, I put the food in the woks and dispose of the carry-out containers. When the guests come through the door, I am standing by the stove, stirring. It works every time.

On this night, we invited another speaker friend, Linda Pulliam, and her husband Charles from nearby Chapel Hill. They arrived first, and Linda burst out laughing when she saw me stirring at the stove, me in an apron no less. "Where'd you buy the dinner?"

While I could not fool Linda and Charles, I figured Lola and Hank would not be as savvy, never having been to our home. What Linda could not figure out was why I was going to so much trouble and expense for people I barely knew. I told her the truth; Jerry talked to them a lot at every convention.

Lola and Hank appeared and chitchatted as they passed me in the kitchen, stirring and looking gourmet. Everyone else sat on the porch for polite conversation while I occasionally clunked my wooden spoon on the side of the wok in the kitchen. (Like Aunt Bee, I just use an ordinary wooden spoon.) Minutes later, in my best hostess voice, I sang out, "I hope you like Chinese food." Lola's answer caused me to drop the spoon into the hot and sour soup. "I will eat anything, as long as it doesn't have sesame seeds in it," she said. "Sesame seeds make my throat bloat up so big you would have to put a straw down it for me to breathe."

Holy jumping catfish! Lola's got a "lergic!"

Linda's feet hit the porch floor running. "I will see if I can help Jeanne," she mumbled and headed in my direction. She found me staring blankly into the woks and stirring slowly, having absolutely no idea what went into Chinese food. What WAS all that stuff? I had not even put in a few odds and ends to pick it up. "Are sesame seeds in Chinese food?" I mouthed. A shrug of Linda's shoulders said she did not know either, and a hot flash shot through my body. We could hear Lola on the porch.

"The last time I accidentally ate sesame seeds, I wound up in the hospital soaking in a tub all night long. I thought I was going to die." Linda and I stared at each other. My mouth was suddenly dry, and my heart rate doubled. Four woks of interesting-looking food continued to cook in front of us.

Now Jerry's feet landed on the porch floor. "They may need me in the kitchen," he announced, leaving Charles to carry the conversational ball. Within seconds, Jerry was talking on the telephone in muffled tones to someone at the Chinese restaurant who spoke very little English. "No, NOT Szechuan. SESAME seeds! Not number THREE. SEEDS! Do you put SESAME SEEDS in any of your dishes?" He soon gave up.

Then a strange, unexplainable thing happened. Linda, who does not care that her stove door will not open because of the way the kitchen cabinets were built, suddenly proclaimed there were no sesame seeds in Chinese food. Linda! One of the few people in North

Carolina who may cook "worster" than I. And to show how flustered I was by that point, I believed her!

Soon six people sat down for dinner, four of them rather hesitantly. (Charles had been equally concerned, although he could not leave his conversation assignment on the porch. Someone had to talk to Lola and Hank.) The visiting couple raved over the lovely dinner with the varied assortment of difficult-to-cook Chinese dishes. They were amazed at my culinary skills. And with every forkful Lola ate, Linda, Charles, Jerry and I inhaled mid-sentence or mid-bite to stare in her direction. With her every swallow, we exhaled, feeling a little safer that her throat had not bloated and swollen shut. Straws lay in nearby drawers, just in case.

When dinner was over, we moved to the game room where Lola and Hank thought we talked for three hours about the speaking profession. Incorrect. For three hours, we watched Lola's every move with eagle eyes. If she shifted her weight, we leaned with her. When she bent down and scratched her ankle, Charles almost fell out of his chair. If she had rubbed her neck, one of us would have called 911 while the others shoved straws down her throat.

In hindsight, it was almost a nice evening. The conversation was interesting and Lola and Hank turned out to be delightful people who are now good friends. But I was worn to a frazzle from the stress of waiting and watching for Lola to bloat.

That is why I was limp when we closed the front door and Lola and Hank went on their merry way. And it was THEN that Jerry turned his ashen face toward me and said, "They were really nice, but . . . it was not the couple I thought it was. I had never seen them before tonight."

Eat Your Heart Out!

Briscoe Darling: Oh, we're knowed as a family of hearty-eatin' men and beautiful delicate women.

- Episode #96, "Briscoe Declares for Aunt Bee"

I am certainly not kin to the musical Darling family on *TAGS*, but maybe they would let me sit around as the standby ukulele player. Of course, the way I play the ukulele, all my songs would make them cry. While my musical abilities might not qualify me as a "Darling" I am sure not "delicate." A fellow in Florida might say I fit into the family as a "hearty-eatin' woman."

The vice-president of the hospital where I was to speak met my plane in Pensacola, FL. He was not in charge of the event but made a special trip to the airport just to welcome me to town because we were at Auburn at the same time. He thought it was the hospitable thing to do. I felt like he was serving way above and beyond the call of duty, but I appreciated it.

I did not remember him, but when he said he was one of the guys who worked in the women's dining hall, the scenario rang a bell. "Oh, sure, I do remember y'all," I told him truthfully. "Y'all always seemed to have such a good time."

He replied, "We did, and I certainly remember you too, Jeanne. In the four years I worked in the dining hall, I do not believe you ever missed a meal."

It's a Surprise!

Ernest T. Bass: Surprise, surprise! I can see it in your eyes.

- Episode #113, "My Fair Ernest T. Bass"

Some birthdays are just more "special" than others, and on these occasions, the gift-giver has to figure on going a little strong. Of course, like Aunt Bee in "The Bed Jacket," some people profess they will be upset if others do anything foolish about their birthday because birthdays are for children. In reality . . . .

"What time are you coming over here with my present?" My sister Katherine's question over the telephone early one afternoon jolted my system. It was her birthday! HER FIFTIETH BIRTHDAY! And I had forgotten it. Nothing to do but try to "cover."

"Oh, Katherine, I have been meaning to call but did not get back until late. I want to take you out to dinner tonight."

She was excited, but the thrill disappeared quickly when she learned "out to dinner" meant accompanying me to a banquet speech for the local Habitat for Humanity. Her exact, deliberate response expressed her sentiments. "Drive to Hollywood, California, with a two-year-old? Maybe. Walk across a bed of pure iron nails? Perhaps. But listen to you give another speech down at the church on my fiftieth birthday? It'll be a cold day in August. What time are you coming over here with my present?"

"I was on my way when you called," I lied. "Be there soon."

I panicked. This gift had to be special. Maybe a stainless-steel watch? No, too late to have "50" engraved on the back. My idea bank was empty. I knew our younger sister Andrea had probably sent the ultimate, never-to-be-forgotten gift from Portland, OR a week earlier. If I did not come up with something pronto, I knew I was in for what Barney called "the big freeze." Maybe I should go wander around in the mall until the right gift appeared in a window. Nope, not enough time. Then it hit me. Why hadn't I thought of it earlier? I would give Katherine a piece of her good china. Not a jump-up-and-down-about-it gift, but it WAS something she could use and would not buy for herself. At that point, it was the lone idea in a vacant sea where my ship was sinking with every tick of the clock. I did not even have to leave the house. We have the same china pattern. I would give her one of my plates.

Sisters having the identical china pattern was Mother's idea. She figured we could borrow from each other when we had pure gala events like sit-down dinners for twenty-four. Mother did not dream that twenty-four people eating at my house would be balancing paper plates. Mother also strongly suggested white china. I believe her point was that with white china we would be able to change the color of our tablecloths, napkins, and candles for entirely new effects. She was "Old South." Thought we would have tablecloths and napkins stacked according to color. Ha! We do not even own any "gracious-living" candles. The last time we used candles was during a bad storm.

I headed into the dining room to find a plate that was not chipped. When I pulled out one, my conscience immediately started bothering me. This gift was for my sister. MY SISTER! It was her fiftieth birthday, a benchmark in any woman's life. Nooooo. A dinner plate in her good china was not enough. I'D GIVE HER MY BIG SERVING PLATTER! Megabucks. It had to be worth a hundred and fifty dollars. Guaranteed to beat the Portland sister's gift.

I pulled out the platter and raked the dust off with my arm, shoved it into a grocery sack, and slapped a stick-on Christmas bow on top. And off to Graham I went.

Katherine likes presents, and her eyes lit up when I walked in with the big brown sack. "For me," she said, in faked surprise. The platter was a good decision. A plate definitely would not have been enough. Like Aunt Bee when she received her bed jacket, Katherine would have a birthday she would never forget.

We sat down together on her sofa, and she tore into the sack. "Be careful," I said. "It will break."

"Ohhhhhhh," she teased. "Breakable? Well, what COULD it be?"

Within seconds, Katherine lifted the newspaper to reveal the gorgeous, 11" by 14" white serving platter. Her hands stopped moving as she stared downward, obviously shocked at the enormity of the gift. Seconds later, she slowly turned her head upward and our eyes met. She stared, speechless. I smiled, thinking she was overcome. It was a touching sisterly moment. (Was this that "bonding" everyone was talking about?) She looked back down at the gift, and when a few more seconds passed, she again lifted her head in my direction. This time her eyes were squinting at me and her brow was wrinkled as though she were trying to remember something. For the first time, I had an inkling that maybe this was not a good idea.

Suddenly, Katherine flipped the platter over and pointed to a small piece of masking tape on the back. "Look at that name. This is MY platter! I LENT IT TO YOU LAST CHRISTMAS!"

It was all Mother's fault.

The Ayes Have It!

Andy: I just happened to notice that you like for things to stay the same.

Barney: Well, lots of people are like that. I just happen to be one of them, that's all. I like things to just, well, stay the way they are, and if something happens to change it, well, it upsets me.

                                        - **Episode #14, "The Horse Trader"**

Warren is hired as a deputy by Sheriff Andrew Taylor, and being Floyd's nephew has nothing to do with it. Nothing. Huh? Nothing. Huh? Nothing. Huh? Huh? Huh? He goes by the book, especially in "The Bazaar," when he arrests the entire Ladies Auxiliary for conducting gambling at their annual charity event. He just closes down their bingo game, and hauls them to the courthouse in the back of Goober's red truck, Aunt Bee included.

This leads Andy to tell Warren about the Mayberry Rules For a Long Happy Life. There are just three. "Don't play leapfrog with elephants. Don't pet a tiger unless its tail is wagging. And NEVER, EVER mess with the Ladies Auxiliary." The same thing might go for the Graham Book Club.

How is it said? You can please some of the people all of the time. And you can please all of the people some of the time. But the Graham Book Club? That may be another story.

There is no question about it, you go. When a woman grows up in a small town, and the members of the local Book Club ask her to "do us a little program," the only question is, "When?"

The year I was President of the National Speakers Association I was up to my ears in work. I had responsibilities that accompany the presidency of a national association in addition to my regular speaking schedule. I had writing deadlines. It was Beaver's senior year in high school. I was a busy bee. Busy, busy, busy. Andy would have said, "busier than a cow's tail in fly season." And THAT was the year the Graham Book Club requested a "little program."

My mother had been a charter member of the club when it formed in the fifties. She had passed away, but the membership had not changed much. They heard I had a book coming out and asked if I could drop by one afternoon and "do one of your little programs." One does not turn down an invitation such as that, not if she plans to continue living in the area.

The club had twenty-four members, each of whom bought a book every two years. They met monthly to swap books through a complicated exchange system monitored by extensive charts with a conglomeration of lines on them. It was worth the afternoon to watch the process: high-tech on poster boards. The government should run a tenth as well.

After coffee and cake, and the mandatory discussion of the cake recipe, a reminder was made to "puhhh leaase" make sure to send the books to the meetings if they could not attend. "That's how we lose books," the presiding officer chided, "and we lose several a year. As a matter of fact, ladies, *Annie Laurie* has still not been found, and we continue to look for her."

I leaned over and whispered to Sara Mitchell, the member who had invited me to come, "If someone loses a book, is she responsible for replacing it?"

"Oh, yes," she assured me. "In all these years, though, no one in the club has ever admitted to losing a book."

The treasurer rose to give her report. "We have six dollars." Rolling her eyes in my direction she added, "Of course, we usually do not have a treasurer's report, but we want our speaker to know we do not have any money, so she won't expect a fee."

But the highlight of the afternoon for me came with the reading of the minutes.

When Sara had invited me, she had suggested a specific Wednesday afternoon in October, a hectic time for professional speakers. I would be home only a few days that month. I begged off, but then discovered I was booked to speak in Winston-Salem the morning of the day she wanted. I would have to do some fancy driving, but I could make it back to Graham by early afternoon.

The timing was so close that I asked Sara if the Book Club could meet at 2:00 p.m. rather than 1:30 p.m., which would assure me of being on time as well as making my flight later that day. It did not seem like an unusual request for someone who was doing a "little favor" by giving a "little program," but Sara hedged. She would have to let me know after the September meeting. The members did not like to ever change the time. It threw off other appointments. They would have to vote on it. I understood. Book club ladies like to vote on changes, and some people just like for things to stay the way they are.

After the September meeting, Sara called to report that the time had been changed. For this ONE TIME, the meeting would begin at 2:00 p.m.

Therefore, it was interesting a month later to sit with the twenty-four women in a circle around the hostess's living room and hear the reading of the minutes. The secretary said, "It was moved and seconded that the meeting time be shifted thirty minutes later for our October meeting to accommodate the speaker for that day. The motion passed, 21 to 3."

I looked around the room and wondered . . . who?

Pen Pride

Andy, proudly to Helen's publisher:
> She wrote every word of it herself.
>> - **Episode #213, "Helen, the Authoress"**

Until he thinks he is relegated to a second-fiddle role, Andy is extremely proud of Helen for writing *Amusing Tales of Tiny Tots*. I know this makes her feel good. Right, wrong, or southern, I agonize over every word in my books also. Therefore, I know how pleased Helen Crump is when her publisher says, "I just can't begin to compliment you enough on your book." Jeanne Robertson is no Helane Alexian Dubois, but love me, please love my books.[13]

Do you want to give me tips on how to dress? No problem. Suggestions on a new way to cut my hair? Hey, I am receptive. Criticisms about my child? Whoa. You have just gone too far. And to an author, a book is like a child. We conceive it, carry it, deliver it, and love it. We never get it just like we want it, but generally, we are proud when it goes out into the world on its own. Like our children, sometimes we get so wrapped up in our creations that we often forget they are not quite as important to others.

A client bought copies of my book, *HUMOR: The Magic of Genie*, to give as favors at a spouses' brunch.[14] After I spoke, people lined up to get their gifts autographed. I was "tickled pink."

Many of them asked where I got my speech material, and as I signed books, I explained that the humorous material finds me. I just keep my ears and eyes open so I will notice it when it comes by.

Seconds later, a woman stepped up to shake hands and commented that she had enjoyed the program. "Oh, you don't have a book," I said,

---

13 Helaine Alexian DuBois is the pen name Harold Mosby suggests for Helen.

14 *Humor: the Magic of Genie* was the original title of Jeanne's book. It has been reissued as *Humor: the Magic of Jeanne.*

noticing that she was empty-handed. "The association has them for you as a gift."

"No, that's OK," she responded. "I am in the process of moving, and that is EXACTLY the kind of JUNK I am throwing out."

Spring Chickens

Emma Watson: I'm going downhill fast, and you're the one that pushed me.

- Episode #6, "Ellie Comes to Town"

In "Aunt Bee's Medicine Man," a sideshow guy named Col. Harvey comes through Mayberry looking for the tired and rundown. He wants the undivided attention of those who have to drag themselves out of bed in the morning. His solution to their problem is a tonic—"an elixir to purge the body and lift the spirits." He urges those who want to put a light in their eyes and a spring in their steps to fork over the price: only one dollar a bottle. And he inquires, "Breathes there a man with soul so dead that he can say he is not interested?"

I am right in there with Aunt Bee when she shouts, "I'll take two!" Oh, Aunt Bee, Aunt Bee, I know how you feel. I do not want to hear the doctor say it either, but just between us, we are not spring chickens anymore. I do not know how old you are supposed to be when you buy the magic elixir in this episode and get so tipsy singing "Toot Toot Tootsie" that you almost twirl off the piano stool as I recall. (I believe you say it was the greatest experience of your life "since being baptized.") But your age is none of my business. I do know about my age, of course. Time is jumping right along on me. I am past fifty years old. At this point, I lie in the bed at night and HEAR myself wrinkling.

It wakes me up. The wrinkling comes in loud and clear because it is happening so near my ears. Sounds like a door squeaking open all night long. Creak. CReeeAK. CaREEEEEEak! One night my husband sat right up in the bed and whispered, "The house is settling . . . or is that you wrinkling again?" He is so funny. (He ought to go on the radio.)

If there were some sort of miracle salve for the wrinkling, I would purchase it, but crow's-feet are not my only problem. At this stage in my life, it also seems that a bit of that zest and vigor is disappearing. Some days, I seem to have the "twinges and cricks." Oh, why am I beating around the bush? The truth is, I am falling apart section by section.

For example, my "twenty-twenty eyes" have left me. I can still feel the telephone book in my hand, but I cannot read anything in it. I went to my eye doctor about the situation, and she said I needed something to help me read. I figured it was bifocal time. No, she suggested that I wear one—only one—contact lens. A reading lens. That was fine with me, but I had always thought if I ever wore contact lenses, I would like blue ones. There was something about that one blue eye . . . . So, I got the one blue contact and went home to learn how to put it in.

Soon after that, I went to my dentist, and he informed me that I was grinding my teeth. This was a relief! I thought I was wrinkling, but teeth grinding explained it all. So THAT was the noise we heard every night. It was not my skin crinkling up after all. I mentioned all this to the dentist, and I noticed an odd look on his face as he and his assistant cut their eyes toward each other. (Yet another local establishment where they shake their heads when I pass by.) He assured me that grinding my teeth should not wake up the household and insisted I be fitted for a plastic mouthpiece to wear at night. They took a mold and told me to come back the next time I was in town.

As long as I am 'fessing up, you might as well know that it was right along there that I got a dose of what Floyd calls "the barber's claw." My right hand was hurting and had swollen up to twice its size. I looked like the "crab monster" and I knew why. Jerry and I were learning to sign for the hearing impaired which meant working my right hand to the limit. Added to that, I was working at the computer, practicing a new song on the ukulele, and autographing books. Yep, I began to look like a big lobster carrying around one enormous, oversized claw.

That was not all. One of my shoulders was killing me too. Weeks earlier I had lifted my hand to show my buddy Linda how puffy it was, and she had called to my attention that skin was beginning to hang loosely below my upper arm. Her exact words were, "My gosh! There's something hanging from your arm!" Well, what are friends for? She had suggested putting tiny barbells next to the telephone and doing repetitions any time I was talking. I did that. Within two weeks I had bursitis—also known in some circles as "versitas"—in my left shoulder. Of course, I could have gotten it from sleeping with the window open. Or maybe it was sciatica or neuralgia? If either of those were the case, I would have to buy a dime's worth of sugar pills and get the heating pad fixed because that stuff really hangs on. I was just glad I do not have to suffer the way some people do. Specifically, I could not put my left hand over my head. Because our canned goods are on a high shelf, this kept me from cooking. So, we were not eating. Even though I was able to lift my right arm over my head, I could not pick up a can with my claw hand. I could easily live with the non-cooking, but I was beginning to have trouble lifting my carry-on luggage into the overhead bin. A trip to another doctor was in order. Specialized medicine.

The next time I whipped through town, I went to the doctor that handles these sorts of things and said, "Squirt something in my hand and shoulder and make me feel forty-eight." He said that he could not do that, but he gave me a prescription and said, "I want you to sleep in a glove."

"A glove?" I repeated slowly, trying to take all this in. "Just . . . a glove?" It seemed slightly peculiar to me, and I told him so. "My husband is 57 years old. He won't know what to think if I get in the bed and all I have on is a glove. It seems like I might get cold and Jerry might have a heart attack." I have always supposed a sense of humor has its place in medicine, but apparently, the doctor never found sickness to be a funny subject. He said I knew what he meant—just keep my shoulder and hand warm at night. He gave me a prescription, and I left. On the way home, I swung by the dentist and picked up my plastic mouthpiece.

That night I greased my body up with lotion and got in the bed. This takes a while because, at my age, my skin acts like a vacuum cleaner sucking it in. Whooooosh! Twice I slipped out onto the floor but finally climbed back in the bed and got myself perched in front of the pillows. I had one of my mother's little white church gloves on my right hand. On my left arm from the hand up, was a pillowcase that eventually was pinned to my nightgown at the shoulder. Last but not least, I popped in my plastic mouthpiece. And I waited on him. In a few minutes, Jerry came in, and I turned my blue eye right at him.

You would think a man would say something in a situation like this, but he just turned out the light and pulled the covers up over his head. But in a few seconds, I heard him say in the dark, "Why are you trying to scare me?"

He made sure to tell all his golfing buddies about this, and one of them told me about an acquaintance in Wilson, North Carolina, who was approaching her fiftieth birthday. Her husband had made all the usual comments in jest about never thinking he would sleep with such an old woman. He was a shriveled-up old prune himself, but that was beside the point. This lady planned ahead and bought one of those Halloween rubber masks that fit over the entire head. Past presidents are particularly popular, but she figured waking up with Jimmy Carter or Richard Nixon lying next to him might be too much. She settled for a mask of a very old, ugly woman about a hundred and seventeen years old. It was so ugly, a person could wear it and trick or treat on the telephone. Barney would call it a real "Beasto Maristo."

The morning of her big day, she awoke earlier than her husband and reached under her pillow where she had hidden the mask all night. She pulled it over her head and curled back under the covers, head out of sight. And SHE waited.

A few minutes later he woke up and leaned over for the usual "Happy Birthday, Honey." When she turned that ugly, wrinkled face in his direction to return his kiss, he jumped back so fast that he slipped out onto the floor!

Now THAT is what can truly be called scaring your husband!

***

OK, it is time to slow down a few minutes and let the truck cool off while we get our bearings. We might want to have a piece of apple pie or sit quietly for a few minutes wherever our personal "front porches" are located. Maybe we will hear crickets or a dog howling in the distance.

In this section, I have offered evidence that Mayberry-type humor can still be found today, and a good place to start looking is in the mirror. You have even taken a peek in mine. We are indeed funny creatures who do humorous things, and humorous things are done to us. In both instances, we need to laugh at ourselves.

But it is time to expand our search a little, and the next place to look for current examples of nearby Mayberry humor is in our families. Let's go! Up on the truck one more time!

In Our Families

Aunt Bee: They're just here for a weekend.

Andy:　　　Yeah, I guess we can stand our loved ones that long.

- Episode #129, "Family Visit"

The citizens of Mayberry have a few kin sprinkled here and there who are sources of pride and embarrassment. Don't we all? We meet them when they pass through town as subjects of an episode and thus become forever etched in our memories: people like Otis's brother, Ralph; Aunt Bee's cousin, Bradford J. Taylor; and Thelma Lou's cousin, Karen Moore, a perfect female from Arkansas.

After meeting some of these characters, we might be reassured that as far as family is concerned, "they" are not always like "us." Barney puts it well in "Cousin Virgil": "You know, it's a funny thing. Now here's Virgil and me from the same family, and yet look at the difference. There's Virgil—clumsy, awkward, and uncoordinated. And here's me, if I do say so myself, completely coordinated. Keen. Sharp. Alert."

Usually, these extended family members are unlike the main Mayberry characters, but they serve to illustrate what we all should know: every family is made up of a wide variety of personalities who do all sorts of things, good and bad. And when it comes to relatives, we will do well to do as they do in Mayberry. Love the members of our family, accept them as they are, and hope for the same in return. And for heaven's sake, keep a sense of humor.

Although we are introduced to a variety of out-of-town Mayberry family members, more often we meet relatives only through the casual conversations of the main characters, an element that contributes greatly to the realism of the show. They sit around and talk about family like the rest of us do. Sometimes they relate a long family story. Other times they just drop in a sentence that lets us know the role family plays in their lives. Casually, oh so casually, the importance of extended family is made evident. Andy mentions once going to Asheville, and Aunt Bee interjects that it was when his cousin became a Mason.[15] Helen tells Andy that the University of North Carolina is a state college and less expensive than a private school, and Andy is relieved because Opie can stay at Aunt Martha's. Floyd looks at his nephew Warren and sees the image of his sister. Warren has the same high forehead and pointed nose. Family is so much a part of the lives of Mayberry citizens, that even though we do not meet all the cousins, in-laws, uncles or sisters face to face, we know them.

There is a whole lot of serious, deep-meaning stuff that could be written about the role of family *on TAGS*. Edith Gibson, the character with a doctorate in psychology who appears in "A Girl for Goober," could probably write a thick book about it and come up with a theory on the Taylors being one of today's "dysfunctional families": a single father with a son, old maid aunt living with them, and bachelor deputy hanging around the house so much. Dr. Gibson would make the talk show rounds because there is no doubt about it, the family is quite a complex matter. But even if it were a thick book, I would not buy it. It might take three weeks to read, and I agree with Goober on this. I like thin books.

Mayberry Humor Across the USA is certainly not a fat book or a study of the complexities of the family.

We are looking for humor here, folks! This physical education major sure could not write anything like that. If I did, I could not answer the talk show questions. "Tell us, Jeanne, did the town of Mayberry serve

---

15 Freemasons are members of a fraternity of men dedicated to charity work.

as the surrogate family on *The Andy Griffith Show*?" "Mrs. Robertson, wouldn't it have been better for Opie to sleep on the ironing board rather than in the SAME BED with his out-of-town cousins Roger and Bruce?" "As a North Carolinian, do you agree that Sheriff Andrew Taylor and Deputy Bernard P. Fife should be indicted for misuse of government property in the matter of dating in the official squad car?"

I do not understand this type of talk show hype, and I do not want to. And how dare anyone ask questions like that about *The Andy Griffith Show*! Of all the unmitigated gall!

WHAT I DO KNOW IS . . . that when I hear all the references to family on the episodes, I laugh because they remind me of similar conversations or incidents in my family. Here again, the creative team did a superb job. Mayberry families—immediate or extended—reflect our families; and, in turn, they pass along family information and anecdotes from generation to generation. I burst out laughing when in "Helen's Past" Aunt Bee recalls, "I was standing next to my mother in the kitchen, and she told me that one of my great-uncles used to rustle cattle." Well, Aunt Bee, I have always figured that if a family did not have at least one cattle rustler back in there somewhere, it was simply because they did not live near cows.

Opie wants to know in "Family Visit" why his Uncle Todd never comes to America, and Aunt Bee shushes Andy when he starts to explain. (It has to do with a girl in Cleveland.) In "The Battle of Mayberry," it is a great shock when Mayberrians discover that their revered ancestors were not battle heroes, but a bunch of fellows scared to tell their wives they chose to drink rather than fight. It reminds me of the pride my family had in discovering an ancestor's Civil War diary until we realized that he was a Yankee soldier! A Yankee soldier? In OUR family? Well, we were still proud of the old book, until further reading led to the discovery of not only troop activity, but also visits to "fancy ladies" at night. (Either of these revelations was enough to make us want to . . . blush.)

Our friends in Mayberry keep their families alive by handing down stories about them, stories that are not farfetched when we think of our own relatives. In "A Plaque for Mayberry," Barney is convinced he is a descendant of Duncan Phyfe, the one who was "a carpenter or something."[16] It does not bother Deputy Fife that the last names are spelled differently because "sooner or later, somebody had to spell it right."

My grandmother was one of eleven children in a family named "Flinn." They all grew up in the same area around Luverne, Alabama. Somewhere along the way, several of them became concerned that the spelling of their name was confusing. They called a family meeting, and a number of the siblings decided to change the spelling to the more conventional "Flynn." Others held their ground. Surely it was a pleasant, happy, little family discussion. (I would have loved to have been a wall in THAT room.) The result was that those first cousins who did not spell their last names the same way we did were sitting in classrooms together, and brothers and sisters no longer appeared to be kin to one another. It took the word "confusion" to new unprecedented levels. (note: My grandmother not only stuck with the original spelling but held her head even higher when Mother and Daddy named me Jeanne Flinn, with an i. So there!)

Yep, watching the characters on *TAGS* only serves as a reminder that in the search for Mayberry humor, once we have laughed at ourselves, another very good place to look is within our families. So here goes . . . .

---

16 Duncan Phyfe (1768 –1854) was one of nineteenth-century America's leading furniture makers.

Not a Leg to Stand On

Mr. Brian Jackson, who sculptured ninety percent of the Mayberry
        headstones and a statue of Seth Taylor: You and your kin-
        folk must be very proud.[17]

- **Episode #208, "The Statue"**

When Opie needs to write an essay in "Opie's Most Unforgettable
Character," Andy tries to help him by sharing a few of his unforgettable experiences—like the time he caught a wildcat barehanded.
But Aunt Bee says the cat was sick and just put his head on Andy's
shoulder and went to sleep. Well, how about the time he pitched a
no-hit game with his wobble ball? Goober remembers that one. They
still lost because Andy walked seventeen men. It is in all the record
books. Sometimes, however, we do get away with stretching a story.
Meet Grandma Freddie . . . .

"You got your speaking ability from your Grandmother Freddie."
Matriarch after matriarch made this comment to me after a speech
at Auburn University in celebration of 100 years of women at the
school. I had often been told by those who knew her that I inherited
my grandmother's "showmanship"—a nice word for "enjoying being
the center of attention"—but her speaking ability?

No, this was the first time I had heard it put that way, and I had
spoken in Auburn dozens of times. Of course, people in their nineties—the ones who would have known my grandmother—were not
usually in Chamber of Commerce or Touchdown Club audiences, but
they packed in for a centennial celebration. Their comments interested me, and that afternoon I asked my Aunt Carolyn about them. I
found her in her kitchen preparing Chicken Divan.

"Oh yes, honey, your Grandma Freddie was quite a speaker," she
drawled, moving dishes around on the counter. "Not like you. She was

---

17 The local civic improvement committee decides that Mayberry should com-
memorate one of its illustrious citizens by erecting a statue. They only discover later
that Seth Taylor was a swindler and a fraud.

not a professional. She didn't make a living at it, but for her era, she was something else."

Fascinating. I remembered my grandmother very well. She lived until I was in my thirties, but no one ever told me she gave speeches. She told me she traveled around the country during "thuh war" (as in World War I) and entertained the troops by playing the harp. Even showed me her pictures, and once tried to get me to take harp lessons. I am glad I did not. The harp will not fit in an overhead bin of an airplane.

I also knew that Grandma Freddie's mother had been president of the Alabama Women's Christian Temperance Union and had spoken out loudly against the evils of the dreaded demon alcohol. It was usually mentioned around the punch bowl at family weddings, which we consider special occasions and thereby suitable for social nipping. "If your great-grandmother (giggle, giggle, giggle) had lived to see this. . . . I will have a little more of that supreme punch (giggle, giggle, giggle)." But Grandma Freddie giving speeches? This was news. Funny the things you don't know.

"Oh yes," Aunt Carolyn continued. "She went all over Auburn giving little programs at churches and civic clubs and when she was president of the Alabama Methodist Women, she spoke all over the state. I guess when her friends heard you speak at the centennial, it reminded them. I am surprised you did not know this."

Perhaps I had heard this when I was younger, back when I did not care about such things as much. Time changes that. I wanted to know more. "What did she speak about?"

"Various topics. She was just a good speaker and was willing to put together programs. She did not have videos and brochures like speakers today, but I guess she had that 'word-of mouth' you are always talking about. Word just spread and she received invitations." As Aunt Carolyn placed pieces of chicken on top of broccoli, she continued nonchalantly, "You know, Jeanne, there's always a need for a good program."

She was telling ME this! A professional speaker? If there were not always a need for a good program, my friends and I in the National

Speakers Association might be selling vacuum cleaners or aluminum siding, or managing laundromats.

But back to Grandma Freddie. I wanted to know the rest of the story. Aunt Carolyn was willing to tell me.

"Grandma Freddie's last little program - and maybe her best- was on her trip to the Holy Land. It was better than the others because she had slides. She would show a slide and tell a story about something that happened in that location. Her first program was for the Auburn Methodist Women. Then she spoke to the Baptists, and the Catholics, and eventually went to the civic clubs."

The chicken dish in the oven, we sat down with coffee at that point. I was trying to take all of this in. At my age, it was interesting to hear new information about my grandmother. I wished that I could have talked to Grandma Freddie and learned more. Wished I had taken the time when I could have. What an amazing woman. Probably a feminist and did not know the word. The discussion continued, and finally, I said, "I'm sure the family was VERY proud of her?"

Aunt Carolyn thought back, "Yes," she nodded pensively. "Yes, the family was very proud of her. Of course, the family would have been so much more proud . . . if she had actually ever BEEN to the Holy Land."

"Aunt Carolyn!" I exclaimed. "Grandma Freddie went all over town giving programs on her trip to the Holy Land, and she NEVER HAD BEEN to the Holy Land?" (Grandma Freddie, say it isn't so!)

"Well, she went on a trip," Aunt Carolyn explained. "I know she went on a trip because I booked the tickets, but she did not go to the Holy Land. She never got that far. She went down the Rhine, but she thought it was the Nile. When she came back to Auburn, however, she had a box of slides on the area that she purchased along the way, and that was that. She had a program on her trip to the Holy Land."

"I cannot believe she did that!"

"Well, you, OF ALL PEOPLE, should know how it happened," Aunt Carolyn replied, raising her eyebrows and cutting her eyes in my direction. Stretch a story? Me? Could she have me confused with someone else in the family? Perhaps cousin Mac. He spins some pretty wild tales.

Aunt Carolyn continued. "At first Grandma Freddie pointed to the slides and said, 'This is the such and such.' Then, somewhere between the Baptists and the Catholics, she started saying, 'When I was here. . . .'"

I loved it. It was that "showmanship" rearing its head again. I had one more question. "Oh, Aunt Carolyn, what if people in Auburn had found out?"

"Oh, honey," my aunt drawled. "Everybody knew. But in a town this size, it just didn't matter. There is always a need for a good program, and Grandma Freddie DID HAVE the slides."

Beep! Beep!

Floyd: Oh, but that traffic jam. Yeah. Oh, that was a big one.
                    - Episode #137, "Goodbye, Sheriff Taylor"

They never thought they would see him owning wheels, but in "Hot Rod Otis," the lovable town drunk buys himself a car. This is terrible! Right away Barney figures they are in a disaster area. He cannot stop Otis from driving, but he sure can make him take a driver's test. On the floor with little toy cars and make-believe streets, the arguing twosome never gets further than pulling up at the same imaginary intersection. That is when Otis proclaims, "But we didn't come up at the very same time. I got there first!" This will slow down traffic.

Traffic did more than slow down with Grandma Freddie during an all-day shopping trip to Montgomery. This is remembered as the day she single-handedly brought the state capital to a halt. This happens when someone gets discombobulated dead center in the middle of Five Points, one of the busiest intersections in the state.

The other Auburn ladies in the car retold the incident for years. Exactly in the center of the intersection, they stared helplessly out the windows at motorists in various stages of anger or amusement. Some blew their horns while others smiled and shook their heads. A couple waved. The Auburn ladies, with predictable southern charm, waved back. They were from a friendly town, and it was the friendly thing to do.

If the intersection had been a dartboard, Grandma Freddie's car would have been positioned as a direct hit, but it would not have been the only missile on the target. If that had been the case, she could have steered her vehicle backwards and gotten out of the trouble. No, a bevy of other drivers had followed her, attempting to make the turn through the long light. When Grandma Freddie stopped suddenly, they maneuvered quickly to avoid crashes. From other lanes, with the right of way to turn in an opposite direction, people had also pulled into the flow, only to stop. They veered left and right into mass confusion. The only thing that could have made it worse was snow, which always causes southerners to drive their cars amuck.

The situation, already dangerously close to pandemonium, grew more complicated with each horn blast. Grandma Freddie frantically shifted the gears back and forth, only going inches in an array of directions. Like Aunt Bee when she learned to drive, instead of going up and down and over, she was going down, up, over, and then . . . . Well, it is a clear picture. Her gray hair bounced back and forth as she surveyed the dashboard for an answer and struggled to hold back unladylike, non-Methodist phrases.

Just when all appeared hopeless, a policeman walked through the backed-up traffic, took one look at the scene, and made a beeline for the group from Auburn. It was not a crime wave, but he had a situation on his hands. The ladies were not shouting like Aunt Bee and her protesting friends do in "Aunt Bee the Crusader." "We will NOT move! We will NOT move!" The Auburn ladies COULD NOT move. When the officer was just a few feet away, Grandma Freddie flung open her door and slid to the center of the front seat. "It is ABOUT TIME you got here, young man," she scolded. "Do your job! Get in here and get us out of this mess!" (Naughty Deputy!)

After I shared this story with an audience in Montgomery years later, a man approached me after the program to ask Grandma Freddie's last name. "Lipscomb," I told him. "Did you know her?"

He shook his head. "No, but I believe I was in her traffic jam."

Don't Look Back

Andy: You know I don't think that's a friendly wave. I think he wants us.

                                    - **Episode #117, "The Shoplifters"**

Judd Fletcher, one of Mayberry's solder citizens, is offended when Andy releases him from jail after one of Barney's overzealous charges in "Andy Saves Barney's Morale." He storms back to the courthouse to turn himself in. "Just because I'm old don't mean I don't know my rights!" Yessiree. Judd makes it clear, "Seventy-four or no, I can still disturb the peace with the best of them!" Grandma Freddie could do that too.

It is the kind of true story that spreads around a small town quicker than butter on hot hominy grits. (As if the traffic jam in the Montgomery story had not traveled fast enough.) In her later years, my Grandma Freddie drove the wrong way down Tichenor Avenue in Auburn. It was a new one-way street in the small college town. She noticed that people waved and blew their horns, but since she knew everybody in Auburn, she smiled and nodded in return. She was lucky she did not have a heck of a wreck.

When she got home and thought about it, Grandma Freddie realized she had gone the wrong way on a one-way street. She did the only thing her conscience would let her do. She got back into her car, went down to the Auburn police station, and turned herself in. The sergeant had time for her.

At the family drugstore later, she told her son what happened. Standing proudly with her good name restored, she recounted the experience, but a hint of agitation also surfaced. "I told the first policeman what I had done. That was hard enough. Then he started laughing and called in the other policemen and the clerical help, and I had to tell the WHOLE THING over again."

With a sigh of relief, she added, "But son, they were very nice. The sergeant said, 'Don't worry, Miss Freddie. It doesn't count if we don't see you.'"

A Cultured Gentleman

Jennifer Morrison: Don't think we're old-fashioned, Sheriff. We
　　　　believe a body has a right to a nip now and then.
Clarabelle Morrison: But it should always be for an occasion, is what
　　　　we think.

- Episode #17, "Alcohol and Old Lace"

Mayberry folks do not cuss much, at least not when cameras, ladies, children, or ministers are around. In several episodes, they seem about to let an expletive fly, but hold back. We get the message. In "Howard the Bowler" Aunt Bee suggests the pastor as a fill-in on the bowling team, but Andy nixes the idea because, "You know sometimes in the heat of the game, we, uh, say, you know, say something." In "The Bazaar," Opie wants to go down to the courthouse with his father when the "prisoners" have been on the telephone for three hours. Andy tells his son, "No, you'd better stay here. I'm not sure I'M old enough to hear what I'm going to say." In "The Lucky Letter" Barney says to Norbett, "I ought to write you a citation for speeding, reckless driving, and failure to observe an officer! What's the matter with you? . . . You'd better go back inside, Opie. You're cramping my language."

My great-grandmother, Cora McAdory, would have been pleased with the way Mayberry citizens watched their language. She was president of the Alabama Women's Christian Temperance Union when Big Jim Folsom was elected governor of the state. Big Jim was something of a character. He served two terms and probably would have been re-elected if he had not gone on TV drunk and without shoes. Apparently, he did not need a special occasion or celebration like National Potato Week or Sir Walter Raleigh Landing Day for an excuse to drink the elixir. Maybe he just had a lot to celebrate.

The WCTU was adamantly opposed to Big Jim's drinking and use of profanity, so they implored their president to talk to him. Mamadie, as I called her, drove to Montgomery with my Aunt Lettie and several other ladies for the appointed rendezvous. According to a reliable source—Aunt Lettie, of course—Mamadie got right down to business as soon as they were ushered into the governor's office.

"I am Cora McAdory, President of the Alabama Women's Christian Temperance Union," she announced with authority. "Our members, as well as I, are quite concerned over the rumors of your drinking, womanizing, and use of bad language."

Governor Folsom immediately slammed his hand down on his desk. "Mrs. McAdory, I'd like to know the name of the sumphab@*#h who told you such a d*@# lie!"

Before Madam President could recover, the governor strode to where she was seated and put his arms tenderly around her shoulders. "Can't you tell by looking at me that I am not the type of man who would do such things?"

She gazed upward and smiled demurely. "Why, yes I can." And THAT is what she reported to the Women's Christian Temperance Union.

Chicken Coop Casanova

Barney: One night Thelma Lou, the next night somebody else. You know, keep 'em guessing.

                              - Episode #67, "Andy's Rich Girlfriend"

Oh, that Barney. He is so "swave." How can Juanita resist ol' Foxy Fife on the telephone in "The Great Filling Station Robbery," when he says, "I just thought I'd be the first to say good morning. Cock-a-doodle-do. No, I just made that up. . . . You want to hear that again? You kinda like that, huh? Cock-a-doodle-do. Cock-a-doodle-do."

Barney is not the only one who makes "interesting" comments during telephone calls.

My sister Katherine is a career woman who recently earned a master's degree in business. The mother of grown children, she is now single and a new participant in the WOD—World Of Dating. Neither of us knows much about the nineties WOD, but through Katherine's research, she has concluded it to be infiltrated with many middle-aged men who border on being, at least mildly, socially dysfunctional.

"Throwbacks," according to Katherine's terminology. She does not see herself in this category, of course, because her situation in life is by her choice. Certainly, she has gone out with some very nice men, definitely "keepers" for some women. And she has been able to see the humor when that was not the case. Take the fellow I will call Clyde.

Katherine met Clyde at a golf tournament, and he asked if he could call her sometime. He was recently divorced, and he emphasized several times that he was not involved in a serious relationship and did not want to be. He would enjoy playing golf with Katherine occasionally. Sure. Why not?

At the next tournament they talked again, and he again emphasized he was not in a relationship, did not want to be, etc. Could he come by her house that night? Sure. That would be fine.

After a pleasant visit, Mr. Not-involved-in-a-serious-relationship-and-not-interested-in-one attempted a major teenage move, and Katherine quickly set him straight. (Gomer would say he got "fresh.") He apologized profusely and left. Later that night, he called to apologize again. He did not know what made him act that way. (At his age, raging hormones are no longer a viable excuse.) Again, he emphasized that he was not in a relationship and did not want to be, just wanted to be friends.

Much later that same night, Katherine's telephone rang again. After she answered with the standard "hello," a voice she recognized as her earlier visitor said slowly, "I—love—you."

"What?"

"I said, I—love—you," came the reply in an attempted sensuous tone.

Katherine said hesitantly, "Clyde?"

Clyde paused, recognizing her voice. "Oh, Katherine, I'm sorry. I must have hit the re-dial button by mistake."

For Those of Us Who Like to Watch It

Andy: Well, a diet is a diet!

- Episode #206, "Dinner at Eight"

Houston's was my sister Andrea's favorite restaurant when she lived in Atlanta.[18] She loved it so much that not only did she insist her visitors eat there, but she also pressured us to select her favorites from the menu. Houston's had the BEST margaritas **in** the world. We HAD to have a certain salad with the unique house dressing. The heaped-high, baked potato was a MUST. The GREATEST dessert we would ever eat was the such-and-such.

Andrea left Atlanta for law school in Portland, Oregon, and as one rotund cousin put it, "She got into that healthy living, West Coast stuff where they eat bean sprouts." Barney might say she was watching the "ol' carbs and glucose." More accurately, she went on a fat-free diet.

Returning to Atlanta for a visit with niece Elizabeth, Andrea was dying to eat at her favorite place. She had stopped drinking, so she ordered lemonade when the others got margaritas. Then a baked potato, plain. Then her favorite salad, but for the first time, she asked the waitress what was in it. Hold the ham and steak strips. No chicken chunks either. Was the cheese low-fat? No? Leave it off. Niece Elizabeth swears that by the time Andrea finished changing the salad, all that they put in front of her was a bed of lettuce, a few carrots, and the special dressing. Andrea pushed the latter aside and brought out a bottle of fat-free stuff from her purse.

---

18 Houston's Restaurant is part of a group of upscale American casual dining restaurants, owned by Hillstone Restaurant Group. They have numerous locations throughout the US.

Elizabeth watched all this, thinking her aunt was perhaps saving room for dessert. No, Andrea was full. No dessert, except for the one spoonful she ate from someone else's plate just to see if it was as good as she remembered. So much for watching the "ol' carbs and glucose."

The crowning comment came on the freeway going home. That was when Andrea sighed and announced casually, "Well, I am glad we went, but I don't think Houston's is as good as it used to be."

Two Sugars

Andy: Awwww, that's nice. A little sugar on the jaw.
- Episode #36, "Barney on the Rebound"

Unable to foresee that one day I would forget her fiftieth birthday, my sister Katherine named one of her children after me. This was smart, very smart. After all, I do not have daughters and my jewelry has to eventually go somewhere. (Don't tell my daughter-in-law.) My niece, "Little Jeanne," as she is referred to by the family, and "Big Jeanne," as I am referred to by people out of earshot, are alike in many ways. She even said to forget the jewelry and send frequent flyer points. But then, she has seen some of the stuff I wear. So has my daughter-in-law who, being a wonderful young woman, did her best to stifle her laughter and said, "Give it to Little Jeanne." (I did have one nice antique pin, but I lost it.)

Niece Jeanne grew up in Graham, North Carolina, and pulled for the local high school Red Devils as I did, and she is southern. Extremely southern. In her first year out of Auburn University (another similarity) she worked for Alpha Gamma Delta Sorority (yet another one) and traveled around the country as a Chapter Consultant. It was a way to eeeeease into the real world after college life.

At an airport in Michigan, she was approached by a man who had been standing behind her at the ticket counter. Would she mind saying a couple of words for him? Small-town, savvy young women often have the knack of sensing when a situation is harmless, and

Jeanne knew this one was. "Well, sure. I'd be happy to. What couple of words do you want me to say?"

"I'll close my eyes and you say, 'Hey sugar.' S-U-G-A-R," the stranger who was her grandfather's age, spelled correctly.

Jeanne knew exactly where he was headed. What he wanted was an h on the end of that word. She put her arm around his shoulder and slowly drawled, "Hey, sug'ah."

The man opened his eyes and sighed. "Ah, that's it. Thank you. I was once stationed in the South, and you just brought back some mighty good memories."

Don't You Repeat That!

Goober: Howard, ever been any comedians in your family?

Howard: No, no, not really, although my Uncle Carl used to come out with some good quips from time to time.

- Episode #216, "Howard, the Comedian"

After a series of small strokes, my Uncle Lan's thinking became confused. Against advice from doctors, Aunt Carolyn was determined to keep him at home in Auburn, Alabama, as long as possible. Fortunately, they both had a sense of humor.

Toward the end of his life, even near-rational statements from Uncle Lan were few and far between. Then just when the family would think he just was not "in there," he would make an astonishing statement or review with great accuracy things that had happened to him during World War II. When this occurred, his children and Aunt Carolyn shook their heads. Somewhere—down in there SOME-WHERE—was the fun-loving and often mischievous man they knew and loved so much.

Several weeks before he had a stroke that was to take his life, Aunt Carolyn took Uncle Lan for a ride around town. Walking was a major accomplishment for him, so car trips were a way to get him out of the house. As they rode through Auburn, Aunt Carolyn mindlessly chitchatted, "Look, Lan, we are riding by the college library. Look, Lan, there is the drugstore. Look, Lan, here we are at a stop sign." But Lan rode along without response.

Then they passed the gigantic lot where the largest Baptist church in Auburn, maybe in the world, was being built. All souls in the community could be saved at the same time in such a colossal building. One subject you can never talk enough about is sin, but this massive project was running a close second. The size of the project was the talk of the small town, at least among the reserved Methodists, Presbyterians, and Episcopalians. After she inspected the sprawling development, Aunt Carolyn turned to her husband. "Look, Lan. There's the new Baptist church. Isn't it huge?"

Uncle Lan slowly turned his head and looked out the window a few seconds then returned to his straight-ahead stare. But this time he felt obliged to comment. Aunt Carolyn drove off the road laughing when he drawled, "Six Flags Over Jesus."

Wonderful Husband Material

Daphne: Well, he may be cheap, but he's sincere.
                    - Episode #68, "Barney Mends a Broken Heart"

Barney Fife is frugal and practical when it came to spending money. This is evident in "Barney's First Car" when he tells of buying a septic tank for his parents. Understandably, Andy questions, "For their anniversary?" Barney explains, "Yeah. Oh, they're really hard to buy for. Besides, it was something they could use. They'll be thrilled. Two tons of concrete, all steel reinforced." Barney is a good son. I may be married to his cousin.

My husband Jerry is my best friend, and there are many of Barney's "ad-jact-tives" that describe him—words such as dependable, honest, funny, quiet, and likable. Floyd could describe Jerry too, just like in "The Case of the Punch in the Nose" when he described Charlie Foley—"a nice person, but he's a cheapskate. Now you know that yourself."

On one of our first dates in 1963, Jerry and I went to what was then named "Jim's Tastee Freeze" in my hometown of Graham. I remember it well because the Tastee Freeze was an order-at-the-window place, which meant I could not walk inside and show off how tall my out-of-town date was. (Out of town? Burlington. Two miles away.) When friends passed my side of the car, I mouthed, "He's TALL!"

Ordering was the most memorable thing about the date and should have been a clue. I got a hamburger with cheese; Jerry did not. "You don't like cheese?" I asked. Oh no, he loved cheese, but the hamburger cost 25¢ and the cheeseburger 35¢. "The ten-cent difference is a 40% increase in price," he explained. "I have never seen a cheeseburger that was 40% better." I was not out with one of the last of the big-time spenders. No siree. When it came to money, Jerry was on the conservative side. Older women would have picked up on something like this instantly, but I was young and falling in love, so this clue went over my head. After that, although we never actually went Dutch treat, we had a number of low-budget evenings.[19]

Lest you think he is some sort of a Scrooge or Ben Weaver, please understand that Jerry will give someone in need the shirt off his back, but he keeps that kind of giving quiet.[20] He says if no one knows, then we are giving for the right reasons. It is times like this that he reminds me, "I am just glad we are in a position to help. AND WE GOT THAT WAY FROM . . . (yep, you've got it) . . . NOT ALWAYS GETTING CHEESE ON OUR HAMBURGERS!" It is symbolic. Quite frankly, sometimes, he and his symbolism and practicality get on my nerves. I identify with Thelma Lou in "Man in the Middle" when she tells Barney, "If you tell me once more that the best things in life are free, I'll scream!"

When it comes to special gift-giving days (birthdays, Christmas, Valentine's Day, wedding anniversaries, etc.), Jerry thinks like Frugal Fife. There is no reason to go overboard because these days happen

---

19 Dutch treat refers to an outing, meal, or other special occasion at which each participant pays for their share of the expenses.

20 Ben Weaver was the owner and proprietor of Weaver's Department Store in Mayberry. He had the reputation of being a stingy miser.

annually. Let's take Christmas, for example. For a long time, Jerry and I had a ten-dollar limit on our gifts to each other. It was a cheapskate game called "Tightwad" that he talked me into playing. I agreed, because I declare, it made him so happy not to spend money. The winner was the person who could sque-e-e-eze the best gift out of ten dollars. There was no prize. One of us just "won" for the year. Wowee.

After several holidays of gifts like pineapple skinners and place-mats (only three so as to stay under the monetary limit), I called a halt to the game. We could afford for him to give me more expensive, personal items, and I told him so. The next year I received a top-of-the-line drip coffee maker. According to Jerry, drinking a cup of coffee is a very personal thing. Nylons are personal too, but I did not want them either. (Sometimes I think we live in the same house, but not on the same street.) I do love him though. YOU KNOW THAT.

It became apparent I needed to select my own gift and openly HINT! My hinting was not as blatant as what we hear about Opie in "Opie and the Carnival." That is when we learn he recently had written an essay titled "What I Would Do If I Had A Tool Chest," and had left it out for Andy to see. Well, for crying out loud, Jerry would have bought me a tool chest, but I WANTED an exercise bike. From exercising in hotel health clubs, I knew I preferred a Schwinn Airdyne—top of the line, creme de la creme, expensive, but that's what I wanted. To avoid any possible error—like getting a kid's used bike from the want ads—I shopped around town and found exactly where the piece of equipment I wanted was located. I wrote down the place and the price, and when Jerry saw the amount, he immediately changed his opinion of out-of-shape thighs. He simply could not justify spending THAT MUCH MONEY on something he thought I would use "about a month."

Knowing this little bit about his make-up, one can imagine my surprise when Jerry pulled into the driveway on December 21st with the expensive bike in the trunk of his car. I was just dazzled.

I carried on so much about Jerry's apparent change of attitude that several hours passed before he sheepishly told me the truth. He had

RENTED the bike for one month! His reasoning was that if I really used it during January, we could then buy it and apply that month's rent toward the purchase price. It was his own version of buying on the "never-never" plan and killing two birds with one stone. The second bird was that by the end of January, it could double as a Valentine's gift.

Like I said. Dependable. Honest. Funny. Nice. And CHEAP! EVERY-BODY KNOWS THAT!

A Living Legend

Warren to Goober: The things that happened to this guy, things we only dream about. You know what I mean?

- Episode #166, "Off to Hollywood"

The search for Mayberry humor in our family would not be complete without mentioning our son Beaver. See, he is somewhat of a character. (A little bit of it may have come from his mother's side.) Some of Beaver's escapades during his teenage years were in my first book, so I will just update what he has been doing lately.

Beaver finally stopped growing at 6'8" and admits he never saw a biscuit he did not like. (Aw, big IS the word for it!) This meant that as a family, we are 6'2", 6'6", and a large 6'8". THREE BIGS! People on our street are not referring to the size of our home when they say we live in "the big house." (We are just thankful the government has not thought of taxing tall.)

With children, you mold them, shape them, and send them away to college, and I will be darn if they do not come back on you sometimes. This should not have been a total shock in our case. Beaver had always been a strong advocate of that old saying about all work and no play, and he put it into overdrive on the collegiate level. We refer to that era as his "animal stage" because like Clara Edwards discussing her brother in "Opie's Group," we had every reason to suspect he was not living a "well-rounded life." Beaver swears to this day, however, that his college days were six of the best four years of his life.

In his fourth year in college (or his sophomore year, same thing) Jerry called Beaver aside to tell him we were past fed up. "You are playing a little basketball and doing a LOT of partying. You have membership in one fraternity and apparently social privileges in two others. Meanwhile, your mother and I have been to THREE freshman teas. The college thinks we have got a slew of students enrolled. You are the only one, and you are still a sophomore. Do you have any idea what you want to be?"

Beaver said, "Yes sir. I want to be . . . a junior. I believe if I can ever be a junior, I can get out."

Because we were unable to impress upon Beaver the value of studying, and because his parents were beginning to feel like grab bags for cash, he took a sabbatical soon after that to view college life from afar while he washed dishes in a restaurant. I am proud to report he went from sink duty to salad server to maitre d' within six months. It was his version of climbing up the corporate ladder. With this perspective, Beaver returned to higher education, buckled down a little, and by the grace of God graduated from a fine school—Elon College.[21] In honor of the occasion, students named a booth after him at a place near the campus called "The Lighthouse." It was where he had hosted his own version of the Mayberry social club, "The Regal Order of the Golden Door to Good Fellowship." This did not command great parental pride on our part.

The problem was that Beaver was plenty smart, but was not acting like he had any "smarts." And then the strangest thing happened. Right before we were about to get his head looked into, Beaver settled down as sons usually do and became solid as a rock. I wish I had back all the time I spent worrying about it and delivering my sermons of the day. Oh, he has not joined the Lions Club yet, but he's solid. These things usually have a way of adjusting themselves, and his mother KNEW all along it would happen. (Ha! Ha!) Marriage played a big part in it. Read on. . . .

---

21 In 2001 Elon College became Elon University.

News From the Altar

Briscoe Darling, about his sons: Each and every one of 'em is going to
   get himself nuptialed.

- Episode #193, "The Darling Fortune"

Ramona Ankrum seems a bit peculiar when we meet her at Mrs.
Wiley's tea in "My Fair Ernest T. Bass." She winds up playing leapfrog
with Ernest T. in the front yard. Where I come from, that is slightly
peculiar for a grown person.

Barney is especially surprised at Ramona's behavior because she
is from a respectable family. But Andy explains that her grandfather,
Rotten Ray Ankrum, came down from the hills in 1870, burned down
Mayberry, and went into the charcoal business. It is Barney's response
to that information that makes me nervous. "Blood will tell, breeding
will out." Oh, dear.

For the humorist, marching to a "different beat" has nothing to
do with anything. Often, we do not even hear the beat because we
are fascinated by the drummer's hat with the doodads on top. It has
occurred to me—and other humorists—that our strange ways may be
passed along to our children. Very scary. For years, Beaver dated an
interesting assortment of young women ranging from "girls a mother
would like" to "she brings tequila with her." Then, to our delight, he
settled down and married our best friends' daughter, Dayna. In truth,
it was one of the great natural romances of all time. They had been in
love since the sixth grade, but it just took a while to put it all together.
The parents were thrilled!

There was discussion of having a short, sweet event so that leftover
money could go toward furniture, but it did not work that way. It did
not work that way at all. Beaver and Dayna figured they could get a
starter set of furniture out of the attics of both sets of parents and
opted for a big wedding rather than a small affair with a few friends.

Mercifully, I will spare most of the wedding details, but a few are necessary to clarify why I fear this "blood will tell, breeding will out" thing.

It was a typical, small-town, southern "happening"—parties for several months, luncheons and dinners days before the event, and relatives everywhere inhaling food. Beaver fell right in line as a typical groom and had little to do with the overall planning, but he was granted one request. He wanted a band that often played at The Lighthouse (where he had his booth) to play at the after-rehearsal party. They were called "Big Bump and the Stun Gunz." Big Bump could play the electric guitar with his teeth from the parking lot while the dancers remained inside. What a talent! Or, what in tarnation? It just depended on a person's perspective.

FINALLY, six hundred and forty-eight people all "gussied up" crammed into the Front Street United Methodist Church for the thirteen-minute ceremony. Contributing to the size of the crowd were many "interesting" speaker friends from around the country. A "motivator" wanted to sit in the pulpit, and a "trainer" pushed cassettes at the reception. One neighbor said it was the first time she had left a social gathering with over a hundred dollars in books and tapes. (The humorists watched all this with sharp eyes and knew they would later tell about it.)

But back to this business about the blood and breeding, and its scary effect on me. When Beaver was younger, I often played that old "gotcha last" bit on him. I would trick him, grin and proclaim, "Gotcha last!" It frustrated him as a child, but that was years earlier and long forgotten by me. Children never forget.

The couple was pronounced husband and wife and proceeded up the aisle as their high school buddy blared forth on his trumpet. (He had "quaintened" it up a shade for the day. He was accustomed to running off "perboles."[22]) I choked back a tear because I did not want to walk out crying and have people mumble, "I bet she wishes she had not traveled so much when he was growing up."

---

22 Or hyperbole – an obvious and intentional exaggeration or amplification in order to create an effect.

The twelve bridesmaids and groomsmen walked out by twos. Why twelve? I had asked the same thing. Dayna had explained innocently, "The church won't let you have fourteen." I love her!

My husband, the best man, escorted the maid of honor up the aisle. Everything was progressing in strictest Methodist tradition, just the way we like things in North Carolina and the way our minister preferred in particular. I had been reminded REPEATEDLY that it was not a time to be funny. What did people think I would do? Stand up at my son's wedding and start dropping one-liners?

The bride's mother, my good buddy Gray Long, was escorted out, and husband Gene, in his lesser role as father of the bride, trailed along behind. Before she left, Gray smiled at me. WE HAD DONE IT! Looking back on it, I am surprised we did not exchange high-fives at the front of the church before she was escorted up the aisle. Now I waited for my turn . . . and waited . . . and then waited some more.

When the trumpeter started the "perboles" the second time, beads of perspiration popped out on my forehead. I glanced backwards at my two sisters, who shrugged. It was not their wedding. Relatives from Alabama arched their eyebrows and whispered, "THIS is different."

More seconds ticked by and my mind was racing. Where was Michael, Beaver's friend who was to escort me? Hmm, in the tenth grade, he WAS the one who . . . . Nah, he has forgotten I told his mother about that. He will come. This is a religious ceremony. All these people, months of planning, and the groom's mother—certainly a prime player even dressed in pale—is waiting. Come on, Michael. Come onnnn.

A murmur started faintly through the congregation and grew louder. Then, commotion! What in the world? Suddenly, there was a huge tuxedo standing next to my pew. I looked up in relief . . . expecting the usher. Instead, there was a big ol' 6'8" grinning groom looking down at his mama.

A "transport of emotion" ran through my heart. A great deal of strict, southern, Methodist tradition had been tossed aside by my son and his bride. We do not often "step out of the lines" at our church, and I was so startled that the guests laughed. By the time I was able to get to my feet—fighting back the onslaught of tears—and take my "little boy" by the arm, the congregation broke into applause. Applause! And mother and son walked proudly up the long aisle toward the bride waiting at the rear of the church with outstretched arms. Her mother and father were standing beside her, laughing. All of them had set me up!

Five feet from the door, Beaver looked down at me and said, "OK, once and for all. GOTCHA LAST!"

Blood will tell. Breeding will out. Ain't it scary?

It's an American Name

Ernest T. Bass: I tried courting ol' Hog Winslow's daughter, Hogette.
Barney: Pretty name.
Ernest T. Bass: Hogette? Yeah, it's French.

- Episode #113, "My Fair Ernest T. Bass"

Humorous names that filter in and out of conversations on *TAGS* are a continuing source of humor to viewers. There are names like Hogette Winslow, who married the taxidermist "what sewed up her head"; and Halcyon Loretta Winslow, who went to finishing school but was still "ugly, single, and pitting prunes"; and Hasty Buford and Charlene Darling Wash's husband Dud, who drank hard cider and punched each other in the arm while hollarin' "flinch!"

At a casual glance, one might think the writers took names over the believable boundaries in order to produce laughs. Don't you believe it! They got their desired effect all right, but once again, this part of Mayberry reflects the world as I see it in my family and travels.

We will begin with a sampling of names in my family. You read several stories about my Grandma Freddie, whose name is not a shortened version of something like Fredrika. It is just plain Freddie. And since our family is big on "naming after," there is a female cousin named Freddie. We also have "kin" named Verl, Nimrod, Honky, Aunt Winney, and Aunt Willie. Being from the South, we also have our "belles," specifically Aunt Rubybelle and Aunt Linniebelle.

Growing up in the *Howdy Doody* era, my cousin Clara is thankful that she was not named Clarabelle.[23] I think that would have been fun, though, and then the family could have had a singing group known as "The Three Belles." We had a distant family relative a generation back named "Alabama Belle." Yes, I am telling the truth. However, because this book is an attempt to illustrate that Mayberry humor is prevalent today, I will also add that we have current family friends named Lovelybelle and Libbylove. Incidentally, I did have one routinely-named relative, Aunt Sue, but after rheumatic fever, she had a history of mental problems. I knew her as "Poor Aunt Sue" because that is all anybody ever called her after she got sick- "Poor Aunt Sue."

Of course, when a person calls her son "Beaver," she cannot say too much about anyone's name. I do so only to point out the believability of the humorous names on my favorite television show. Hey, there was even a woman in Mayberry called "The Beaver." She was tagged with the nickname because of a gum condition that caused her to have long teeth.

Son Beaver and his generation proclaim that our unusual family names are archaic. He and wife Dayna produced an "issue" several years after they were married. (Paraphrasing Briscoe Darling, it gave me a feeling of "immortal.") We knew right away the baby was a boy because of the blue blanket, and the proud parents were determined not to give him a funny name. No siree. It was the mid-nineties and they were so much more sophisticated. They named their son . . . Ryder. (Goober would have been happy. He always wanted a name with a "Y" in it.) I do not know where they got that name—a yellow truck going down the highway? The Ryder Cup? Red Ryder?—and I did not ask. What would I say? "Why in the world did you name him Ryder, Beaver?" (By the way, Ryder is darn cute, especially when he grabs your finger.)

---

23 *Howdy Doody* was a popular children's show that was on NBC from 1947-1960. The character, Clarabell, was a mute clown on the show who communicated in mime, by honking his horn and squirting seltzer water.

My husband swears these names are indigenous to my family and characters on *TAGS*, but not HIS family. So, I asked his mother, RUBY LOU, why she named her twins JERRY RAY and GINGER FAY. She said, "They rhymed." Made sense to me.

Situations that writers on *The Andy Griffith Show* set up to revolve around names are also true to life. For example, when Andy considers taking a second job to accumulate money for Opie's college education, he sees an ad for a tailor. It will not work out, though, because then he would be "Tailor Taylor." This reminds me of a similar situation that happened to a contact person for one of my speeches. She had hoped to use three names after she married like so many career women, but her maiden name was Mueller, and she married Don Heitmuller. Both Mueller and 'muller were pronounced the same. That made her Patty Mueller-Heitmuller. When she tried it, people laughed. I am not surprised.

In Livingston, Montana, I met a teenager named "Utanana." Silly me, I asked about it. She said her parents came from Utah and Montana, so . . . . I figured her parents were hippies, but she said no. They were just from Utah and Montana. Welllll, Charlene Darling Wash's baby girl on *TAGS* was named "Andelina." I have always wondered. Andy and Carolina? It is just a thought.

In Mayberry, the Beamon family passes the Taylors on Sunday morning in "Family Visit." There is Claude, Sr., Claude, Jr., Plain Claude Beamon, and Claudette. Plain Claude is so called because he is not a junior or a senior, not because he is so homely. He is just Plain Claude. Well, a friend of mine interviewed a man for a job named Last One Jones, Jr. She asked if he were the youngest in a very large family. No, he was not. His father had been, however, and therefore was named Last One Jones. That made the interviewee Last One Jones, Jr.

These examples could go on for pages. Meeting new people every day and autographing books gives one the opportunity to run into people named Putter, Blossom Citter, and Sister Eulalia Estep. (Why would I make something like this up?) As I was finishing this book, I spoke in Atlanta and a man in the audience told me that he named his daughters "War Eagle" and "Tiger." (No, not in honor of Barney Fife's nicknames: "Eagle eye" and "Tiger" Fife.) [24] His friends standing nearby assured me this was correct. I even saw the girls' photos. I guess it is better than a Georgia fan naming his daughter "Bulldog." The funny thing was that "War Eagle" was attending the University of Georgia. Is this a strange world, or what?

The all-time favorite name to cross my path, however, came from a woman who approached me after a speech to school office personnel. She said she used to work for a superintendent in eastern North Carolina named Dr. Travis Twiford. Every time she said it three times in a row, it reminded her of Elmer Fudd. [25] "Twy it."

***

At this point, I had better curtail all the family stories, lest I am not invited to the next cousin's wedding. (A low probability) By now, I hope you are thinking, "Jeanne's family is not so funny. She ought to learn about mine." Ah, THAT IS THE POINT! Just like the characters on *The Andy Griffith Show*, each of us has our own traditional anecdotes to pass along. All family trunks are packed with cherished stories that occasionally grow in the retelling as well as several that have to wait a few years to be told in public. It is not an option to pass these stories along. It is a duty! An obligation! And recalling these yarns and taking a good look at our relatives is an excellent reminder that the family humor we see in Mayberry still exists. It is really nearby.

There is another humor source that is also close at hand—our friends. We can see many of them by just walking around, so that is how we will travel this time. We'll leave the truck parked. Oh, wait. WAIT! Perhaps we should follow Aunt Bee's advice in "Andy and Barney in the Big City" and step off on our right foot so all will go well! Ready? Let's go!

---

24 "War Eagle" and the Tiger mascot are both associated with Auburn University, Jeanne's Alma mater.

25 The cartoon character, Elmer Fudd, is the archenemy of Bugs Bunny.

In Our Friends

Goober: Even sometimes these great philosophers can be wrong.
Floyd: They can?
Goober: Uh-huh. A man's best friend is not his dog. It's people.
Floyd: Oh, you really get to the meat of things, Goober. Go on, boy.
Goober: Of course, I still love dogs.

- Episode #196, "Goober Makes History"

Goober is right. Man's best friend sure ain't his dog, it is people all right. And in his Goober-like way, this much-loved character offers another memorable comment from the same show. "Andy, did you ever stop to think that people need friends just like they need air for breathing?"

Andy gives Goober a long, quiet look after the breathing line, but nowhere on earth have friendships ever been more important than in Mayberry, North Carolina. They are right up there under breathing. Being a friend is not a sideline or an accidental development with these folks. It is more than a sometimes thing. Friendship is not cultivated to serve as a rung on the social ladder or for business purposes. For Mayberrians, "networking" means their fish does not slip back in the water; and "time-sharing" means spending a few minutes together. The people in Mayberry are good friends because they believe it is important. Not only do they want to have friends, but they want to be thought of as a good friend. They live by an unprinted code of laws that govern how friendships should be conducted, and this information is taught to each generation, mainly by example.

Actually, one of Mayberry's laws of friendship is spelled out quite clearly in a touching scene in "The Case of the Punch in the Nose" when Andy tries to mend a tiff between Floyd and Mr. Foley. Andy says: "You've both known one another much too long to talk to each other like that. Now, I mean it. You've been friends for twenty years. More than friends, you, you've been neighbors. You must have seen one another through a lot of trouble in that time. Now you're not kids, either one of you, and you both know the value of old friends, and the first law of friendship is to be ready to forgive."

The first law of friendship—TO FORGIVE—may be the only one stated so explicitly on the show, but others are presented subtly. Sitting in those hotel rooms with remote controls and concentrating, I have spotted a bunch of them and offer several as reminders of the flavor of the town.

FRIENDS TAKE TIME FOR EACH OTHER.

Aunt Bee: Hello, Katherine. How do you feel? . . . Katherine, I've saved you a little supper, and I'll bring it right over.

- Episode #64, "Opie's Rival"

FRIENDS DO NOT PURPOSELY HURT FRIENDS.

Gomer: Well, I never would have gone if I thought it was going to hurt Barney. Heck, I wouldn't do anything to hurt Barney.

- Episode #126, "Barney and Thelma Lou, Phfftt"

FRIENDS KNOW WHEN TO TELL FRIENDS THE TRUTH AND WHEN NOT TO!

Andy: You're making a fool of yourself.
Barney: Do you think so? Do you really think so? Honestly and truly, is that what you think?
Andy: Yes, I think so.

- Episode #106, "Citizen's Arrest"

Andy to Barney after they clean out the criminals working at Floyd's: Let's hope he never has to find out.

- **Episode #60, "The Bookie Barber"**

FRIENDS ACCEPT FRIENDS AS THEY ARE.

Andy to Aunt Bee, when she is angry because her longtime friend always has to be "the best": Well, maybe that's just one of the things you have to overlook about Clara.

- **Episode #203, "Only a Rose"**

FRIENDS CARE ABOUT FRIENDS' FEELINGS. FRIENDS MAY KID, BUT THEY DO NOT EMBARRASS.

Andy, to Gomer: The laugh will be on Barney, and I'm afraid it'd be the kind of laugh that would hurt him pretty bad. I'd hate to see that, wouldn't you?

- **Episode #127, "Back to Nature"**

FRIENDS DO NOT GLOAT.

Goober: I'm glad you ain't the type to rub it in, Andy. Cause you could sure do some rubbing.

- **Episode #205, "Don't Miss a Good Bet"**

FRIENDS UNDERSTAND FRIENDS.

Andy: . . . Barney, in spite of getting little things like getting carried away with himself and going off the deep end, is underneath a very proud and sensitive person.

- **Episode #148, "Barney Runs for Sheriff"**

FRIENDS DO NOT LET FRIENDS DRIVE DRUNK
(Yep, even in Mayberry!).

Andy to Barney: I believe we can fix it so Otis will never want to drive
again.

- Episode #115, "Hot Rod Otis"

All of these unstated laws are significant, but none is more important
or prevalent than the one discussed in this book. It is the law that
seduces us back to Mayberry. Sound the trumpet! Clang the Cymbal
City cymbals! FRIENDS SHARE LAUGHTER WITH FRIENDS!
Examples abound.

The Mayberry laws of friendship as I see them on *TAGS* could be
an entire book, but this book is about the search for Mayberry-type
humor. So, why is all this friendship discussion important? Simple.
If the Mayberry residents were not truly good friends, so much of
the gentle kidding, hilarious rapport, and shared laughter would not
be possible. THE STRONG FRIENDSHIPS IN THE COMMUNITY
LET MAYBERRY HUMOR FLOURISH.

Remember, Mayberry humor is not put-down humor. It is kind.
Any fun the characters enjoy immediately ceases if they think they
hurt a friend's feelings. They genuinely love and care for one another
and accept things they cannot change about their friends, which gives
everyone more freedom to be the people we find so hilarious.

A beginning speaker once asked me if she could get rich in professional speaking. I told her I was rich when I started speaking and get
richer every day. My answer was honest because I agree with Barney's
response in "Opie and His Merry Men" when he overhears Opie ask
his father if they are poor. Barney answers, "You see, Ope, it ain't only
the materialistic things in this world that makes a person rich. There's
love and friendship. That can make a person rich."

That is why I am loaded. I have always figured if I did not have
good friends, it is time to check my pulse because I might be dead. I
have a bunch of genuine, full-size, regulation friends who accept me

as I am, and they know I will do the same in return. Along with all the other important stuff, we share a lot of laughter. That is why I know that a very good place to continue the search for Mayberry humor is to take a good look at some of your friends. With their permission, I will tell you about a few of mine.

Guest of Honor

Andy: Uh, I wonder if you wouldn't mention this any more'n you
          have to.

- Episode #13, "Mayberry Goes Hollywood"

Soon after my search for Mayberry humor began, I heard about Mayberry Days held in Mt. Airy, North Carolina. Although *The Andy Griffith Show* is not patterned after this particular small town, Andy Griffith did grow up there, so whether by design or chance, the flavor of the community shows up in the series. I had spoken at the Mt. Airy Chamber of Commerce banquet a few years earlier and had always remembered a comment from the evening. A man at the head table could not remember who had spoken the previous year, but said that the speaker grew up in Mt. Airy, then left and made a million dollars. "He was not a professional speaker," he added, "but people around here just like to look at someone who has made a million dollars."

When I learned about Mayberry Days, I naturally wanted to widen my scope and experience it firsthand. A clue that Jerry and I were in for an interesting time came when I called for rooms. Mt. Airy is not far, but we wanted to stay in the thick of things.

The lady with the Surry Arts Council in Mt. Airy was nice, but scared me when she said that rooms were going fast, and advised, "Y'all better call soon." It was 1993, but The Calloway Motel advertised rooms for $38. Jerry was thrilled with the price, so I "rung up" Blanche Calloway, the lady listed as proprietor. No local telephone operator was involved. I dialed direct, and Blanche was in.

The voice on the other end shouted into the phone, "HELLO!"

"I must have the wrong number. I thought I was calling The Calloway Motel in Mt. Airy, North Carolina."

"This is it, hon. Whatcha want?"

"Oh, OK, I'd like to see about getting a room during Mayberry Days."

She sighed. "How many nights you gonna be staying?" (I believe I had caught Blanche off duty.)

"We'd like one room for two nights if that's possible."

"Uh," she started, and paused before speaking again. "Look hon, could you call me back in 'bout twenty minutes? I'm cleaning the bathroom."

I did call back and we stayed at The Calloway Motel for our first trip to Mayberry Days. It was delightful, and so was Blanche.

Man's Entitled to an Opinion

Mr. Wheeler: It's a pleasure meeting up with folks like you.

- Episode #38, "Aunt Bee's Brief Encounter"

During the Mayberry Days weekend, I wandered off by myself while Jerry was getting another pork chop sandwich at the Snappy Lunch. (I had already eaten two.) I wanted to see the goat tied up outside the old jail, a funny reminder of a terrific episode. (OF COURSE, it is not there ALL the time.) Everyone was real friendly, and I lingered to chat with a fellow whose name I wish I had gotten. The low-key, laid-back approach to the whole weekend was impressive, and I told him so.

He said it would not be the same the next month at their Autumn Leaves Festival when 250,000 people arrived in town. Mayberry Days pulls about 3,000. "But we like you Mayberry folks," he added. "I call you the 'Scuse Me—Go Ahead People.'"

"The what?"

"The 'Scuse Me—Go Ahead People.' It's just something I have noticed. When two or more Mayberry Days visitors arrive at a door at the same time, they always stop, nod, and say, 'Scuse me. Go ahead.'"

I do not believe that the people attending Mayberry Days could be described any better. I knew that I would be back the next year.

Birds of a Feather

Andy: Barney, I'll tell you the truth, you are a bird in this world.
- Episode #14, "The Horse Trader"

Earlier I mentioned joining the Barney Chapter of *The Andy Griffith Show* Rerun Watchers Club (*TAGSRWC*). I attend every meeting my speaking schedule will allow, which unfortunately is not nearly enough. The members are truly examples of "Scuse me—Go ahead" folks.

My second year at Mayberry Days, I was right in there with the Barney Chapter members as they gathered at the Andy Griffith Playhouse around 8:00 a.m. to get on our truck for the parade. About this time, member Phyllis Rollins realized she did not have her big, black shoulder bag that held all her doodads, including her billfold. She remembered having it with her when she left the Mayberry Motel, and the only other place she had been was the Snappy Lunch for breakfast. We deduced that the bag was there.

We had no phone, but the Snappy Lunch was only two blocks away. Several people offered to walk over and see if the bag was there, but then we decided this would be unnecessary. During the parade, we could just stop at the restaurant and have someone run in and check.

So, a good two hours after breakfast and in the middle of the Mayberry Days parade, we stopped our truck right in front of the Snappy Lunch and backed up the procession. None of the parade participants seemed to mind. Hungry fans still stretched up the sidewalk waiting to get in the restaurant, and they did not seem to mind that either. Club member Jim Ballance hopped out and headed inside, and within seconds came out grinning and carrying the bag. It was wide open with billfold exposed and nothing missing. My theory is that people who drive from places like New York, Michigan, and Alabama to go to Mayberry Days and wait in line to eat pork chop sandwiches, do not bother with pocketbooks that do not belong to them.

Back to this search for Mayberry humor. A main attraction my second year at Mayberry Days was a cockatiel bird named Chipper who could whistle *The Fishin 'Hole*, the theme song from *TAGS*. He is famous. Won $10,000 on "America's Funniest Home Videos" and was instantly catapulted into a life of bird fame. Chipper appeared with his owner, Larry Faulk, on stage at the local movie house every couple of hours and at Colonel Tim's Talent Time on Saturday night. It was the durndest thing I have ever seen.

On cue—the strum of Larry's guitar—Chipper launched into the familiar tune and whistled it all the way through . . . unless he was interrupted. Apparently, Chipper is not a deep thinker, and if stopped anywhere during the song, he cannot go back and pick up where he left off. (I have seen speakers like that. They have to take it from the introduction.) Anyway, the audience was instructed not to laugh or take pictures, and we complied. However, several times the back door was opened or commotion came from the popcorn area. When this happened, sure enough, Chipper's little head snapped in the direction of the noise and the whistling stopped. He would have to take it from the top.

Chipper was good, but the Mayberry humor for me came from his owner before the whistling commenced. There we were, fans crowded into this grand little theater in Mt. Airy, North Carolina, on a Saturday afternoon, waiting with bated breath to hear this bird whistle. Finally, owner/trainer Larry walked down the aisle carrying the covered birdcage. We watched as he quietly put the cage in position on stage, adjusted the microphone, and removed the cloth. The excitement mounted as we were given instructions on how to act while Chipper whistled. Then, the bird's owner picked up his guitar and drawled to the captive crowd, "Chipper likes for me to sing a song before he whistles." And he did. We listened and applauded wildly. It's the Mayberry way.

Before we leave Mayberry Days and my friends in the Barney Chapter, let me make sure you do not think we are completely nuts. We are "into" this, but keep things in proper perspective. Like the time we went to Siler City to visit Aunt Bee's grave. (Of course, it was actually Frances Bavier's grave, the actress who made Aunt Bee the nation's favorite aunt.) We got out of our cars and walked with reverence toward the gravesite, mumbling, "Scuse me. Go ahead." Neal Brower, known as "The Professor" because of his classes and columns on *TAGS* that appear in *The Bullet* newsletter, was president of the chapter that year and is a United Methodist minister. I expected him to say a little prayer or at least a few moving words. SOMETHING. But no one spoke. We just all stood there in respectful silence about two minutes, looking at the words "AUNT BEE" on the headstone. Finally, the quiet was interrupted when someone said something that stirred all of us: "Let's go eat."

Like I said, it's the Mayberry way.

Perfectly "Mannerized"

Reading one of those fat etiquette books is one way to learn all about good manners and social graces. Attending Mrs. Wellington's School for Girls up in Raleigh is another.[26] But a fun way to learn more "ah men na tees" than a person will ever need to know is to watch all 249 episodes of *TAGS*. In several shows, Andy and Barney try their best to teach etiquette to people like Gomer, the Darlings, Jeff Pruitt, and even Ernest T. Bass. But the real lessons of manners and social graces are worked in through casual conversations, as illustrated by the examples below.

Aunt Bee: Opie, you can't come to breakfast like that, a naked savage! You go back and put your shirt on.

- **Episode #120, "Bargain Day"**

***

---

26 Mrs. Wellington's School for Girls is a fictitious school referenced on *TAGS*.

Opie: Shoot the sugar, Pa.
Andy: How's that again?
Opie: May I please have the sugar?
Andy: That's better.

                                    - **Episode #120, "Bargain Day"**

***

Andy: Of course, wash your hands! You don't sit down at the
            table with dirty hands.

                                    - **Episode #161, "Opie's Job"**

***

Andy: Opie, I believe Aunt Bee's trying to tell you that worms
            ain't exactly a good subject for the breakfast table.
Opie: Then can I tell you about the bugs?
Aunt Bee: No!

                                    - **Episode #101, "Opie the Birdman"**

***

Andy and Opie at the kitchen table -
Andy: Is the sun a little hot for you?
Opie: What?
(Andy nods toward Opie and the boy removes his cowboy hat.)
Opie: Oh. Sorry, Pa.

                                    - **Episode #66, "Mr. McBeevee"**

***

Opie: It's Old Lady Crump.
Andy: Well, to start with you'd better call her Miss Crump.

                                    - **Episode #86, "Andy Discovers America"**

***

Andy pulls out Peggy's chair at the table -

Opie: Ain't ya gonna do me, Pa?

Andy: Hum? Oh, only ladies. (Opie starts to eat.) . . . Wait for
           Miss Peggy.

- Episode #65, "Andy and Opie—Bachelors"

***

Andy to Opie: Let me put it to you this way. In this country, more particular in this house, when we have company, we entertain them. Now I don't care if it's a girl, a two-headed monster, or a dragon with a long tail, we entertain them. Now Miss Crump is bringing her niece over here. I'm sorry she's a girl, and I'm sorry it's Saturday, but we're GONNA entertain them.

- Episode #190, "Opie's Girlfriend"

***

The examples could flow for pages. Lessons on proper manners are in almost every episode of *TAGS* because there are just some things you do and some things you do not do, and these manners need to be constantly taught. In the South, these "rules" are etched in our memories forever, and they are with us . . . until the end.

The lady I will tell about could have been my mother. She could have been almost ANY SOUTHERN mother. Dana Gribben, a speaker friend, lives in California but was originally from the South. She tells me that her mother was a casting director's dream of the traditional southern lady. She never quite understood why her daughter chose to live "out there" on the West Coast. For that matter, the older woman never understood why her daughter chose to run her own business and own a motorcycle. I have a little trouble with that last one myself unless she had a sidecar for her friends.

When her mother was terminally ill, Dana went home to stay a few weeks. She was needed to help out; but more importantly, she was hoping for last-minute bonding.

Dana stayed at the hospital round-the-clock during her mom's final days, and at one point the sick woman regained consciousness and seemed to recognize her. Imagine how the younger woman felt when her mother motioned for her to draw nearer. Some final words of love or approval? Prophetic words to live by? Where she had hidden the silver?

Dana fought back the tears as she leaned over the bed. The older woman reached up and weakly clutched her daughter's arm as she looked into her eyes and whispered, "Don't forget to write each of these nurses a thank-you note."

Off We Go!

Malcolm Merriweather: You notice I don't drive on the left anymore. Of course, I don't drive on the right quite yet, but I'm halfway there.

- Episode #124, "The Return of Malcolm Merriweather"

In order to see her mother daily and oversee her care, a friend in Auburn, Alabama, moved her mother from the small town of Evergreen to a nearby nursing home. The older lady's numerous daily telephone calls became predictable, and one morning the daughter's line jingled before breakfast. Would her daughter drive her to Evergreen that day? She had "a little business to tend to."

The daughter had a full schedule but promised she would call back if she could work in the trip. The younger woman proceeded with her day and did not think about the request again until lunch when the telephone rang, and her mother sang out proudly, "I'm in Evergreen."

"Mothhherr! What are you doing in Evergreen?"

"I told you. I had a little business to do today. When you didn't come, I got another ride."

The daughter was dumbfounded. "Ah-another ride?"

"Yes, during breakfast I mentioned that I needed to go to Evergreen. A gentleman who lives at the Manor said he thought he could find the keys to his car and would be happy to drive me. So here we are."

Visions of the elderly men who shuffled tediously through the halls near her mother's quarters came to mind. One certainly would not want to wax the steps in that building. "Mother, who is the man?"

"Just a minute, darling," the senior citizen replied, and then turned from the telephone to inquire, "What did you say your name was?"

The residents of the Manor were all watching when the couple drove up slowly several hours later, their white heads barely visible bobbing above the dash. They loved it when their peer told her daughter, "We had NO TROUBLE at all. People seemed to stay out of our way."

I Had a Dog and His Name was Spot

Andy: Barney, you want my honest opinion? I don't believe that dog could find his own food dish.

                              - Episode #128, "Barney's Bloodhound"

Goober is so proud of his new, fine dog in "A Man's Best Friend." He names him Spot because "he hadn't got any spots on him." (He made that up himself.) He tries to get the dog to do tricks for Andy, but to no avail. Spot just is not a showoff. I cannot say the same for our dog by the same name.

Actually, Spot was a rather routine name for a boy called "Beaver" to give his dog. One would think he could have come up with something more original, like Blue, Mack, or Gulliver. My husband and I had a few other names for the mongrel, but they were not words we could shout around the neighborhood, much less put in print. I am sure the neighbors wished our Spot had been like Otis's dog Spot. That dog was usually invisible.

Every time our dog Spot bolted out of an open door, he ran off, only to return later dragging an item from the surrounding two-block area. Shoes were his favorite, but he was not selective. Gloves. Tennis rackets. Umbrellas with broken handles. Small garden tools. If Spot could get a bite on it, he brought it home.

Every few days, our son made a pilgrimage up and down the nearby streets with his arms full of Spot's treasures. Beaver went to each house, laid the stuff out on the front steps, and summoned folks to identify their belongings. It was an interesting glimpse into human nature. People scooped up their property with one hand and examined the remaining items with the other. Their comments were insightful. "If no one claims such and such, I'll take it." "Hey, nice umbrella. I don't mind the broken handle. How many more houses do you have to go?" "I'll give you fifty cents for that T-shirt." One lady asked Beaver to add a couple of things she found in her yard to the collection. "As long as you are going around." Beaver obliged because it was the neighborly thing. Spot's antics got to be a joke on our block, but I did not realize to what extent until early one Sunday morning. Like parents of teenagers, dog owners are often the last to know.

We returned home late Saturday night with a truckload of furniture after closing on my parents' home. We were able to carry all the pieces inside except an upright piano, which we managed only to roll out of the truck. (I could not wait to get inside and have someone bang out "Chinatown, My Chinatown" on the keys. [27]) It was too heavy for us to maneuver up steps, so we just left it in the carport for the night.

When I went out early the next morning to get the paper, I threw my hand up to a neighbor in her yard several houses down. She waved back, cupped her hand around her mouth, and shouted, "WHERE DID SPOT FIND THE PIANO?"

---

27 The song was made popular by the Mills Brothers.

We're Brothers Together

Barney: This just happens to be a very delicate piece of machinery
that's been treated with kid gloves, and I intend to continue to give it that same kind of care.

- Episode #90, "Barney's First Car"

The first time *TAGS* viewers meet the Darling family is in "The
Darlings Are Coming," when they come down from the mountains
and pull into Mayberry in their truck. The machine is "half-mad with
thirst," and Briscoe Darling proceeds to dip water for the radiator out
of the memorial horse trough with his hat. She is always good for
"eleven hats full." Unfortunately for Briscoe, parking a truck in front
of the memorial horse trough and dipping water out of it are illegal
acts in Mayberry. It does not matter that he is willing to give a horse
the right of way if one happens along. Whatever they do to keep the
old truck going, it works. The Darlings ride it into town during six
episodes and again in "Return to Mayberry," the ultimate reunion
show that first aired on NBC-TV in 1986. Sometimes though, vehicles need to be put out to pasture. Case in point.

The 1969 automobile known as "The Brown Bomber" was already
old when the family brought it with them to North Carolina from
New York in 1976. The young Kathleen Flanagan, my friend, was not
even born when the car was new. Her father commuted to Greensboro
with four other men, always driving his pride and joy when it was his
turn or when he could get it started.

In the eighties, "The Brown Bomber" was still running, although
less and less reliably and usually sounding like either a bantam rooster's
"pucker, pucker, pucker" or a child's bicycle bell—"pa-ding, pa-ding."
Oh, who am I kidding? It had a whine like a crying child. Too bad
Goober was not there to fix it. Finally, when a local mechanic looked
under the hood and just closed her up, the commuters convinced
their friend it was time to put the car to rest. He balked for months,
saying he would not get any money on a trade-in. They assured him

someone would give him a few dollars for the metal if nothing else. Amazingly, a junk dealer in town made an offer on the parts, which the commuters feared they would have to haul to him in burlap sacks.

The day arrived for Mr. Flanagan to end this era of his life. The family watched from the house as he started "The Brown Bomber" one last time and puckered out of his driveway for the final trip. It was an emotional experience, and he wanted to do it alone. I guess macho was involved, like when a cowboy shoots his crippled horse—"It's mine. I'll do it."

Mr. Flanagan drove his "horse" slowly along the street. A block away from home he glanced in his rearview mirror and discovered that his four commuter friends were driving in single file behind him. Their lights were on as if they were in a funeral procession.

The entourage followed Mr. Flanagan all the way to the junkyard, where they pulled in. They then got out of their cars and stood, dressed in dark suits with their heads bowed.

All of this reminds me of "hitmen" attending their victims' funerals. Not only did they show their respect for a friend's "loss" of a loved one, but it was rumored that they also paid the junk dealer to buy the parts.

Symbol of My Profession

Ernest T. Bass: You done took my cap, which is the symbol of my
    profession.

- Episode #164, "Malcolm at the Crossroads"

Ernest T. Bass may not look like it, but he takes his attire seriously. In "Ernest T. Bass Joins the Army," all he wants is a uniform. In "My Fair Ernest T. Bass," he dons a suit to go to tea at Mrs. Wiley's. And in "Malcolm at the Crossroads," the cap he wears as a school crossing guard becomes very important. Most viewers understand how he feels about outfits, caps, and uniforms.

A game was scheduled between the fledgling, younger, and less experienced Little League baseball team from Elon College, North

Carolina, and the semi-pro Little League team from the neighboring community of Altamahaw-Ossipee. Our friend, Jim Powell, does not remember how the lopsided match came about but declares that he will never forget the incident. He and his Elon buddies were tossing the ball around on their regular field one Saturday morning, and the coach rode up in a big truck and told them to hop on. They were heading for a game.

The Elon boys had heard about the big boys over in Altamahaw-Ossipee but had no idea just HOW BIG they were until the truck pulled into foreign territory. The opponent was already on the field, and Jim recalls his coach having to coax most of the Elon guys to get off the truck.

Not only were the opposing players much bigger, but they had uniforms. UNIFORMS! The Elon players had on dungarees and dirty T-shirts. But their coach was not assigned his position for nothing. He knew the secret to motivating a team. He surprised them by reaching into a big sack and pulling out new caps. Yep, one of the Elon College merchants had swung for each boy to have a brand-new baseball cap with "E" stitched on the front. Not the same thing as a complete uniform, but enough to entice the boys to get off the truck. At that stage of their young lives, a baseball cap was the symbol of their profession.

Intimidation was part of the Altamahaw-Ossipee team's strategy. Jim recalls hoots from the big boys as he took the field for the first time. He thought they were laughing at the large, lobster-claw-sized mitt on his hand, but no, it was the uniforms. They practically rolled on the ground as they hollered, "Hey, where'd ya 'git' those uniforms?" Jim took his place way out in distant center field, as far from any action as he could get. That is when the shout occurred that he will never forget.

"Hey! You out there in centerfield! You with the baseball cap over your eyes! What's that "E" stand for? Ignorant?"

The Story That's Going Around

Howard Sprague: Sarah, will you get me my mother, please. (pause) Oh, she's fine.

- Episode #185, "The County Clerk"

The Information Highway seems to be running through our front door, but Mayberry has always been "online." The head of the Internet is Sarah, the town's telephone operator. Never seen, but mentioned in numerous shows, she keeps her headset on the pulse of the community. No call is so important that it cannot be interrupted with a question or exchange of pleasantries. We only hear one side of the conversations, but we know exactly what Sarah says.

But a small town does not need a central switchboard with an operator like Sarah to have a hotline system. In the South, this is never truer than when someone dies.

Andy says it well in "Ellie Comes to Town." "Oh, ain't it wonderful how the folks help a body out in time of need." Potato salad. Pound cakes. Fried chicken. It all comes pouring in to the grieving family when someone in small-town America goes on to their "everlasting calling." Information spreads through a community via the dependable small-town hotline that is generally faster than CNN, FAX, or even e-mail.[28] Long viewed as simply an avenue for gossip, this communication system serves other purposes equally as well. It is known as "word of mouth," and it works with phenomenal speed and usually with a high degree of accuracy.

Within hours of a "passing," friends and even general acquaintances arrive at the dear departed's back door. They are carrying food on dishes marked with identifying strips of masking tape for easy return. In the smallest of towns, the names are unnecessary. Women

---

28 FAX (short for facsimile) is a machine that transmits scanned printed material (both text and images) to a telephone number connected to a printer or other output device. It has been rendered nearly obsolete by the internet.

know one another's china patterns or standard burial casseroles. "Oh, that Pyrex dish must belong to Ginger. She always brings her squash thing in that." "That's Ruby's cake plate." "Isn't that Dovie's platter?" Word spreads so quickly in close-knit communities that plates of ham biscuits and chicken wings often are found on the kitchen table before cousins living down in the county can get to the house. (Of course, pulling a U-Haul slows them down.) Sometimes even the hotline can be given assistance, much to the chagrin of my good friend, Nan Perkins.

Nan has a good sense of humor but is not a clown. She is more likely to enjoy a good story than to instigate a practical joke. She would never start a false rumor, although she would not be above sharing an interesting tidbit of information with a select group of good friends. That is why she was horrified when one of . . . well, here is what happened.

On a Saturday night, Nan's eight-year-old son Edward returned from a birthday party and mentioned that one of his friends, whom I will call Arnold, after one of Opie's buddies, had not been there. Nan thought she might know the reason and explained that Arnold's grandmother was very sick. "What's wrong with her?" little Edward wanted to know. "She's just old, honey, and I do not think she is going to live much longer. I've heard she may not make it through the night." End of conversation.

The next morning in Sunday School, Edward's friend was again absent, which led the teacher to inquire, "Does anyone know why Arnold is not here? Has anything happened to his grandmother?"

Upon hearing those questions, Edward jumped right in and offered what he thought to be factual information. "His grandmother died during the night," he said. "My mother told me." In fact, the lady I will call Mrs. Hooper had not died, although she was near death's door.

The teacher mumbled, "I need to let someone know about this," and scurried out. She found the minister before the church service began. By then, of course, the information "came from Nan Perkins."

Mrs. Hooper was a longtime member of the church. The congregation needed to be informed.

The news spread through the official church channels between Sunday School and church—the precise time Edward joined his mother in their regular pew for the worship service. Mother and son were sitting there when the minister announced to the congregation that he had sad news. "It is my understanding that Mrs. Hooper passed away during the night. As you know, she has been a member of this church her entire life. I am sure . . . . "

His words trailed off in Nan's mind as she shook her head and said to Edward, "What a shame. I didn't know she died." Edward was perplexed. "Yes, you did, Mama. You told me that last night."

At the front of the sanctuary, which suddenly seemed several miles away, the minister prayed on. "And so, our Heavenly Father, please be with the family . . . . "

Nan swears that ten women combined could never experience a hot flash like the one that flew through her body at that moment. She was not having a religious experience. "No, Edward. I did not say she had died," she whispered emphatically as perspiration appeared on her forehead. "I SAID, she was dying."

"In the name of the Father, the Son . . . . "

Edward's eyes widened. Nan's heart sank.

"and the Holy Ghost. Amen."

The members of the congregation lifted their heads. Nan lowered hers to within an inch of Edward's face. "Did you tell your Sunday School teacher Mrs. Hooper had died?"

A response was unnecessary. Tears that welled up in little Edward's eyes answered for him. Mother and son stared at each other for a few seconds, and then abruptly turned toward the minister.

"Please turn in your hymnals to page #292, 'Leaning On the Everlasting Arms.'"

Nan blankly followed the instructions while she contemplated interrupting the service. No, not a possibility. What if poor Mrs. Hooper had indeed passed away? Edward might not have caused a problem at all. If lucky, maybe she could fall over dead right then. How convenient, when she would be at the church. By that point, my friend was not clutching at straws. She was grasping for them.

"Lean'ing. LEAN'ing . . . ."

Several blocks away Mrs. Hooper lay in the hospital with family members gathered around as she clung to life. Back at the church, Nan was also clinging. When the blur of the service concluded, her knees almost buckled as she walked out of the sanctuary. "The longest church service I have ever attended," she later recalled.

Church let out a little after twelve and ladies hurried home to call friends and put chicken casseroles together. In times like these, small towns shine. By one o'clock, food poured into the Hooper home. Much to the family's surprise, people were carrying dishes up the driveway when they returned from the hospital. The elderly lady actually had died shortly before noon.

For years, members of the Hooper family talked about the spontaneous outpouring of affection from their friends who arrived with food within minutes of their mother's death. It was amazing. AMAZING. "What good friends," they commented over and over that week and later. "They were here with fried chicken and cornbread before we could get in the house and take off our coats."

As reported, Nan has a terrific sense of humor, but she has an even stronger sense of right and wrong. At the beach several years later, she shared the story with close friends. We told her that she got lucky. "Oh, I know," she agreed, and then confided, "But I have to be honest. It has always bothered me that I sat in church that morning and prayed, 'Oh, God, if she's going to die soon, why not let it be sooner?'"

And if the small-town hotline knew THAT . . . .

Photographic Mind

Goober: I was saying there sure are a lot of people walking around
            who need eyeglasses.
Floyd: Strong ones.

- Episode #195, "The Ball Game"

Lest you think Nan Perkins and son Edward are the only ones in that
family to live Mayberry humor . . .

Sally, one of the "Convicts-at-Large" calls Floyd "Four Eyes." I
wonder what she would have come up with for Jerry's longtime tennis
partner, Ed Perkins (yes, Nan's husband). The time came for Ed to
get his driver's license renewed. Hoping for four more years without
the provision of "needs glasses for driving," he planned to bluff when
the patrol officer pointed to a line on the eye chart. He was treading
on thin ice. With some fancy memory work from his last visit to the
eye doctor and faked deliberation, Ed squinted in the direction of the
eye chart and slowly recited the correct letters, "Teeee. Zeeee. Veeee.
Eeeee . . . "

The officer interrupted and said, "Mr. Perkins, would it help if I
told you they were numerals?"

Share and Share Alike

Barney, pretending to be a criminal in order to elicit information: I've
            been in stir plenty. Yeah, the bulls used everything, tried
            everything on me. Bright lights, rubber hose, I never cracked.
            Yeah, I've been called plenty, everything from Chopper to
            Mad Dog, but one name they never called me, Tattletale.

- Episode #50, "Jailbreak"

Andy has a way of cutting to the quick of a situation. For example, in
"Opie's Charity," he makes another of his many simple sentences that
say so much. "It just ain't nice to be selfish." That pretty much sums

it up without any further discussion. It ain't nice to tattletale either. Most of the time.

A sales rep, Dave, who came to my office, recalled the time he took his daughter and son, then eight and four, for a ride. When they piled in the car, the young girl tightly clutched a little box of Tic Tacs her father had bought her the day before. When she "picked one" off the bunch to eat, Dave noticed that all the little mints were stuck together in one big blob.

"What happened? Drop the box in some water?"

Little brother jumped in to tattletale. Maybe one could not blame him on this occasion. "No! She didn't drop them in water! She licked each one of them, and put them all back in the box so she wouldn't have to share."

She did not have to.

Hello, Doll

Andy: Oh, now Elinor, you're putting words in my mouth.

Ellie: Well, let me put in a few more. I am not withdrawing! I have every intention of running for council!

- Episode #12, "Ellie for Council"

The men in Mayberry can be sexist. No doubt about it. But they do not mean any harm by it, and it is not their fault. They are products of their time. This is all pre-Phil and Oprah and the poor fellows simply have not been enlightened.[29] It is a treat to watch them become less sexist as the series progresses. From the initial shock of a lady druggist to Aunt Bee flying a plane, we watch people grow in the way they think and act.

Oh, there are several episodes that can throw into a rage a rabid feminist who chooses to look at the world through blinders. A show

---

29 Phil is Dr. Phil McGraw, an author, television personality, and host of the popular *Dr. Phil* television show.

like "Ellie Saves a Female," where Barney, Andy, and Ellie Walker help a young woman "fix up" so she can attract guys and eventually produce farmhands, can get a goat or two. Or how about "Opie's Girlfriend" when Helen practically advises her niece to lose to boys? Those and several other shows could be painful to me if I put on those blinders. But Andy knows there are often two ways to look at something. Take off the blinders and notice that helping the young farm woman is an excellent example of people caring, and observe in "Opie's Girlfriend" the concern for a friend's self-esteem. It is all in the way we choose to look at something.

With that said, though, I have to admit that I enjoy watching the women of Mayberry "help" the men along in their enlightenment process. In "Ellie for Council," I love it when the druggist runs for the town council and announces her intentions to encourage other women to do likewise. And I cheer every time Ellie says to Andy, "Who knows, the day may come when the city council of Mayberry is comprised entirely of women. Put that in your soda and sip it!"

Elinor Walker could tell my buddy Robert Henry a thing or two.

Diversity. Sexist remarks. Harassment. These terms have burst into our consciousness with new, important meanings since *TAGS* first aired. And just as in Mayberry, they demand we adjust our thinking. While the majority of caring people are trying to do so, sometimes even the most conscientious professional can slip back into long-held habits. Speakers are in prime positions to subtly influence through our remarks and attitudes, but first, we have to correct our own thinking. We have been as guilty as others in poor selection of terms. Just ask Robert Henry.

Professional humorist Robert Henry is a very funny man and a past president of the National Speakers Association. He grew up in the South, graduated from Southern Mississippi, and was Assistant Dean of the Pharmacy School at Auburn University when he stopped teaching and went into full-time professional speaking. He certainly knows not to call waitresses names like "Honey" and "Baby Doll," like Bobby Fleet does when he comes through Mayberry with his "Band with a Beat." But years of good ol' boy do slip out occasionally. I cut him some slack because I know his heart is in the right place and that he keeps trying to improve.

Several years ago, Robert was giving a three-hour seminar to sales-people. When he announced a break halfway through the session, a professional-looking woman in the audience charged to the front of the room. While Mr. McBeevee and Colonel Harvey pretend to make smoke come out of their ears during their visits to Mayberry, real smoke practically seeped out of her ears as she pushed by others to get within inches of Robert's face.

"I have almost walked out of this program several times and taken my sales force with me," she spat out for an opener. "There is no reason we should have to sit here and be offended."

Robert's world started spinning. "Offended?" he managed to mumble while his mind raced for an explanation. What could he have said? What story could have possibly caused such a reaction?

"Yes, offended! I own my company, and I brought my entire sales force here today to hear this program. Every time you have referred to a manager or salesperson, you have used the word 'he.' What is your problem? Don't you think women can be in management or effective in sales? Are you not aware that half the people sitting in here are women?"

Robert felt weak in the knees because he knew she was right. OF COURSE, she was right, he remembered thinking as other questions raced through his mind. How could he have made such an error? Why did she have to get right in his face? Could he fake a heart attack? Wonder what the hospital stay would cost?

Robert should not have made this mistake; he did know better. He was caught up in the content of his program and lapsed into old habits. There was nothing to do but learn from the error and move on as Barney tries to do in "Andy Saves Barney's Morale." That is when Deputy Fife makes the big error of arresting half the town and laments, "Once burnt is a lesson learnt. One mistake, a better cake. Once bit, best forgit."

"I am so sorry. OF COURSE, you are correct," Robert began. "I do not know how I could have been so insensitive. I certainly know better, and I appreciate you calling it to my attention. PLEASE give me a chance to make amends. I hope you and your sales force will stay for the remainder of the seminar. Perhaps I can use this as an example of how well-meaning people can be insensitive."

The woman stood taller. "I will be sitting in the front row," she announced. "Make the correction or we are gone." Her next seminar should have been on how to work with people to obtain your desired goals. She did not need a course on assertiveness. It was as though she warned Robert as Barney warns Otis in "The Loaded Goat" when they thought the animal had swallowed dynamite. "Yeah, one wrong move and everything goes BLEWEY!"

When Robert began the second half of the program, he immediately attempted to make amends by saying, "Before we get started, I want to apologize for something. During the first half of this seminar, I have referred to salespeople and management only in male terms. It was insensitive on my part and certainly unprofessional. I stand corrected and have learned a valuable lesson today."

The response was terrific because they knew Robert was sincere. The group burst into applause, especially the women. Of course, several of the men asked, "What's he talking about?" but Robert could see everyone was smiling. A wave of relief shot through his body. They still liked him. Everything was going to be OK. And RIGHT THEN is when he should have shut up and gone straight into his seminar material. But no, he continued with his confession. It illustrates that one should quit when he/she is ahead.

Basking in the applause, Robert smiled broadly and stepped in the direction of the woman on the front row. He wanted to give credit where credit was due. "Quite frankly, I would not have realized I was doing this," he said, "if it hadn't been called to my attention by this cute little thing in the front row."

He should not have done that. BLEWEY!

Is There No Mercy?

Andy: I never will forget that fine canteen that you and the club
           got up for the boys when they was coming back from the
           war. Giving up your time to dance with them.
Annabelle Silby, proudly: Every Saturday night.
Andy: Course, I always did figure the boys had been through
           enough.

- Episode #5, "Opie's Charity"

A family acquaintance, Pearl Jean, was an active member of her church
choir, and desperately wanted the group to perform during Christmas
at the prison where her brother was the warden. She extolled the
group's hard work and accomplishments. Wouldn't it be wonderful
for the inmates to benefit from the joyous sounds of her friends from
the church?

Perhaps her brother had seen Barney in "The Inspector" when he
shouts, "Stop that singing! This is a prison, not a hotel!" or maybe he was
just a real smart warden. In either case, he listened to his sister's offer and
slowly shook his head. "No, Pearl Jean, I do not think it's a good idea."

"And why not?" she persisted.

"Because," he answered, "some of the prisoners might not be guilty."

Valuables

Frank: Oh, now there is a real sentimental relic. Did I ever show
           that to you, Andy?

- Episode #39, "Mayberry Goes Bankrupt"

When Andy has to evict Frank Myers from his home in "Mayberry
Goes Bankrupt," he winds up inviting him to come and stay with the
Taylors. Frank brings along some of his important stuff in a little box:
a brass medallion from the St. Louis World's Fair; a spoon with the
skyline of Milwaukee on it; a "gen-u-ine" whalebone napkin ring; a

red, white, and blue sleeve garter; and a bond issued by the town of Mayberry in 1861. They are "valuables" to Frank, but they are not worth a tiddlyboo. This collecting reminds me of a good friend of mine, but it would have taken more than a small box to load up his sentimental relics.

During a speech on Marco Island, Florida, I had a chance to visit with Ira Hayes. Ira had been around a long time, and his tremendous success in the speaking profession was due not only to his talent but also to the fact that he was a genuinely nice person. People liked to be around him. He relished his travels and adventures and was thankful for the opportunities he had been given. Nowhere was this more evident than in his office.

Having lived in the house with a teenage son, and having clunked through thousands of flea markets and rummage sales in my time, one would think I had seen the upper limit on mess. Not so. Ira Hayes had the junkiest office I have had the pleasure to wade through, but it was junk with charm and a true monument to the word "memorabilia." The office was in his home: a small room set aside for, as his wife Carol called it, "Ira's stuff."

On this visit, Ira stood next to me in the middle of the room as we gazed at the walls covered with over four thousand name tags. Four thousand! And the name tags were just the beginning. Ira pointed out specific items of interest. "This one is a little unusual," he said in his low-key style. "It's from a convention in 1948. And look at this one. Ever see a name tag that big?" I had not.

Plaques from audiences everywhere thanked or honored Ira. Gimmicks representing thousands of meetings poured out of every nook and cranny. Photos punctuated the piles of name badges.

"Remember this?" he quizzed with a glint in his eye. It was a 1978 photo of the two of us. We looked funny, but not just because of the change in style and hair. Unlike gymnastics, there is no "correct size" for professional speakers. Stretching and standing on his toes, Ira came to my shoulder. In the picture, I am kissing him on the top of the head, and he is grinning his great Ira Hayes grin.

Standing there with him, staring at the walls, I could sense that Ira was happy in his room. Quite honestly, I was thinking that one lighted match would make the place convention history. But we do not always say what we think. "This is . . . overwhelming, Ira."

Ira smiled his nice-person smile and continued to gaze lovingly from wall to wall. "The memories of my lifetime," he said after a slow sigh. "Everything in here is a reminder of one of the places I got to go and of the nice things people did for me." I nodded in understanding, and then I noticed a long rack holding tiny bottles high on one wall. "What's that?"

Ira fixed his attention on the small objects for several moments before replying. "Oh, that is very special," he said. "That's my dirt collection."

I nodded to give myself time to think about what he said. "Hmmmmmmm."

"Those bottles hold dirt from each of the states and countries where I have spoken," this leader in the speaking profession for decades explained, staring upward.

"Dirt? You did say dirt?"

"Yep. I just took a sack and spoon and would ask my client to pull over on the side of the road so I could scoop up a little dirt. Then I would bring the dirt back home in the sack, fill up one of the empty airplane miniature bottles and label it." He smiled as he remembered gathering the dirt. "See. Montana, New Jersey. There's your state— North Carolina." We looked at North Carolina together. "It's quite a collection, isn't it?" he commented.

Ira was quiet. I was speechless. We continued to gaze from tiny bottle to tiny bottle. White dirt, black dirt, tan dirt, red dirt. It was all there. It struck me that somebody could go around his local county and gather dirt of various colors, put it in bottles, and say it came from far-off places, but I did not mention it. There was no question in my mind that Ira had painstakingly scooped up all the dirt and stuffed it in his bag for the trip home. The mental picture of him—crouched over on the side of the road, spoon in hand, while others waited in a car—made me smile.

After a few moments, I threw in the appropriate comments such as "Well, that is really something," and "It must have taken a long time to get it all." I did not know what else to say. Finally, I commented sincerely, "You know what, Ira? You may have the only fifty-state collection of dirt in little bottles in the entire country."

Ira turned and smiled his great, nice, Ira Hayes smile. "Nope," he said proudly. "I made a set for each of the children."

(Note: Ira Hayes passed away as this book was being completed. He was one of the GREATS in the speaking profession. There is a pain in the hearts of all speakers for we lost a true "valuable.")

Calendar Come to Life

Floyd: That's a female all right. Right, Andy?
Andy: Yep, that's definitely not a boy.

- Episode #48, "The Manicurist"

The Nashville bus is right on time when it brings Ellen Brown to Mayberry in "The Manicurist." Nature has been good to her—real good—and she creates quite a stir among the gang hanging around Floyd's barbershop. From Andy to Mayor Pike, they gawk out the window as she walks across the street. Barney's exact words sum up their thoughts. "Ring a ding ding." Seconds later they realize she is coming their way and frantically scatter back to their places to act nonchalant. That scenario could have happened one morning at the Oak Grove Cafe in my town.

It all started when I returned from a speaking trip and my assistant Toni brought me up-to-date on all the office communication. "Mary Beth Roach called yesterday."

"Who?"

"A speaker from Houston. The one who impersonates Mae West. You know her."

"I have never heard of her."

"Yes, you have. She was at the speakers' convention last week. I met her."

"I don't know her. Am I supposed to call her back?"

"No, she had questions about running a speaker's office, but I answered them," Toni explained. "Just keeping you informed."

Months later in wrapping up her report to me, it was a Yogi Berra "dé·jà vu all over again." "Oh, by the way. Mary Beth Roach called while you were gone."

"Mary Beth Roach?" I searched my memory.

"The woman from Texas. You remember. I talked to her last summer. She has called several times since, but I always answered her questions and did not tell you. You don't have to return her call. Just keeping you informed," she said, drawing a line through an item on her list.

This scenario revisited us several more times. Mary Beth always called when I was gone and always talked to Toni, who answered her inquiries. I never needed to call back.

Then one day in June, an excited Toni burst into the office. "Mary Beth Roach is coming to Burlington next week, and she's staying with you!"

"With me? Staying WITH ME! I don't even know Mary Beth Roach!"

Toni was bewildered. "Of course you do. She is ONE OF OUR VERY BEST FRIENDS!" (If you work with a woman long enough, you get as goofy as she is.)

But Southern Hospitality (capitalized on purpose to indicate respect and importance) rules. One week later, I rolled out the red carpet for my VERY GOOD FRIEND, Mary Beth. I did not know I was hosting two for the price of one.

Mary Beth Roach is a speaker who incorporates an imitation of Mae West into her programs. "Imitation" is an understatement. Mary Beth "becomes" the famous sex symbol.

For her master's degree in speech, Mary Beth wrote a thesis on the lady with the clever lines. After researching and studying all of Mae's famous quotes, Mary Beth discovered she could deliver those lines with amazing similarity in voice and body language. Friends begged her to "do your Mae West thing" and with very little encouragement,

Mary Beth did. When she started speaking professionally, Mae popped up in programs, to the howling delight of audiences.

Since there was no holding Mae West back, Mary Beth produced a stunning replica of the celebrity's famous outfit: a black velveteen gown that swirls on the floor around her feet; a black and white feathered boa that drapes over the shoulders and runs across cleavage; a wig of cascading white curls, topped by a hat that is a nest of black feathers extending a foot and a half around her head. This astonishing outfit completes Mary Beth's reincarnation of Mae West.

But a perfect costume does not capture and holds the attention and admiration of an audience. It is Mary Beth's knowledge of the person she portrays drawn from years of studying film footage, and her mastering Mae's mannerisms that captivate people. Those who see Mary Beth as Mae don't just say, "Well, wasn't that cute." The overall effect usually leaves them speechless, especially if it is early in the morning and she comes swooping into the Oak Grove Cafe in Burlington, North Carolina.

The Oak Grove Cafe was a "leave-your-hat-on-if-you-want-to" restaurant that was a town fixture until its owner passed away. Similar places—like the Snappy Lunch and Bluebird Diner in Mayberry—abound across America. Locals gather for breakfast or just coffee, discuss the United Nations or an umpire's call at a local ball game, and world problem-solving before heading to work. During the week, most of the regulars are men who pull tables together to accommodate the fluctuating size of the crowd. My VERY GOOD FRIEND, Mary Beth Roach, was to arrive in Burlington in the evening and leave after breakfast the next day. Toni and I decided to round up several women friends to meet us early that morning at the Oak Grove Cafe. Why not show an out-of-towner a little local color? Our buddies enjoy meeting my speaker friends whom they believe to be a strange and interesting breed. Mary Beth did not let them down.

She arrived late in the evening and turned in after we talked a while. I woke her at 5:45 a.m. "I'll be ready to go by 6:30," she sang out. It did not occur to me that she might not be putting on normal, regular, run-of-the-day clothes.

My husband went down to put out the garbage and passed a strange figure in the kitchen. Jerry's a quiet man, and he is also accustomed to eccentric speakers, so he nodded politely, but hustled back upstairs. "Your friend either went out on the town after we went to bed and is just coming in, or she is going down to the Oak Grove Cafe with more on her mind than a cup of coffee."

He did not have to say more. I knew that Mary Beth was standing in my kitchen dressed in black velveteen and feathers. "Did she have on a long white wig?" I asked unnecessarily. "Either a white wig or she had a frightful night," Jerry answered, and then added, "I only caught a glimpse of her, but there's cleavage too." (He is quiet but observant.)

Toni pulled up right on schedule, and Mary Beth swept out of the house like a Grand Dame making a ballroom entrance. I hovered behind, carrying her black velveteen train. I missed Toni's expression because I could not see through the plumage. It took a few minutes, but we finally maneuvered our very good friend, the gown, the hat, and the feathers into the back seat. "Mae" sat perfectly straight, hat against the roof, arms spread across the back of the seat. She projected an aura of self-confidence, but Mae was having fun. Before I got in the car, a neighbor jogging by called out, "Morning, Jeanne! Is one of your speaker friends in town?"

We proceeded to the Oak Grove Cafe, and on the way devised a pre-breakfast strategy. Mae West would swoop into the Oak Grove Cafe by herself and "work the breakfast crowd." No warning. No announcement. No explanation. After she walked around the room, she was to swoop out and join us in a side room. It is astonishing what people will do under the anonymity of a wig and costume.

The hat preceded Mae into the main dining area. Toni and I watched through the door, expecting the place to "break up." But no, I guess they had seen about everything down at the Oak Grove Cafe. A hush fell over the patrons until a voice mumbled, "What is it? Somebody's birthday?" Everyone in the restaurant looked up except an older fellow at a cluster of tables where a large group was gathered. He kept right on eating. Mae headed straight for those tables.

As she worked the crowd, all the men grinned and reared back in their chairs except this one fellow. He kept sliding a biscuit around on his plate as she walked from man to man, gushing famous lines such as "When I'm good, I'm very good. And when I'm bad, I'm better." The diners greeted each remark with hoots and laughter, all except this one guy who continued to look straight down as though Mae was not hovering. In truth, his eyes slowly followed Mae's feet as she moved around the table dropping her lines and rubbing her hands through each man's hair.

But when she lingered to run her hands across the top of the head beside him, Mr. Nonchalant became Mr. Transparent. Without looking up or ever saying a word, this "uninterested" gentleman quietly took off his hat and slowly leaned his head in her direction.

Partin' is Such Sweet Sorrow

Barney: Oh, I tell you, Ange, you move to the big city and get on that culture kick, you just want nothing but the best.

- Episode #211, "A Visit to Barney Fife"

Shakespeare has always been considered one of the best, but Andy Taylor knows that even Shakespeare is best understood when explained in a down-home style. In "A Feud Is a Feud," he tries to explain to Opie the story of *Romeo and Juliet:* "Goodbye. Goodbye. Partin' is such sweet sorrow, that I would say goodbye, 'til it be 'morrow. What did it mean? Well, that means, I'd love to sit and jaw with you a little longer, but I got to be amoving on."

Well, not everybody needs Andy to explain it. Some people, like my buddy Margaret Parham, understand Shakespeare very well. That is why she wanted just one thing for her birthday: to see *Hamlet* when it came to nearby Elon College. Her husband Tom, the tennis coach at the college, could have cared less about seeing a Shakespearean production, but he wanted to please Margaret. *Hamlet* it was.

On the big night, professors from what they consider the more "academic departments" smiled and exchanged glances as Tom, the tennis coach, took his seat among them. Because Tom is so well-liked, they felt comfortable in tapping him on the shoulder with their rolled programs and saying what they thought. "Did not know you were a Shakespeare fan, Tom?"

Tom leaned his head backward and whispered out of the side of his mouth, "I have been following him since he was on the junior circuit. Nice serve."

"Haven't seen you at many of the campus plays, Tom."

"I usually sit in the back," he divulged. "The acoustics are better, and it gives me a better perspective on the soliloquies and overall plot."

The good-natured ribbing stopped only when the curtain went up. This also meant the lights went down, along with Tom's head. Within seconds, he was sound asleep. Margaret let him doze, only elbowing when he started to snore.

Toward the close of Act One, there was a sudden loud sound from the stage. Tom bolted straight in his seat, eyes blinking, but quickly got his bearings. In a voice that spread throughout the auditorium, he turned to Margaret and said, "Doth anyone knowith whatith going onith?"

"Partin' is such sweet sorrow." Tom parted.

***

In this chapter, you have met buddies like Mary Beth in her Mae West outfit and Coach Parham at the Shakespearean production, to name a few. It is with everyone's permission that I share these accounts. These friends believe in the important "law of friendship" which is portrayed throughout *The Andy Griffith Show*: FRIENDS SHARE LAUGHTER WITH FRIENDS. They also understand that in today's world, as in Mayberry, STRONG FRIENDSHIPS LET HUMOR FLOURISH.

Well, it is time to keep moving. There is a lot more ground to cover on our search for Mayberry humor. I am tired of truck traveling and walking, so this time we will catch the next bus. After all, according to Floyd in "Guest in the House," a bus is a lot like life. "Coming and going. The bus bringeth and the bus taketh away." Go with me in the next chapter while it "taketh" us to a few of my "comings and goings."

You'd better hurry, or the bus will leave us!

In Our Comings and Goings

Opie: When I get older, can I loaf around the barbershop too?
Andy: Oh, I wouldn't call it loafing, Opie.
Opie: Gee, Pa, you don't do anything there. You just sit around and play checkers and talk and grunt.
Andy: Well, there's a lot more to it than THAT.
Opie: A lot of times when I go in there, everybody's just leaning back in the chairs sleeping.

- Episode #210, "Floyd's Barbershop"

One of the endearing features of *The Andy Griffith Show* is that the characters are developed through mundane interaction that often has little to do with the main storyline. Because the humor evolves from characters rather than jokes, time is allotted to develop these personalities. We need to know them just like we know our friends. It is important that we can anticipate how they will act in certain situations and relationships. Viewers need to see Mayberry people as they go about their daily routines—their "comings and goings"—and the writers, producers, and actors were clever enough to let us peek in on that. We see our Mayberry friends "hanging out," exchanging nonchalant conversation, and in general, going through the casual sameness of each day. Because we see this side of life in Mayberry, the people of the town become "real."

We chuckle at the idle chitchat and good-natured kidding that goes on in places like the barbershop. That is how we find out that as long as it stays below 65 degrees, Floyd will wear winter underwear. Even if it goes up to 70 degrees, he will not change unless it holds for a while. On the sidewalk bench or chairs, even the most seemingly insignificant comments about the weather bring smiles to our faces. On a hot day, Andy says "Howdy, Floyd" and sits down. The response is "92." Barney and Andy gossip in the squad car as their friends and neighbors walk by, and we laugh. After all, you have to tell SOMEBODY when you know that Cecil Gurney has two sets of false teeth, but will not admit it. We feel at peace when Andy and Barney absentmindedly harmonize on their high school song or a familiar hymn such as "Tell My Darling Mother I'll Be There." It is all so believable, so "every day."

The producers and writers not only realized the importance of portraying these daily happenings, but also the significance of "dead time" when the actors say very little or nothing at all. Some of the quiet times are the most potent because they stir our memories with uncanny accuracy. In the community church on Sunday, heads slowly nod forward before suddenly snapping back. We see the Taylors spend evenings on their front porch; Aunt Bee rocking and mending; Andy strumming his guitar, and Opie occasionally breaking the silence with a question like, "Pa, can I ask you something?" During the week Sheriff Taylor and Barney quietly work at the courthouse, and we watch as if bystanders at a window. The creative team connected with the series knew what very few television sports commentators have discovered through the years. The scene speaks for itself. Just let us watch.

Most people can easily relate to the everyday interaction of the characters on *TAGS*, regardless of their lifestyle or occupation. This is even true for a professional speaker. Every career has its pros and cons. Perhaps a downside to what I do is that, unlike Mayberryians, I do not have my daily "comings and goings" in the same place with the same people. Quite frankly, I miss that. I miss that a lot. But it is difficult to hang out in the familiar places and swap comments about the weather when one's whereabouts are apt to change daily. It is not possible to mosey down to the local diner to share stories with friends over lunch when you are a thousand miles from the friends and the diner. Taking a stroll over to the local filling station for a Nectarine Crush or a Huckleberry Smash is not an option if you do not know where to find the filling station. And discussing the weather on a sidewalk bench is not possible without a bench. If you could find one, all the bench mates might not be as nice as the guys hanging around Floyd's barbershop.

But just because one is not in the same location or with familiar people day after day does not mean there is a lack of routine. Nooooo siree. I hang out and swap my share of idle chitchat. I mosey. I stroll. I discuss the weather. There is a sameness to my daily ritual. It may take place in a variety of locations with people I may never see again, but do not think for a second there is a lack of predictability to my "comings and goings."

For me, idle chitchat and casual conversations occur in airplanes, hotels, and taxis. The comments make about as much sense as some in Floyd's barbershop, but I enjoy them. I am not like Lydia Crosswaith, Andy's fixed-up "date" from Greensboro in "Barney Mends a Broken Heart." She is the one who monotones, "I hate to chitchat. I don't mind ordinary conversation, but I hate chitchat." Even with the recent extraordinary emphasis on political correctness, I still see brave souls who dare to kid one another like they do in Emmett's Fix-It Shop, and take it when it comes their way. I amble on down to local establishments for a tub of non-fat yogurt or a Snickers and engage in tidbit conversations with folks. Mayberryites do the same at Wally's Fillin' Station when they want a bottle of pop.

In most cases, however, I never see the people I encounter again. Like the many visitors who go through Mayberry and are seen only once, I am the stranger who passes through many towns. Just a face in the local crowd.

My assistant Toni and I have worked together since 1979, so when I am home, we may sit right there in the office—our squad car—and gossip. Well, actually, paraphrasing Mayberry's Emma Brand, we do not actually gossip, but we do feel obligated to pass along news. Keeping me informed is in Toni's job description, but it is a company policy to always abide by a rule espoused by Clara Edwards in "Aunt Bee and the Lecturer," which is, "Anything you tell me I'll try to keep from going any further." Because we both went to Auburn University, Toni and I might even start singing the Alma Mater slowly, reminiscent of Andy and Barney joining in on "Mayberry Union High." (When that happens, I close the door. Like Barney, Toni cannot sing. Not a lick.)

I have always looked at the people I encountered in my "comings and goings" as possible sources for speech material. For years I have kept an organized system of collecting humor that occurs around me. The system has the clever name of "Jeanne's Journals." (I believe this reflects Howard Sprague, don't you?) After the banquet that prompted this search for Mayberry humor, I decided to take a more deliberate look at my "comings and goings." I wish I could say I spent a lot of time researching the subject on benches in front of courthouses, or in barbers' chairs across the country, or even cooking with friends for an annual bazaar. But that is just not my lifestyle. Occasionally, my "comings and goings" humor occurs in my office, but most of the time it revolves around travel.

By keeping my ears open, I laugh daily at comments made by people I meet: comments that remind me of things Andy, Barney, Floyd, Aunt Bee, Opie, Goober, and the other characters might say. And by keeping my eyes open, I see people doing things that would have played well on *TAGS*. We do not have to live in mythical Mayberry or watch *TAGS* reruns to experience this side of Mayberry humor. Checking the chitchat and conversational exchanges in our own daily "comings and goings" works quite well.

Join me as I recall a few of mine.

You're Gonna Bust Something!

Emma Watson: I came looking for justice, and it's blind.
                          - Episode #6, "Ellie Comes to Town"

Older Mayberry citizen, Emma Watson, complains to Andy that the lady druggist will not sell her the pills she needs for her sciatica in "Ellie Comes to Town." Andy tries to explain that he cannot force Ellie to comply, but Emma is perturbed. Before she leaves the courthouse, she gives Sheriff Taylor a piece of her mind, "And to think I even voted for you in the last election. Never even considered anybody else! Bad, bad sheriff!"

Perhaps a flight attendant I heard about had Emma in the back of her mind when an unhappy, rude passenger complained about everything. The flight attendants reluctantly took turns waiting on the uppity woman, and one by one, she singlehandedly offended every person who tried to help her. There was not enough overhead space. She did not get the seat she wanted. The plane was too hot. Nothing suited her, and with each grievance, she punched the call button. When dinner was served, it contained a baked potato wrapped in aluminum foil. Within seconds, the woman pushed the button yet again and sarcastically told the flight attendant, "This is a BAD potato."

The attendant picked up the spud and spanked it three times. "BAD, BAD, BAD potato!"

One Phone Call Under the Law

Andy: No, by dog. There's more than one way to pluck a buzzard. Yes sir.
                          - Episode #11, "The Christmas Story"

The plane did not have telephones, but the rude passenger insisted he be allowed to use the one on board for airline personnel. He needed to make a car reservation. The flight attendant told him there was no such telephone, but he was adamant. He was a "million miler" at the "platinum level," and he KNEW the plane had a telephone. He needed some "niceness" lessons. After repeated confrontations, the flight attendant realized that she had a superego buzzard on her hands. Creative plucking was in order.

"Sir, you are correct. We do have a telephone on board," she finally told him. "It's just for airline personnel, but if your car reservation is THAT important, I will let you use it. Which rental agency do you want to call?"

Puffing out his chest, he responded, "Hertz," and she went to supposedly place the call. He gave the passengers around him a "they-know-better-than-to-fool-with-me" look. I am sure they were impressed.

Minutes later the young woman returned, "I have put that call through to Hertz for you, sir." He followed her to the front of the plane, and she handed him the intercom, which did resemble a telephone receiver. Putting it to his ear, he heard a flight attendant in the back of the plane say "Hertz Rental Car." He made his reservation—he thought—and with a smug smile returned to his seat.

Two flight attendants in the back of the plane and one at the front laughed and giggled until the end of the flight. Not sure about the people at the upcoming Hertz counter.

Chain Reaction

Andy: How'd you come up with an idea like this anyway? It's the kinda thing we used to do in high school.
                              - Episode #134, "Man in the Middle"

It was at the end of a long week. As I boarded, the flight attendants were still laughing because of the previous flight. A man and his wife had been seated across the aisle and two rows apart from each other. During dinner he wanted her roll, but rather than hand it, she heaved it at him. Unfortunately, she missed, hitting another passenger several rows up. This fellow sat up a little, looked over the top of his seat to see the originator of the roll toss, then glanced back down. A few seconds later, he inched his head back up over the seat like a child peering around a tree in a game of hide-and-seek. Suddenly, this adult—possibly a CEO—threw a roll at the woman, then ducked out of view. Retaliating, the husband threw his roll at the man. Within minutes, rolls were flying all over the plane. People were stirred up and did not even know what they were stirred up about.

Aunt Bee would have rapped their hands with a spoon like she did to Briscoe Darling's. After all, it was she who once admonished Ernest T. Bass, "Throwing food is a sin!" But Aunt Bee was not there, on the plane.

I asked the flight attendant what they did about it, and she replied, "Nothing. We were too busy handing out rolls."

One Volunteer

Barney to Andy: Oh, you're funny, aren't you? Oh, you're real funny. You ought to get a cane and a cigar and work in a carnival.
- **Episode #28, "Andy Forecloses"**

He just would not have it any other way. We were waiting to depart Atlanta when the gate agent announced over the public address system, "Ladies and gentlemen, we are oversold by one seat. If anyone is willing to take the next flight to Salt Lake City, we will be happy to book you on that flight and give you a round-trip coach ticket to anywhere in the continental United States." There was no activity from the passengers, so in a few seconds, he tried again. "If there is someone—ANYONE—who does not mind getting off this flight, PLEASE let us know."

Quickly, he clicked the PA on again and added, "No, this offer is NOT available for flight attendants. Don't even THINK about it!"

Fun Girl

Andy: If you don't mind my saying so, you ought to be ashamed
          of yourselves.

          - Episode #201, "A New Doctor in Town"

Howard and Floyd are concerned when Andy has a date with Mavis
Neff in "Helen, the Authoress." They hope he is made of sterner stuff
than another fellow they know. Floyd recalls it well. "You remember
what happened to Harvey Bunker when he started going with her.
They made him give up his job as scoutmaster."

In my search for Mayberry humor, a flight attendant told me
something that stirred my memory of ol' Mavis Neff and the major
move she tries to put on Andy. There had been a streaker on one of
her flights. A woman! The passenger was sitting in the rear of the
plane, and she just went into the lavatory, took off all her clothes, and
STREAKED to the front of the plane and back. (Where is a "genu-
wine" Therma weave bathrobe when you need one?)

She should have been ashamed of herself! But imagining the passengers' reactions. I started laughing, "What did you do?"

"Well, obviously, we cut off her drinks . . . but that is not the funny
story." The flight attendant leaned closer. "A little later, an elderly man
who had been drinking apple juice pushed his call button and ordered
a cup of black coffee. No sugar. No cream. Just strong, black coffee. He
said he needed something to wake him up."

With a wink, he also explained to the flight attendant, "My wife
tells me I slept through something very exciting, and I do not want to
miss it if it happens again. Which one of you girls was it?"

Folding Up In Combat

Gomer: I'd feel better if someone of a more official nature than you
was in charge.

- Episode #118, "Andy's Vacation"

The flight attendant explained that when she worked in reservations, she grew accustomed to giving the same information over and over: "Be at the airport forty-five-minutes before the flight." "No, there is not a movie shown on a thirty-five- minute flight." "You are allowed three pieces of checked luggage." One day, just when the job got boring, a very angry passenger-to-be announced, "I wanna speak to the supervisor! Now!" Clearly, she was frosted.

We might have called the reservationist a "trouble checker." Her job was to try to ward off the call to her superior, so she responded with what she learned in receptionist training. "Why don't you tell me the problem. Perhaps I can help you?"

"No. Who's in charge? THAT'S the person I want to speak to. You gave me wrong information once, and it cost me a lot of money. I am not talking to anybody but a supervisor!"

Still trying to head off a supervisor-directed call, the reservationist asked, "What wrong information? How did it cost you money?"

"I'm going on a trip next month. I called y'all last week and asked how much luggage I could take on my trip, and the woman told me PLAIN AS DAY—'three checked bags.' And I went out, and I bought three expensive, red and black checked bags! Now a friend of mine says I did not have to do that at all. And THAT IS WHY I want to talk to a supervisor!"

"At that point, I transferred her call," the flight attendant related to me with a shrug, "Hey, that's why supervisors get paid more."

Eye Witness Identification

Andy: Do you know what would make it a fine picture? If you had brought your uniform. Of course, I don't imagine you brought that.

Barney: Well, it just so happens I DID pack it.

Andy: You didn't.

Barney: Well, it was hanging in the closet, and I had room in the suitcase. I didn't know if there'd be any occasion.

- Episode #177, "The Legend of Barney Fife"

In Toronto, I went straight to the airport after my speech, not knowing how long it would take to go through customs. I like to travel in comfortable clothes, but this time, I wore my new "speakin' suit" rather than chance missing the flight. Floyd Lawson believes that to get a good suit, people have to go to Mt. Pilot, but I found mine in Atlanta in a shop for tall women. It was very tailored and I had not worn it much. However, I had never worn it in an airport, or I might have picked up on the fact that the navy was identical to the color of the Delta Air Lines flight crews. (I had wanted a suit the color of salt and pepper mixed together, but I could not find it.) The similarity to the flight crew's uniforms slipped by me. Nor did I notice that I was walking directly behind a flight crew as I approached the security checkpoint.

At the scanning machine, I stopped and bent over to put my rolling cart on the moving belt. "That's OK," the woman said casually. "You do not have to do that."

"Ohhhh," I thought. "She has read my book."

I continued my procedure out of habit, placing the travel bag on the machine. Maybe she was not talking to me? But her eyes were fixed in my direction, so I finally said, "I beg your pardon?"

She flipped off the conveyer belt, placed her hand on my bag, and hoisted it up and over to the floor. "YOU do not have to do that," she explained again with a hint of impatience.

Maybe southerners have to go through a special interpreter?

The lady motioned toward a guard about ten feet away. "Just show that man your picture."

I was confused. "My picture?"

"Yes, just let him see your picture and get a good look at your face." It did not seem right to me, but, hey, I was in a foreign country. Maybe they did things differently.

Rolling my cart behind me, I reached in my purse and pulled out one of my speaking brochures. A few feet away, I handed it to the man in uniform. "I understand that you want to see this."

Clearly perplexed, he looked at the picture on the brochure and then gazed back at me. Thinking he was making a comparison, I tilted my head and smiled, just like in the photo.

"Very impressive," he nodded, "but take a look at this."

He whipped out his wallet and showed me a picture of his wife!

A Cappella

Barney: Ho, Ho, Ho, Merry Christmas!
                                   - Episode #11, "The Christmas Story"

It is the holiday season in the "The Christmas Story," and Scrooge Ben Weaver puts a damper on everything when he arrests a local fellow for moonshining. Ben has the evidence to prove it, and Andy has to admit it is not "sarsaparilla." The moonshiner is not making his product to sell; he just wants to "merry up" Christmas a little. Too bad he did not think of trying singing.

Several days before Christmas, bad weather turned a normally one-hour flight into a seven-hour odyssey. All airports near my destination closed after we took off, and our flight was shuttled from city to city, refueling along the way. Passengers were kept on board the entire time.

After the initial irritation, frivolity, and humor set in, along with complimentary drinks—MANY complimentary drinks. Toward the end of the ordeal, a passenger asked for one more bourbon and water.

Knowing we had at last found a place to land and fearing he would have to drive home, the flight attendant refused his request. He pleaded, "If you will give me one more drink, I will stand at the front of the plane and sing *Ave Maria.*"

Well, it WAS the Christmas season, and we had been in the air long enough for it to be New Year's Eve, so she took him up on his offer. Getting everyone's attention, she announced to the rest of us that if the guy sang well enough, he could have one last drink. There would be a vote.

I thought the guy was doing the best he could, but everyone did not appreciate his efforts. After a line or two, sung off-key and at the top of his lungs, another passenger stood up and pleaded, "I'll give him my drink if he will just STOP THAT SINGING!"

Watch It!

Floyd: Humph! That insulting attitude of yours isn't getting us anywhere.

- Episode #74, "Convicts-at-Large"

The passenger plopped several enormous pieces of luggage on the floor in front of the flight attendant just inside the airplane door. "Here! YOU find a place for them!" he barked. And then, whoosh, he was gone. It was clearly a case of intimidation.

Her brow wrinkled at his rudeness, but the flight attendant said nothing. Maybe she figured it was good for him to get mad and get a little circulation going early in the morning. When he was out of sight, she got a little circulation going of her own. She picked up the bags and THREW them off the plane onto the jetway, almost hitting the startled gate agent bringing the paperwork down the ramp. "Check these bags, please, and bring me the claim checks."

There was no further mention of the luggage until the plane was about to land. Then Mr. Congeniality became very interested in their location and pushed his call button. Where had she put his bags?

She had been waiting for that question the entire trip. "You told me to find a place for them, sir, and I did. I put them in the jetway before we closed the door. I am sure they are back in Atlanta."

She let him go berserk for a few minutes, and then calmly handed him two claim checks. Their eyes locked in silence. Intimidation a second time. Pure and simple intimidation. He did not say a word. She did not have to. Triumph!

One has to find ways to keep amused while traveling. On this day, I went down to baggage claim just to watch him pace. Paraphrasing Andy, "I wouldn't have taken a dollar and a quarter for it."

On My Word . . .

Andy, quoting from *Othello*: "Oh, what a tangled web we weave when first we practice to deceive."[30]

- Episode #53, "Guest of Honor"

Gentleman Dan Caldwell gives his word often in "Andy and the Gentleman Crook." He tells Aunt Bee he never met a more charming lady—on his word as a gentleman. He promises Opie he will finish a story about John Dillinger the next day—on his word as a gentleman. He assures Barney he will not try to escape—on his word as a gentleman. Of course, the problem is . . . he gives his word a lot, and he is no gentleman.

Two men seated together summoned a flight attendant. "We have a two-dollar bet on something," one of them explained. "Help us settle it."

It sounded like trouble. She knew it and had a whole lot too much "smart" to get pulled into that one. "Oooh, no," she protested. "I am not getting involved. Gambling is illegal on our flights. I'll report you."

"Oh, come on. The bet is on which one of us is uglier looking. We have two dollars riding on it. You decide." Both men lifted their chins

---

30 This phrase, often attributed to Shakespeare, was authored by the Scottish author, Sir Walter Scott.

slightly and flashed runway smiles in her direction. Lots of teeth. (I wondered if one twitched his cute little nose while the other batted his eyes.)

"The uglier? You're both ugly," the attendant announced with a laugh and proceeded up the aisle.

After the grilled chicken on lettuce had been served, one of the two fellows fell asleep, and immediately his friend started motioning for the flight attendant to return. "Now, tell the truth," he whispered. "He will never know. The bet is off. He is uglier than I am, isn't he?"

That is the problem about "smart." Sometimes it can be prodded out of you.

"OK," she agreed and pretended to be sizing up both men. Finally, she proclaimed her choice. "HE . . . is uglier than you."

The instant the words were out of her mouth, the winner—or shall we say the lucky loser—hit his buddy on the arm. "Wake up! You owe me two bucks! She said you are uglier than I am."

"You told me you would not tell him!" the attendant scolded with fake ire.

The con man puffed up his chest to brag, "I am not only better looking, I am a better liar, too!"

Now Cut That Out!

Charlene Darling: Oh, Pa, can't I even look at the pretty man?
                    - Episode #88, "The Darlings Are Coming"

It generated excitement to a routine commuter flight when the attractive, college-age young woman exited through the small door. She wore a sassy cowboy hat that certainly did not have any berries decorating it, and before she could get down the steps, the wind pulled it off and sent it tumbling across the tarmac. She jumped to the ground and took off after it, racing by three other planes and causing a baggage truck to skid to a halt. Within seconds, airplane personnel surrounded her and escorted her back to our plane, hatless. But minutes later, a muscular, good-looking guy (the word is "hunk") ran up with the elusive object. She was so grateful to get her hat back that she gave him a hug and a little "kissy" on the jaw, bringing hoots and whistles from his buddies. Not to be outdone, he grabbed her and laid one back on her, flat on the mouth. (I believe it is called moxie.)

A woman my age standing near me said, "I think I'll drop my purse and see if I can attract him over here."

A Negligee with a Black Nightgown

Andy: I did used to take the *Police Gazette* though, but I had to cut it out when Deputy Fife joined the force. Well see, it had a lot of girlie pictures in it, and Barney, he . . . he's never been married.

- Episode #26, "The Inspector"

A couple I estimated to be in their eighties sat down near me in a gate area in the Atlanta airport. Someone had left a magazine on the next seat, and when the woman picked it up, it fell open at the centerfold. "Humph!" she said in disgust and turned the "girlie" picture toward her husband. (I believe the person in the picture just had a ribbon on her foot.) "Now that is just NOT sexy, is it?" the woman asked her husband.

The guy gave the page a long look, and fought to hold back a grin before he winked at me and answered to his wife, "If you say so, dear."

More Power to You

Goober: Well, being an executive, I decided to wear my suit . . . for the first day anyway.

- Episode #221, "Goober the Executive"

Goober gets in a little over his head in "Goober the Executive." Everybody is after him to do something, including a salesman who thinks that he needs a third gas pump.

The salesman's title is Vice President in Charge of Regional Sales for Northeast North Carolina for the Emblem Oil Company of El Paso, Texas. Whew!

The yuppie seated beside me on a flight back to North Carolina was originally from Asheboro, a small town not far from where I live. He introduced himself as David. I asked him the typical airline conversation question, "What company are you with?"

"RJR," he said, naming one of the biggest companies based in the state.

"What do you do with RJR?" I asked, and a few minutes later, just to make sure I noted it correctly, requested, "Say it again."

In a businesslike manner, he responded, "I am the senior technical manager, corporate information systems audit, responsible for microcomputers, decision support systems, and data communications network audit."

I just looked at him a few seconds, trying to put it all together before I spoke. The world has gotten so complicated. "And tell me something. When your mother goes to her Ladies Auxiliary meeting down in Asheboro, and her friends ask her what little Davey is doing, what does she say?"

He grinned, nodded his head in understanding, and answered my question in small-town talk. "She smiles and says, 'Little Davey has a real gooooood job at RJR'"

Call 'Em as You See 'Em

Aunt Bee: I mended your socks, and I washed those knickers as best I could.

Opie: Not knickers, Aunt Bee.

Aunt Bee: Oh, I know. It's got some technical name like dugout or something. My, I'll be glad when this is all over.

-Episode #195, "The Ball Game"

Mayberry humor at its best!

There is certainly nothing wrong with kids playing baseball. To many people, it is the national pastime. The young executive seated beside me on the plane was getting his boy started early and told about rushing the previous day to get to his son's Little League game. Leaving work, he had called the boy on the car phone and started giving instructions. "Be ready, son. I am running late. We will make it, but it will be close."

"Yes sir."

"Get your glove because we won't have time to look for it."

"Yes sir."

"Be looking for me when I pull in the driveway."

"Yes sir."

"See you in a few minutes."

"Yes sir."

Suddenly remembering that his son needed to wear his baseball uniform, he said, "Oh, wait a second, son. WAIT A SECOND! What do you have on?"

After a pause, the tiny voice said, "Andy Griffith."

A Penny Saved is a Penny Earned

Andy, to Aunt Bee: You go to way yonder too much trouble to save money.

- Episode #120, "Bargain Day"

I was in the ladies' room in the Pittsburgh airport. One traveler was washing her hands, and another woman occupied a stall. Suddenly, a fourth woman burst in and immediately looked under the doors checking for feet.

She was looking for her buddy who had just attended a college reunion with her. Later I learned that the two had been suitemates years earlier and that the housemother had once called a dormitory meeting to announce they were using too much toilet paper. Well, why throw away good money? After all, a penny saved . . . .. This scenario had thrown them into hysterics then, and again when discussed at the reunion. Not knowing the background, I just saw a woman scurry into the restroom, check for feet, and then knock on the closed stall door as she sang out, "Hey! You're using too much toilet paper in there!"

The woman at the sink jumped and asked timidly, "Am I using too much soap?"

Social Security In Action

Aunt Bee: Oh, he's in seventh heaven.

- Episode #184, "A Baby in the House"

Big Jeff Pruitt arrives in Mayberry to find a "female type" in "The Farmer Takes a Wife." Barney's suggestion is to drop in on a hen party at Thelma Lou's. Jeff loves that idea because it lets him "look over the whole crop and pick one out."

A gentleman I saw did not need a whole "crop" of feminine "pulchritude" to make him happy. A few ladies could do the trick.

The passengers were already seated and ready for departure on a Delta flight to Greensboro when the two gate agents escorted one more person down the jetway, an elderly man who needed a great deal of assistance. He had a cane which he attempted to use as he slid his feet along, and he had a big grin that let us know he was basking in the attention.

At the door of the aircraft, the gate agents turned him over to the flight attendants. "Mr. Breeney needs a little help," one of them said. A flight attendant stopped what she was doing and answered, "Well, we are just the people who can help him." Mr. Breeney kept grinning as he moved with great deliberation past the galley. He was in hog heaven. Four women were all hovering around him.

"I'LL GET IN FRONT OF YOU, MR. BREENEY," one of the flight attendants said, raising her voice as we often do around older people. She maneuvered into position while the second attendant stayed behind him. Mr. Breeney kept barely moving—and grinning. "OK,

MR. BREENEY," the first flight attendant said. "YOU PUT YOUR HAND ON MY SHOULDER—AND GRAB HOLD OF MY ELBOW OR ARM."

Mr. Breeney never broke his shuffle or the twinkle in his eye when he shouted, "YOU SHOW ME THE PART . . . AND I'LL GRAB IT!"

No Coffee, Tea, or Punch, Thank You

Cy Hudgins: Well, I sure hope he don't do no damage. You know, that fool goat will eat anything he can get his teeth into.
                    - Episode #81, "The Loaded Goat"

For a minute, I thought Jimmy, the goat, was on a trip with me.

"What can I get you?" the flight attendant asked the woman seated beside me on a nine-hour flight to Honolulu.

"Do you have any drink that tastes like a cigarette?" she replied with a plea.

The attendant smiled. "I would not be working for the airlines if I had the formula for that."

"I tried to quit once," the passenger explained to me when the attendant moved up the aisle. "I gained weight. It was tough. I ate more."

Before I could comment, she explained further, "Well, actually, it was not that I ate more. It is just that I ate strange things, such as pencils, tablets, and pieces of cardboard. I gnawed on chairs during my break." (It sounded to me like she would have eaten anything she could get her teeth into.)

Later I was halfway up the aisle to the lavatory when I turned back to get my papers and pencil. No need to tempt someone.

Somebody's Impression of . . . Something

Howard: You see, Goober, abstract paintings are not representational.
Goober: They ain't?
Howard: No, no, not by any manner or means.

- Episode #246, "The Wedding"

Howard Sprague, Mayberry County Clerk, and a mother's boy, finally gets his swinging bachelor's pad in "The Wedding." He decorates it himself. Goober likes sitting on the bearskin rug, but he just does not understand the paintings. Apparently, somebody at the Atlanta airport found the same off-the-beat place Howard had shopped at in Mt. Pilot.

It took a while, but regular travelers through the Atlanta airport finally accepted the large displays of abstract art over the escalators. More accurately, we got accustomed to it. The neon lights, splashes of color, and strange configurations across large walls still jolt first-timers.

Two men in front of me stepped on a down escalator and immediately stopped talking when they gazed upward. The artwork was . . . different. Incomplete? Upside down maybe? They just could not figure it out.

Sometimes a quiet statement says it best. At the end of the long, wordless ride down, one of the men sighed, "Boy, somebody did a good selling job."

A Pick-Me-Up

Barney: Yeah, I guess I didn't hit the ol' sack 'til almost 10:30. Boy, these late hours are going to kill me dead.

- Episode #36, "Barney on the Rebound"

I took a taxi from O'Hare to downtown Chicago at 2:45 a.m.—the MIDDLE of the night. It had been a long flight with a dull movie, something like *The Anteaters From Outer Space*. (A three-handkerchief picture.) After great discussion, the passengers had deduced that the meal was chicken cacciatore. I was just thankful to finally be in my destination city. As we pulled out onto the freeway, the driver turned slightly and offered me gum, extending one of those jumbo packs in my direction. "I would love some," I responded, pulling out a piece. "Thanks." I am not a slender, high-spirited person like Barney claims to be, but I do like a sugar pick-me-up late in the day.

The driver put the remaining sticks down on the front seat and said casually, "Wish I could offer you more. I tried to get a liquor license, but they said I need a more permanent location."

It was REAL FUNNY at 2:45 a.m. Well, I laughed.

Baseball Costumes

Helen shows Aunt Bee and Andy photos from the baseball game:
Aunt Bee: Oh, yes, there you are in your umpire's costume.
Andy: Uniform, Aunt Bee.
Aunt Bee: All right, uniform.

- Episode #195, "The Ball Game"

Aunt Bee is so excited about sister Nora and Ollie coming to Mayberry in "Family Visit." Andy and Ollie will surely have a lot in common. After all, they used to play baseball together, and according to Aunt Bee, "Once you learn to catch a ball, you never forget." Apparently, all the professional teams did not get the word.

"You'll be met at the airport by a man dressed as a Chicago Cub fan." Those were my exact travel instructions for a speaking trip to Peoria, Illinois. The flight arrived on schedule, but no one fitting that description stepped forward. After fifteen minutes, I went to the ticket counter to have him paged. Fortunately, I had the fellow's name. No telling who would have responded to an announcement of, "Will the person dressed as a Chicago Cub fan please pick up the page phone."

After placing my page, I commented to the airline agents, "He is supposed to be dressed as a Chicago Cub fan." They instantly pounded the counter in laughter. "A Cub fan? Dressed in a Cub outfit? Then look for someone in camouflage. The Cubs have lost the last seven games." (Maybe someone had touched their baseball and jinxed the team.[31]) When they got control, one asked, "And just what do you think a Chicago Cub fan will look like?"

I am from basketball country. To my knowledge, I have never seen an authentic Chicago Cub fan, but why end their fun? "Oh, he'll have on a Cub T-shirt and a Cub hat," I surmised, "and maybe a glove. And he will probably be tossing a baseball and catching it, and . . . "

They laughed so loud at that comment that the supervisor came out to check on them. Finally, one said to me, "You were on the right track until you said he would be tossing a baseball and CATCHING it. CATCHING it? Not a chance!"

My client arrived, wearing a standard dark suit. As we walked away, I said, "I thought you were going to be dressed as a Chicago Cub fan."

He lowered his head and whispered out of the side of his mouth, "It is NOT THE TIME to be dressing in Cub memorabilia."

A Wake-up Call!

Floyd: Yeasaas. By the way, a funny thing happened to me yester-
           day at the shop. Ned Gresham said to me, he said, "Floyd,
           you look tired." And I said, "I'm so tired I can hardly keep
           my mouth open."

- Episode #216, "Howard, the Comedian"

It was 5:05 a.m.—A.M.!—and I was waiting in the gate area for a 5:30 flight out of Nashville. Other passengers in various stages of sleep were stretched out nearby. Their mouths hung open, and their heads snapped upward when they dozed over too far. They would have fit in perfectly on the bench in front of Floyd's barbershop.

---

31 In the episode "The Jinx" Floyd remembers that his son had once been jinxed when Henry Bennett touched the boy's baseball.

A couple of good ol' boys with hanging bags the size of Buicks plodded down the concourse and plopped down in seats across from me. They were not merry men. Later in the day, their attire would be whipped into shape; but at that hour, their shirt collars were open and ties hung randomly around their necks. One of them had missed a spot combing his hair, and it pointed straight out toward the ceiling. I raised a hand to my own head just to check.

The dynamic duo stuck their feet straight out in front of them and hung their heads over the backs of their chairs, balancing cardboard coffee cups on the armrests. Just when I expected snoring, one mumbled, "I didn't know airplanes got up this early. I had to get up at 3:30 to get here."

It took so long for his buddy to respond that I thought he was sound asleep. Finally, he mustered enough strength to say, "My travel agent has been trying to get me on this flight for years." He stayed stretched to the limit for a few more seconds, then slowly sat up and took a swig of his coffee. A sly grin snuck across his face. "I think I'll go call her."

And away he ambled.

Curious Acting

Goober: If a fellow ain't curious about things, he'll never learn nothing.
                    - Episode #205, "Don't Miss a Good Bet"

I flew to New Orleans to speak at the Hyatt Hotel and was met by a hotel driver named Stewart. After settling into the long, black car, I held off until we pulled away before looking for Mayberry humor.

"How long have you been driving for the Hyatt?"

He looked out his side window as he maneuvered into traffic. Without glancing my way, he casually replied, "Oh, several years."

I waited a few seconds, then asked, "What's the funniest thing that has happened to you driving people back and forth?"

Was that such a stupid question? Stewart cocked his head to one side and looked at me through his rearview mirror. Studying me between glances at the road, he finally answered a block later. "The funniest thing is, that is the SAME QUESTION you asked me when I drove you about a year ago."

The next morning, I told the audience about Stewart and his good memory. They loved it, and later I saw several of the convention attendees relating the story to him. Oh, he was enjoying it. He was leaning back, resting his weight on his elbow on the bell stand, and had a smug grin on his face.

I watched silently from afar for a few moments until he suddenly realized I was there. Without shifting his weight, he threw up a hand in my direction as though waving to the masses from a balcony. "Hey, thanks, Mrs. Robertson! You made me a STAR!"

Gluttons, Gluttons, Glut-tons

Opie: Can I have my nickel for milk?
Aunt Bee: Um-hum. Now, remember, this is for milk, not another piece
          of apple pie. You need that milk to make your bones hard.
                              - Episode #34, "Opie and the Bully"

Aunt Bee certainly knows the correct order of eating and takes pains to remind her nephew in "Opie and the Bully." Sandwiches come before apple pie. More than likely, we all had "Aunt Bees" to tell us stuff like this. Even when we know better, though, if our "reminders" are not around . . . .

I shared the forty-minute van drive to Hilton Head Island with four men from a pizza company. They were part of the group I was to address, the Southeastern School Foods Association.

We were all hungry, and the driver agreed to stop at the little "groce-teria" near the airport if we made it snappy. He had to stay on schedule.

The five of us hit the ground running and descended on the store like a busload of teenagers. We scooped up the first snacks that met our eyes, threw down our money, and within minutes scurried out with an assort-ment of chips, candy, beef jerky, and popcorn. All five of us clenched cups of soft drinks between our teeth, and after we had settled back into our places in the van, the only sound was the rattling of wrappers.

On the road again, the driver asked why we were going to Hilton Head. No one answered at first because our mouths were full. Then too, maybe we did not want to respond.

Finally, one of the men mumbled the truth through chocolate and nuts, "A conference on school nutrition."

I've Got the Magazines to Swing It

Aunt Bee to retiring Congressman John Canfield: Oh, my goodness. You make Mayberry sound like a one-horse town. We are not that far behind anymore. We have our social functions just like any big city.

- Episode #160, "Aunt Bee, the Swinger"

Early one morning in Tuscaloosa, Alabama, I shared the hotel shuttle to the airport with two men from Dallas, Texas. They had driven a new truck to Alabama and were flying home. Delivering trucks was a second job. First and foremost, they were firemen, a fact I discovered when we passed a firehouse. As fate would have it, the shuttle driver was a volunteer fireman, and an instant bond was created among the three. I started to break into the conversation and tell them about a fire I caused in the kitchen one time when I was boiling dinner, but decided against it and just rode along, listening.

One man asked, "How many shifts does your fire department run here?" The driver said, "Three. A, B, and C." (I bet Barney would have said something like "1, B, and 3.")

His answer surprised the two big-city keepers of the flame, and they raised their eyebrows at each other. "Really? Three shifts?" We rode on a few seconds while they thought. Soon one commented, "I'm surprised they'd run three shifts, no bigger than Tuscaloosa is."

The driver drawled, "We may be smaller than y'all, but we git the same magazines."

My Big Finish

Gomer: How'd you do that with your voice?

- Episode #122, "A Deal Is a Deal"

The day before the first Martin Luther King national holiday, I was again in the back of an airport shuttle van heading from Savannah to Hilton Head Island. The front two seats were filled with white male sales reps traveling together. They glanced at newspapers and ignored me when the conversation turned to the new holiday. They were against it. I could tell they did not like change very much. Change upset them, and they wanted things to stay the same. (They probably did not even like the government putting stamp machines in the post offices.)

One by one, they listed all of their reasons for opposing the special day, and still ignored the fact that I was present. Eventually, one guy sighed and said, "I am not against blacks or anything; it is just the whole minority issue. This year blacks get a day, and before you know it, next year WOMEN will want a day!"

The instant the words were out of his mouth, a hush spread through the van. I could tell they were cutting their eyes toward one another and signaling in my direction. After a few awkward seconds, the big talker turned to me and said, "I'm sorry. I hope I did not offend you."

"No, you didn't," I replied with a careful mix of sweetness and sarcasm. "But then, I am not black."

He laughed nervously, not knowing what that meant, and turned back to the front. There was another uncomfortable silence which I ended seconds later. Dropping my voice as deep as it would go, I grumbled, "I am not a woman either."

Short-haired Mink

Emmett: I'm not much of an expert on furs. I know you're supposed
to blow on them, but I never knew why.

- Episode #245, "Emmett's Anniversary"

Barney purchases a fur for Thelma Lou in "The Luck of Newton
Monroe." It sets him back thirteen and a quarter. (That is $13.25.)
That does not seem like much money for a fur, but Barney can tell it
is genuine because he blows on it. The "genuine" fur falls out when
Thel' shakes it. This episode always reminds me of a cab ride I once
had in Texas.

"Just push those stuffed animals out of the way," the Austin, Texas
cab driver instructed when he opened the back door. A hoard of little
bears, tigers, and lions peered up from the floorboard. There was even
a pink elephant.

Hey, we are nothing if we are not flexible, and I do know a character when I happen upon one. So, I carefully started the process of
getting into the cab. It is never simple for a 6'2" woman to climb into
the back seat of an automobile, and maneuvering around stacks of
small stuffed animals did not help. I was careful not to step on any of
them as we pulled away from the airport curb. I felt as though I had
boarded Noah's Ark.

"I'm sorry if my little friends are in your way," the driver explained.
"I've got a meeting with the mayor in a few days because the city won't
let me keep 'em across the back window. The powers-that-be think they
fall down on the passengers." I looked down at dozens of little button
eyes staring up at me and picked up a floppy-eared dog. Bless its heart.

"I like to decorate my cab, but the city thinks I can't see out the back,
which is ridiculous," the driver explained further. "I use the mirrors
on the sides. I am taking my case to the top. I'll go to the Supreme
Court if I have to, but I'll start with the mayor."

I put a fierce-looking eagle and a tough-looking tiger on the seat
beside me and reached for several others. I smiled at them. It is a

Miss Congeniality carryover; I smile at everybody and everything. However, I stopped smiling when I noticed the empty gun holster hanging on the rearview mirror.

"What's the purpose of the empty gun holster?" I asked, balancing a pitiful-looking little elephant on my knee.

He drawled, "Makes people wonder where the gun is."

Seconds later, my driver saw a familiar cab and quickly reached for a microphone under his dashboard. He had a loudspeaker system attached to the OUTSIDE of his cab and started making off-the-cuff, friendly remarks when we passed his cab-driving buddies. "You're looking good, John!" "Wash your cab, Jack!" "Hey, whatcha doing over there?" He was having a ball! It reminded me of the time Barney runs for sheriff and hires a man to ride around town in a truck with a PA system. The blaring noise startles people, to say the least. "FIFE FOR SHERIFF!" "WIN WITH FIFE!"

"I'm right behind you," my driver blared as we pulled behind a friend at a light. The friend threw up his hand and laughed, but his startled passenger wheeled around in panic. My driver smiled and saluted. I waved a couple of stuffed animals. The passenger was still staring when we passed him. By then, I had several little animals pressed against the window on his side, waving their little paws in his direction. I just thought I would give him something to talk about when he got home.

My driver seemed like a source for Mayberry humor, so I asked him about something funny that had happened in his cab. I figured it had to do with the loudspeaker or the animals. Wrong.

"It don't get that cold in Texas, but a lot of women down here wear fur because their friends do," he explained. "Once, I had a woman passenger up here in the front seat. In the middle of the trip, I glanced at her and her collar started moving. It was slow at first, but it WAS moving. I thought I had been working too long . . . and then I realized that collar was looking me right in the eyes. She had a pet ferret around her neck!"

The next day I rode with a different cab company as I left Austin. I asked my driver if he knew a guy who liked to line stuffed animals across his back window? Nope. How about a driver who hung an empty gun holster on his rearview mirror? Didn't believe he wanted to.

Then I mentioned the loudspeaker on the outside of the cab. "Oh yeah, I know EXACTLY who you're talking about. We need guys like him because they make us smile. He's the one who shot that ferret!"

Traveling Religion

Andy, to "widow" Annabelle Silby: Yeah, I know. Being run over by a taxi cab ain't the most fitting way for a man to go.
- **Episode #5, "Opie's Charity"**

Well, of course not! Being run over by a taxi cab is definitely not the most fitting way to pass on to our great reward. But if it did happen that way, the town of Gibsonville, North Carolina, might be the place to be.

After traveling over the country asking cab drivers for examples of Mayberry humor, I returned home in November 1992 and picked up a local newspaper. Right there on the front page of the second section was a feature story on a new cab company in Gibsonville, a small community in the county. The owner had two cabs, and their names were "God" and "Jesus." I do not make this stuff up. THE NAMES OF THE CABS WERE . . . "GOD" AND "JESUS!" What does a customer think when the dispatcher says, "We will send God right over?"

Of course, if a person gets run over by either of those cabs, it might lead to an inside track to a better place. And a lot of us need all the help we can get.

Alligator Farm in Florida

Barney: All wild creatures shy away from anything with man smell.
- **Episode #101, "Opie the Birdman"**

The van driver from the Tampa airport to Innisbrook nonchalantly gave us his usual general instructions about the resort. Shuttle buses were available to take us from lodging to the convention building, room service was available if we preferred to eat in our rooms, and then, "If you play golf, be careful of the alligators."

He had MY attention. "Excuse me, are alligators on the golf courses?"

"Oh yes, you will see them out there almost every day. Big ones, up to twelve feet long."

I leaned forward. "Won't they attack people? In the movies, they run fast."

He nodded. "They do, but only for thirty or forty yards. After that, they tire out."

I mumbled, "It would be the fastest FIFTY-yard dash I would ever run. I would breeze across the fairway like greased lightning."

At the next stoplight, the driver twisted around in his seat to tell me quite earnestly, "Well, you would not really want to dash. If an alligator is chasing you, the best thing to do is to zigzag. Cut left to right, left to right. Keep it up and you will be OK Alligators don't zigzag well."

THE MAN SAID, "Alligators don't zigzag well." I am no rocket scientist, but I am not sure one has to be to figure this out. THEY DON'T HAVE TO! All they have to do is run straight forward. If the humans are zigzagging from left to right in front of them, alligators can just stay on a straight path, and before long, they will get us! SNAPAROO!

I had a mental picture of a man running lickety-split across a golf course, trying to get away from a twelve-foot alligator. His friends up at the clubhouse were screaming, "Zigzag! Charlie! Zigzag!"

The headline would have read: ZIGGED WHEN HE SHOULD HAVE ZAGGED.

Gives a Body the Creeps

Andy: What are you going to do tonight?

Barney: Nothing. Sit around in my room. Not much can happen to
            me there.

- Episode #146, "The Lucky Letter"

Do not be so sure, Barney. Remember the young man from out-of-town who walks right up to the hotel counter in "Stranger in Town?" He wants a room and the clerk gives him #209. The visitor knows it well. Wilbur Hennessey got drunk in that room and fell out the window. He wants another room and requests #216, saying, "Not that green is my favorite color, but at least it's been freshly painted." Some hotel rooms do stand out and much CAN HAPPEN in one.

Continuing my search for Mayberry humor, I asked the desk clerks at a hotel in Pennsylvania to tell me something funny about their work. They immediately looked at each other and said in unison, "108."

Months earlier a man had overdosed in that room, but they got help in time to save him. A few weeks later, room 108 caught on fire. It was refurbished. Then the general manager told them that a few years back a man had died in room 108.

So, when a late-night check-in was very, very rude to them earlier that week, they said at the same time from several feet away and without looking at each other, "Put him in room 108."

Say Cheese

Aunt Bee: Well, I'm trying to keep a complete record of our vacation
            for the folks back home. And then I can say to the ladies,
            "That's our bellboy."

- Episode #167, "Taylors in Hollywood"

It is evident the Taylors are not world travelers when they check into the Piedmont Hotel in "Taylors in Hollywood." The instant the bellman steps out of the main room, Aunt Bee, Andy, and Opie do what people do. They dance around and mouth to one another about how nice and large the room is, snapping back into savvy travelers when the bell-man reappears. Probably did not fool the fellow, though, not when they invite him to come back any time for a visit. I often wonder what bellmen say about me, especially a bellman named Alexander.

My client took me to a local restaurant named "Doc Alexander's" after a speech in Texarkana, Texas. (Yes, for you Mayberryholics, I did ask the young man at the desk if he were familiar with Keevy Hazelton's hit song, "Texarkana In The Morning". He was not. Humph!) Anyway, before the meal was over, they gave me a T-shirt that bore the restaurant's logo in bright bold letters. Months later on a cold night in Kansas City, I was wearing the shirt over another T-shirt when a waiter brought room service to my room. He asked where I got the T-shirt. I told him and inquired, "Why?"

"Oh, my name is Alexander, so it just caught my attention."

I did not bat an eye. "Well, here," I said, reaching for the bottom of the shirt to pull it up over my head. "I want you to have this one." Not realizing there was another shirt underneath it, he stepped back quickly. "WAIT A MINUTE!"

When he discovered I had on a second shirt, he let out a long breath and his shoulders relaxed. "You scared me to death," he said. "The other bellmen say stuff like this happens to them, but I have never seen it."

My Lips are Sealed

Aunt Bee: Silence is my game. Mum's my name. Tick-a-lock.
                                    - Episode #118, "Andy's Vacation"

Howard cannot get a taker for a "little drinky" when he sets up his bachelor's pad in "The Wedding." His guests are not interested in grapefruit juice, lemon-lime, or orange sodas, and certainly not the hard stuff. After all, it is the middle of the day. Goober still has to do a carburetor job.

Well, that is the way it ought to be when you are working, and it almost is in one company in particular.

Mary Kay Ash (yes, of cosmetics fame) likes for her associates to dress and act appropriately at all times, but especially when they are representing her organization.[32] She emphasizes the importance of making a good impression. Smart lady. (I bet she could run "Pink Lady Cosmetics" that Andy mentions in "Andy's Investment," and run it very well.)

I was scheduled to speak at a Mary Kay Jamboree in St. Louis. Entering the hotel, I was struck by the fact that the lobby was practically empty—strange for a meeting of several thousand. The sunken bar in the center of the lobby, usually the hub of activity at that hotel, was occupied by a lone bartender, despondently resting his chin in his hand. No tips that night.

Later that evening, dining in the sparsely occupied hotel restaurant, I asked my waitress if the guests were at a banquet. "Nope, no banquet here tonight," she replied, as she put my Swiss cheese sandwich down in front of me. (I seldom order chicken when I am off duty.) "Well, where is everyone? There is a big Mary Kay Cosmetics meeting here, but nobody is in the restaurant or in the lobby."

"The word we got is that Mary Kay does not like for her people to imbibe in public. Two of the bartenders went home because there's no business in the bar."

"Ah, I see," I said, nodding my head.

The waitress looked over her left shoulder, and then her right, to see if anyone was in hearing distance. Seeing no one, she shared a secret, "Room service is BOOMING."

---

32 Mary Kay, Inc. the iconic Beauty Company was started in 1963 by Mary Kay Ash.

Adventure Sleeping

Andy: I'm too tired to eat. I think I'll just go up and see if I can get a little sleep.

- Episode #184, "A Baby in the House"

Aunt Bee insists on keeping her niece's little girl in "A Baby in the House." Then, every time she goes near Evie Joy, the baby cries. AND cries. AND CRIES! Exasperated, Andy begs, "I got to get some sleep! Do something! . . . I got to sleep!"

When I have been up all night, even a crying baby will not keep me awake. But I do prefer a PLACE to lie down.

"Yes, Mrs. Robertson, we have your reservation."

These were wonderful, WONDERFUL words because just me and my luggage arrived at the hotel in Orlando early in the day, and one of us was worn out.

The desk clerk was young, very young. Of course, that seems to be the case more and more these days. My guess was that she had just graduated from high school and was new to the job. Her eyes widened as she read the information on her computer. "Ah, Mrs. Robertson, Toastmasters International is really doing you right. They have you in a two-room suite."

I widened my eyes too, mostly not to disappoint her. "Well, how nice. It is not necessary, but certainly very nice."

Her fingers flew along the keyboard and suddenly stopped as she peered down at the computer. My "extra-sensitive perception," reared its head. "I can't get in, can I?" I asked despondently before she spoke.

"No, not right now. None of our two-room suites are clean, but we should have one for you by two o'clock. You might want to stroll around the hotel and see the sights."

"That is over three hours. Look, I really do not care about a two-room suite," I explained with extra politeness. "I will take any single room that is clean. Give me some sheets, and I will take a broom closet. I have flown all night from the West Coast, and I am beat. I have to get some sleep."

She looked a little disappointed, as though I did not comprehend the significance of this special provision. "Well, other rooms are available, but my instructions indicate you are DEFINITELY to have one of the two-room suites. They are very nice. It will be worth the wait."

I wanted to beg like Andy, "Do Something!" but instead, I just spoke with more determination. "PLEASE. I will take ANY room that is ready. FORGET the two-room suite."

She sensed I was serious. "Just a minute," she said softly and walked away from the counter to another young clerk. They put their heads together as they glanced in my direction, and in a few seconds, the first clerk walked back. "We have solved the problem," she said with a big grin. "I am going to give you two rooms."

"Two rooms?" I almost screamed, "All I want is a bed and a Bible!" But figuring she might not know Briscoe Darling's memorable quote, I let it pass. But I did say, "I don't need two rooms. What would I do with two rooms?"

The young woman thought a few seconds and then her face lit up. "You could dress in one and sleep in the other."

The thought of me running back and forth between adjoining rooms struck me as humorous, but by this time, people behind me were beginning to shift their weight impatiently. "I'll take 'em," I mumbled, and picked up the keys she put on the counter.

It was not until I got to the elevator and glanced in my hand that I made the discovery. One room was on the seventh floor; the other was on the ninth.

One Big Muscle

Barney: Yeah, I turn myself into an obstacle. Suddenly, I'm no longer Barney Fife, the man. I'm Barney Fife, the bulkhead.
                      - Episode #30, "Barney Gets His Man"

I arrived at the hotel in Denver around noon to speak at a banquet that night. Halfheartedly, I called the desk to see if the hotel had an exercise room, and was disappointed to learn that it did. That excuse flew out the window. I pulled on my traveling exercise outfit and trudged to the elevator, still trying to decide whether to exercise or just get a piece of apple crumb pie.

My "traveling exercise outfit" consisted of a pair of baggy Auburn University shorts that were raveling at the hem and a sloppy T-shirt with the words "I believe in AUBURN and love it" right next to several interesting food stains. My power shoes were Keds with the orange and blue Auburn shoestrings falling over the sides. My socks bore orange and blue stripes around the top and were bordered with little blue tigers above the ankles. My husband saw the outfit once and said I looked like a beat-up, college duffel bag. I was in Denver to speak to the National Athletic Trainers Association. Maybe they would want me to do a poster.

I opened the door to the hotel health club-normally a very quiet place in a hotel on a Saturday afternoon—and thought I had stumbled into the filming of an exercise video. Never have I seen so many head-bands, bright-colored, rumpled socks, and elastic outfits. Tiny strips of clothing fit over leotards, excuse me – leggings, and into body crevices that I normally try to keep clothing out of. This elastic stuff is foreign to me, but whoever's selling it is doing well. It is everywhere.

What I DID NOT see were fannies, thighs, or pudgy stomachs, until I passed a mirror. Most people were one big muscle from their toes to their heads. In one corner of the room, people were stretch-ing. Limber, stretch, limber, stretch. In another corner, several were jumping rope nonstop. I remembered Deputy Fife's advice on rope skipping in "A Medal for Opie," and almost started singing, "My mother, your mother, lives across the way. Every night they have a fight and this is what they say. . . ." I could not remember the rest of it. Anyway, I bit my tongue and just nodded to a few folks who stopped jumping and stretching in order to look at me and proceeded to a vacant Stairmaster. (I was afraid if I tried to jump rope, I might strangle myself.) Exactly 8 minutes, 23 seconds later, I climbed off the steps and nodded to the same people as I held my head high, sucked my stomach in, and walked out. I did not want to overdo it and get some of those "torn calciums."

I heard people laughing when I shut the door behind me. It was the only time in my life I ever wished I had on a University of Alabama T-shirt.

Just a Bed and a Bible

Barney: Well, since you're planning to spend such a long weekend with us, maybe I better frisk you and make sure you ain't sneaking in any of that bottled goods of yours.

- Episode #76, "Barney and the Governor"

Aunt Bee is so disappointed in "Aunt Bee the Crusader" when she learns that Otis has been drinking again. She has been praying for him. Otis just cannot explain it. He sees temptation coming, but it sees him coming too. He will try to do better. Well, at least he is in good company.

The young bellman at the Hyatt in Knoxville, Tennessee, started laughing when I asked him if had seen any Mayberry-type humor at the hotel. It turned out he thought he helped Otis Campbell check in one night, and amazingly, it was during a Baptist convention. "A guy with that convention had whiskey hidden in his shoes," he explained in disbelief.

"His shoes?"

"Yeah, can you believe it? A Baptist! I saw a bottle when I was helping him take his belongings upstairs and a shoe fell off my cart. I reached for it, and the guy almost shoved me to the floor to beat me to it."

I have a lot of good Baptist friends, and I knew I was going to tell them this little piece of Mayberry humor as soon as possible. First, though, I shared it with my contact when she picked me up for my speech that night. She did not miss a beat. "Do you know why you should always take two or more Baptists with you on a fishing trip?" she asked quickly.

I had no idea.

"One Baptist will drink ALL your beer. Two or more will not drink ANY of it."

Get Them Girls Outta Here!

Barney waking up Andy: There's a bunch of wild kids in town, just whooping and hollering, and screaming and carrying on. It's wide open, Ange. No telling where it will end up.

- Episode #137, "Goodbye, Sheriff Taylor"

There was a high school convention being held in the hotel, and teenagers were everywhere when I lined up to check in. Quietly standing in front of me was a white-haired senior citizen with a cane. Apparently, he had checked in earlier but had now returned to the registration desk. I overheard his polite explanation to the woman behind the counter.

"I am going to be needing a little help," he explained. "I found the room you assigned to me. But when I put the key in the door and opened it, four teenage girls inside started squealing at the top of their lungs and jumping up and down on beds. I was so startled that I backed into the hall, but by that time, more teenage girls had poured out of the adjacent rooms. They all started screaming and hopping around. I was completely surrounded. It was something like a chain reaction."

The clerk could imagine the scene, and I could also, having taught junior high squealing girls. The man clearly needed some help getting those girls out of there. "Oh, I am so sorry," she told him. "There has been a mix-up. I apologize for the inconvenience."

"Oh, it's all right," he said with a sparkle in his eyes, and a faked, newly found air of importance. "I am accustomed to it. I look like Elvis."

Sprechen Sie Deutsch?

Andy: Curious. Curious. Curious. Curious.

                              - Episode #10, "Stranger in Town"

Ed Sawyer arrives in Mayberry in "Stranger in Town," and seems to know everything about the town and its citizens. Most of the towns-people think it is peculiar, and they do not like it! One lady says it gives a body the creeps. She has seen a show on television where a stranger knew about folks in a new town, and he turned out to be from the supernatural world. Barney does not go that far. . . . He just thinks the guy is a spy and keeps throwing foreign phrases at him. Andy does not think the boy is Tokyo Rose but admits it is curious.[33] Well, a situation like this can jolt you.

I spent a New Orleans afternoon in the French Quarter and stopped to watch two street performers who had attracted a large crowd at Jackson Square. To everyone's delight, they were picking on people who were standing around, finding out their names and including them in the routine. In particular, they raked a guy named "Emmett" over the coals. I was particularly drawn to him. Emmett is not an overly used name, and this fellow even reminded me of Mayberry's Emmett Clark whose Fix-It Shop took the place of Floyd's barbershop when Howard McNear (who played Floyd) had to leave the series for good due to illness. Just like Mayberry's Emmett, the fellow in New Orleans seemed a little shy but played along with the performers. The whole routine was successful, and Emmett beamed a sheepish, slightly mischievous grin the entire time.

Several hours later, I was sitting in the Desire Oyster Bar with a dozen raw oysters right in front of me, when Emmett and his family came in. I saw them about the time he led them by my table,

---

33 Tokyo Rose was the name given by Allied troops serving in the South Pacific during WWII to all female English Speaking Japanese radio broadcasters who were used to spread Japanese propaganda.

and without giving it any thought, reacted and said, "It's Emmett! Emmett!" I startled him so that he took a step backwards, causing a chain reaction of his family bumping into one another right down the line. They looked at me with bewilderment. Not accustomed to having 6'2" women shouting at them in an oyster bar in New Orleans? Emmett's expression said he had never seen me before in his life, and he thought I was a nut. And, as we all know, you never can tell what a nut might do.

I quickly explained. "I saw the street show on Jackson Square. You were great!"

Emmett broke into a broad smile and shook his head. "Boy, that is a relief. I come to New Orleans often on business. I did not know WHERE we had met."

Is He One of Ours?

Barney: We're sort of birds of a feather, you might say. I'd like to stay and talk to you some more, but I've got work to do.
            - Episode #35, "Andy and the Woman Speeder"

Professional speakers are usually outgoing, gregarious, jaw-kissing type folks. A room packed to the walls with them might be a little overbearing, so just imagine a hotel full. It gives new meaning to the phrase "communication center."

During the National Speakers Association Convention, several of us filled an elevator at our hotel in Washington, D.C. Typical of professional speakers, we were all talking. Standing in the corner of the elevator was a man whom I had never seen, but I figured if he were in the hotel, he was attending our meeting. I thrust my hand in his direction. "Hi, I'm Jeanne Robertson. Are you an NSA member?" He cautiously extended a hand, shook mine suspiciously, and stepped back even further into the corner without saying a word. OK, perhaps he was not one of us.

"I'm sorry," I said. "I figured you were attending our convention. A speakers' meeting is here in the hotel."

He grinned. "No, I am not one of you, but I know who you are." Each speaker, assuming the stranger was referring to him/ her personally, stood a little taller and smiled. (At speakers' conventions, you have to move fast or you will catch ego.)

"I am in town by myself," he continued, "and last night I was standing in front of the hotel trying to decide where to eat dinner. Several of your members came out and did what you just did—walked right up, stuck out their hands, and asked if I was a speaker. When I told them I was not, they said it did not matter, to come on and eat with them anyway. And I did."

He flashed a broad smile. "It took me about twenty minutes to figure it out. What you people need . . . is an audience!"

Gracious Living

Barney: It's really pounded too. No question about it. They got one of these open kitchens and you can look right in there and watch 'em pound it right with your own eyes.

- **Episode #132, "Opie Loves Helen"**

The place was like a typical junction cafe, and the teenage waitress sauntered up to my table, pencil, and tablet in hand. "Whut you want?" Those were her only words, certainly not what is taught in customer service school. Whut you want?

I was by myself on a speaking trip and considered the family dinner for one, but finally said, "I'll just have a Caesar salad minus the chicken strips, and I look forward to watching you prepare it at my table, as the menu indicates."

She shifted her weight, slinging a hip to one side. "Well, we don't do that anymore. We fix it in the kitchen now."

I was searching for examples of Mayberry humor, so I was not going to let that pass. "Why?"

She shifted her weight again, "Well, THEY TOLD ME that if we're fixing it at the table, the customers are watching. And if we get to mixin' around in that big bowl, and some of the lettuce falls on the floor, . . . there's nothing we can do with it then but throw it away."

Beat to the Socks!

Andy: I've had it. I'm sick of sheriffing. I'm sick of this room. I'm sick of this town.

- Episode #118, "Andy's Vacation"

Sheriff Taylor, who is usually calm and composed, has HAD IT in "Andy's Vacation." He has been at work since four that morning and has dealt with crisis after crisis. Even though the viewer knows everything will be back to normal by the show's conclusion, it is still painful to hear Andy say he is sick of Mayberry. He is even sick of Barney in a "friendly sort of hoping-you'll-understand way." Barney gets his feelings hurt a little, but Jeanne Robertson understands. It is tough to be Miss Congeniality all the time.

Bad days are yet another realistic feature of *TAGS*. We all have them. Unknown until now, however, is how the humor on the series can help us get through those especially bad days that pop up in our "comings and goings."

When I started looking for Mayberry humor, I subconsciously stored humorous lines from the shows in my brain, or my "petulla abondola" as Barney might call it. Before long, these lines became a tremendous asset.

It seems that when I am the most tired and do not feel like talking, my airline seatmate wants to talk my arm off. I have tried everything to ward off these conversations. Headsets. Pretending to be asleep. Not knowing the language. I have even asked if the person wanted to increase his/her income while I casually drew circles on a tablet. Most people are genuinely nice, just talkative, and I do not want to be rude. This means I am destined to go through life nodding and listening to whatever long, drawn-out tale is being spun. Usually, I am bored, but my face does not let on.

However, when people are rude, and it is one of those days when I have had it, . . . well, that is another thing. That is where the humor of *TAGS* comes in handy. I play what I call "Odd Facts," which is my own in-flight version of "Interstate Pest Control." Rather than get angry, I just launch a Mayberry line and say it real friendly-like. It is surprising how quickly someone will hush when I look up from my airline meal and quote Barney. "Did you know the size of a horse's eyes are the same at birth as they are when he's fully grown?"

That is my personal favorite, but there are hundreds of these humorous lines throughout the series. Five end-the-conversation lines that have worked for me are offered below. Save them for the next time you encounter a beast that has come down out of the forest to sit next to you in flight.

Johnny Paul Jason says that if you put a horse hair into "stagnation" water that it will turn into a snake.
- **Opie, Episode #77, "Man in a Hurry"**

One theory states, if you eat too much polar bear liver, it'll kill you.
-**Andy, Episode #160, "Aunt Bee, the Swinger"**

If a rider dressed in black riding east to west on a white horse in the light of a full moon passes a bridegroom, he is cursed and the union is cursed.
- **Barney, Episode #121, "Divorce, Mountain Style"**

Puta willow chip under a dog's head while he's dreaming, and then put it under your own pillow, you'll have the same dream.
- **Barney, Episode #121, "Divorce, Mountain Style"**

A lot of polliwogs has frogged since last we laid eyes on you.
- **Briscoe Darling, Episode #193, "The Darling Fortune"**

Were the writers on *The Andy Griffith Show* clever, or what?

On one flight, however, I was seated next to the most obnoxious man I had ever met, and it was to be a four-hour trip. He was a pest—a BIG PEST—and was about to drive me out of my mind before we pulled away from the gate. I thought the clown was going to talk my head off. It is called an invasion of privacy. I wanted to scream like Emmett in "Howard the Bowler" when he advertises on the bowling shirts, and someone pulls out of the competition. "Why me? Why does it always have to happen to me?"

I could not "hermitize" myself because I had to work, so pretending to be asleep was not an option. There were no empty seats, so I could not move. I put on a headset, and this nut talked louder. I asked him about horses' eyes, and he told me about the Kentucky Derby. I told him the Dingo Dog was indigenous to Australia, and he had been there. I could have just told him to hush, but he was the kind of fellow who would not notice a muddy elephant in the snow.

Within an hour, I was about to start hollering. Then, miraculously I remembered the Darling family when they came to Mayberry in "Divorce, Mountain Style." What took me so long? I needed to fight fire with fire and outfox the fox.

"Well," I explained to Mr. Obnoxious as I put my computer up and stretched back. "I think I'll meditate." I shut my eyes and after a few seconds, mumbled, "beak of an owl, four tail feathers from a chicken hawk, piece of bacon, and a 'broke' comb." He tapped me on the arm to say, "I beg your pardon."

I continued chanting the Divorce Incantation, my eyes still pinched tight. "BEAK OF OWL, STRIP OF SWINE, TOOTH OF COMB, TAKEMINEFROMTHINE. KINABAIN, KINABA OUT, KINABA IN, AND ROUNDABOUT." Then I opened my eyes and drew a circle on his stomach with my index finger.

He developed an inhibition syndrome and did not speak again. How do you outfox a fox? You outfox him.

***

BUS STOP! We need a little coffee break. We have been traveling around so much reliving Mayberry humor from my routine "comings and goings" that bus lag might be setting in. So why don't we just sit around and do nothing for a short while? It is an excellent opportunity to reflect on the lighter side of daily living, and maybe get a raspberry snow cone. Like Barney, I love to bite the bottom off and suck out the juice.

We will not be at this stop long, because as Aunt Bee reminds us, "Fun is fun, but there's a limit to everything." Eventually, we all have to go to work, and I have permission to take you along to my work to illustrate the prevalence of Mayberry humor.

Let's "finesse" the bus and drive this next leg of our trip. Hey! Why don't we go in the squad car that is right outside? It has not been washed because everybody has been so busy, but that does not matter. Do not just stand there, somebody give me the car keys. If Floyd were around, he might send us off as he did in "Aunt Bee Learns to Drive." Remember? "May this be the start of many hours of smooth driving. May you glide over the highways like a swan skimming across a lake."

And keep your hands off that siren!

In Our Work

Andy: I swear, whenever I start to do anything, I spend eight hours looking for tools and a half hour working.

- Episode #62, "Cousin Virgil"

Andy, I know what you mean. I spend eight hours getting there and forty-five minutes speaking.

By now, it "ort" to be pretty clear that my most regular daily routine—thus, the majority of my time—is spent going from place to place. But traveling is not what I do for a living. I am not a pilot or flight attendant. Too tall. The traveling part is just my commute. It makes it possible for me to do what I do, give speeches.

My workplace is the darnedest assortment of variety you will ever see. ("The darnedest assortment of variety?" I am beginning to sound like Barney.) No matter the extent of prior planning with the client, the speaker never knows what is in store until actually on site.

Now, remember, I am a humorist, not a comedian, whose main goal is to make people laugh. My goal is to make them laugh while sliding in points agreed upon with the person who booked me. The ratio or as little Opie might say, the "horatio" of humor to the message, varies with the slot I am booked to fill. The slot might be the keynote, general session, spouses' program, luncheon, or banquet; and it may be at any time of day or night. I have spoken at 2:00 a.m., and I am not even a politician. My spot on the program changes from day to day, and so do the types of audiences. They range from "big-suits" in the corporate world to slumped-over teenage boys. In most cases, people are excited about hearing a speaker, but occasionally they interpret "coming together for a little bonus" to mean they will be receiving a check. This leads to a lower degree of excitement, or as Gomer would say, "Surprise. Surprise. Surprise."

The length of a presentation varies with what the meeting planner requests. Thirty minutes? Fine. An hour and a half? OK, but that is long enough for me. Trainer-type speakers go for hours, but the humorist generally fills the shorter slots. We opt to finish when they still like us. I prefer this because in longer sessions it is necessary to have a break. Anytime there is a break, I want to leave, so I figure everybody else does too.

And the setups? Well, again, the speaker just never knows. I go from using state-of-the-art sound equipment that is sensitive—very, very sensitive—to a step above a bullhorn, and from seventy-five people spread around a room that seats a thousand to a thousand people jammed into a room that seats seven hundred. (The latter gives new meaning to the words "making ends meet.") I have even worked on an excursion boat, but it made me extremely nervous. My head slapped against the ceiling every time the boat hit a wave. The cramped conditions did not bother the shorter people, but then, they are so close to the ground. The point is, or as Barney might emphasize, THE POINT IS . . . the setup is always a little mystery until I arrive on the scene and a big mystery after I start speaking. Gomer's surprises abound. Lights go out. Head tables collapse. People pass out in the middle of your favorite story. These things just happen when human beings congregate, and that is another reason the work part of my life is a natural place to watch people while they are watching me.

I am not laying all this out to try to impress anyone or get speeches. My purpose here is to explain why I have so many excellent opportunities to look for Mayberry humor. I believe all of us can find the lighter side of our work if we make it a habit to look for it, but I will admit that in this area, I have more chances than others. SUPERB chances. I work with people who are generally away from their normal environments and in situations that lend themselves to mishaps, and I see them—and myself—react like our friends in Mayberry. Because of my desire to tell stories from my life experiences, I have always looked for them during my speaking situations. Like Barney, I am one of those "trained noticers."

Some of my buddies promote the fact that they never present the same speech twice. They swear they put together all new presentations for each client. We humorists are very suspicious about that, but I would not accuse anyone of "falsifying" and I am certainly not making a big "melage" out of it. If some speakers say they plan an entirely new speech for every occasion, then I will simply take their word for it. The first time I heard this, though, I started sweating bullets (more than ONE bullet). Creating a whole new speech for each client is not an option for the humorist. We march to a different cymbal player.

I assure my clients that I will NOT put together a whole new speech for them. I guarantee them the stories I tell will be not only original but finely tuned. It takes time to hone a story and get the timing and little details just right. The series of steps a humorist goes through to develop stories could be the subject of another book, and it would not be as much fun as this one has been for me. But while so much of a presentation is finely tuned, it is important not to be a "push-button" or a "wind-up" speaker who gives a pat program that never deviates. The best way to achieve this—and the most fun for the audience and me—is to use a lot of on-the-spot material. This is where being a "trained noticer" comes in.

The humorist goes to the occasion with a prepared program, all the time searching for on-the-spot material to make the presentation personalized. We are like those secret service agents in front of the President, our eyes darting around the room looking for something that is about to happen. At a reception before a banquet, we float around making small talk, but we are actually hoping someone will fit a great big foot—all of it—in his/her mouth. If a "corsayge" falls into the punch bowl, we call that real good luck. If a flag falls over or the treasurer's slides are upside down—terrific! The audience may see us sitting quietly through an incalculable number of awards, certificates, and introductions, but actually, we are combing the situation and latching on to any confusing statement a recipient might make. Paraphrasing Barney, you laypeople might not pick up on it. It takes a seasoned professional.

Serve the humorist a mysterious entree or an escargot and we get our opening remarks. Let the audience moan at the golf tournament winner's dull joke or the CEO is named Buford, and we start thinking of a way to refer to it. Of course, like Howard Sprague and his attempt at comedy, it is all in the spirit of fun. I do not mean anything personal by it. THE POINT IS, humorists start looking for on-the-spot material as soon as we walk through the door.

So, noticing people and situations during my "work" has always been part of my modus operandi. But when I became enthralled with the humor of *TAGS*, I began to observe even more intently through Mayberry eyes, and I found delightful Mayberry characters everywhere. It turned out that they quite often book me to speak at their banquets and conventions, and always—ALWAYS—they sneak into my audiences. I love them just like I love any family in Mayberry. For years, I have watched people. And when the speeches were over, I have returned to my room and written down notes about the humorous things they said and did. (Heaven only knows what they were thinking about me.) I may not always know the names of these individuals I meet in my work, but they are permanently recorded in my journals and are memories I enjoy sharing with others.

Dry As Dust

Andy to Sam Benson after the preacher walks by: He's a fine man, you
   know that. The town's lucky to have him.

Sam: But those sermons of his do go on.

Andy: Well, he's got a lot that needs to be said. 'Course, now I will
   admit, sometimes he can be dry as dust.

Sam: You said it exactly, Andy. Dry as dust.

          - Episode #153, "Opie's Newspaper"

The meeting planner was seated next to me before a luncheon speech
during an all-day sales meeting. Speakers know we are not the only
pebbles on the beach, and therefore, are always interested in how we
obtain engagements, so as the chicken and dumplings were being
served, I asked, "Have you heard me speak?" He shook his head. "No,
I have never heard you speak."

"Are you a little nervous about it?" I asked with a smile.

He replied, "No. Not at all."

A few seconds ticked by, then he whispered, "Did you hear our
company president speak this morning?" I indicated I had not.

"Well, if you had, you would know why I am not nervous. ANY-
THING will be an improvement."

"Sevenish" It Is

Clara Edwards: Why that's a violation of protocol!

       - Episode #230, "Aunt Bee and the Lecturer"

Clara Edwards is upset when she learns that the Taylors have invited
the speaker for dinner in "Aunt Bee and the Lecturer." Protocol has
been violated! It does not matter that Andy is the sheriff. SHE is
the Chairman of the Hospitality Committee. The problem is solved
by also inviting Clara to dinner, which illustrates once again that

protocol can often be approached in different ways. First, of course, it is important to know the "peckin' order."

We had taken our seats for the 7:00 p.m. banquet. The only empty chair in the room was for the founder of the company, a man referred to as "The Colonel." At 7:10, a vice-president went to the microphone and said, "I want to thank everyone for being seated so promptly. We will begin serving at seven o'clock."

Light laughter spread through the crowd, and someone chimed in, "It is ten after seven now." The vice-president had Andy Taylor "smarts." He looked at his watch and shook his head. "No, it is not seven o'clock until the Colonel gets here, and the Colonel is not here. Why don't we check our watches again? I have six forty-five."

I Can't Hear You!

Floyd: I always knew this would happen! Power-mad! You give a man a little power, and it goes to his head.

                                              - Episode #195, "The Ball Game"

It gave new meaning to the term "bullheadedness." The quiet, private reception for the head table dignitaries was abruptly interrupted when someone on "the committee" clicked on a bullhorn. That is right. Dressed in his best suit at a very nice reception during a state convention, the man whipped out an emergency department bullhorn, flipped the button, and jolted years off our lives. "MAY I HAVE YOUR ATTENTION, PLEASE!" he suddenly boomed. He got it. People jumped.

"ATTENTION! ATTENTION! IT IS TIME TO PROCEED TO THE BALLROOM. FIRST, WE WILL LINE UP IN THE ORDER IN WHICH WE WILL BE SEATED. SO-AND-SO BEHIND SO-AND-SO! THEN SO-AND-SO FOLLOWED BY SO-AND-SO," he blared, methodically going down his clipboard. People did as instructed, and after a while, "NEXT IS THE SPEAKER, JEANNE ROBERTSON. JEANNE ROBERTSON!" I quickly stepped into position. Everyone was happy, so throughout the room, they stifled laughter, fell into place, and paid the bullhorn respect.

When we were lined up and scared to speak for fear of being reprimanded, our drill sergeant moved to the front to double-check everything. When he turned toward us again, people flinched backwards in anticipation. "FOLLOW ME!" he bellowed, the megaphone amplifying his words in our direction. I was reminded of a certain deputy shouting directions through his bullhorn in "Barney and the Cave Rescue." "Approach the cave entrance slowly. SLOWLY! Do not panic. DO NOT PANIC!"

Resembling a caterpillar inching along, the people assigned to the head table wound our way through the hotel corridors until we arrived at the ballroom entrance. The drill instructor with the bullhorn stopped at the door and let us pass as he watched over us every minute and continued to repeat last-minute instructions. "APPROACH THE ROOM SLOWLY. SLOWLY! STAY IN LINE. JUST FOLLOW THE ONE IN FRONT OF YOU. STAY IN LINE! KEEP GOING UNTIL THE ONE IN FRONT OF YOU STOPS! YOU WILL BE AT YOUR ASSIGNED SEAT AT THE HEAD TABLE. STAY IN LINE!" (The man clearly needed to be nipped in the bud.) Someone mumbled, "For Pete's sake, you are gonna burst my eardrum with that thing." Respect for the bullhorn was dwindling.

The thousand people attending the convention stood as we entered the large hall, and they watched in polite silence as we moved up the steps of the stage to the long head table. Seconds later, they burst out laughing when we discovered we were lined up EXACTLY BACK-WARDS from our place cards.

The first person walked to the end of the table, saw it was not his seat, and turned back to look for his card. He bumped into the woman behind him, and it was like a pile-up on a California freeway. People bounced off one another like beach balls as they tried to sort out the whole mess and find their assigned seats. "You are over here." "You are at the other end." "Does anyone see my name?" After a minute of sustained chaos, someone mumbled, "We are playing Fruit Basket

Turnover. Sit down anywhere. We will just swap place cards." The audience roared.

Someone joked under his breath, "What we need is a good bull-horn." No sooner were the words out of his mouth when "JUST TAKE A SEAT! TAKE ANY SEAT! shook water in our glasses. Waiters ran out of the kitchen. The drill instructor had joined us on stage and was standing in front of the head table with that horn pointed in our direction again.

"JUST TAKE . . . "Suddenly, one of the men reached across the table, jerked the bullhorn out of the drill instructor's hand, and turned it back toward him, and the audience.

"STOP SHOUTING AT US THROUGH THIS BLASTED HORN!"

So much for respect . . . and hooray for bud nipping!

Pot Luck and Pot Bellies

Aunt Bee: Have you noticed they're all men?

- Episode #223, "Aunt Bee the Juror"

And I do this for a living. As the male crowd of service station owners meandered into the banquet hall, it was a reasonable question for me to ask my contact, "Do your people know their luncheon speaker is a woman?"

My client would not look me in the eyes; he just stared blankly at the huge overflowing stomachs taking their seats as near their tables as possible. (One of them may have had on a belt with a horseshoe buckle made of imitation mother-of-pearl, but we could not see it.) The meeting planner had made the right decision to have pot roast rather than chicken or tuna salad for his group of hearty-eating men, but at that point, he might have been questioning his speaker choice. Finally, he breathed deeply and said, "Since they do not know there is a speaker, it is safe to say that they do not know the speaker is a woman."

Singing With a Snoot Full

Barney: Well, from all the singing and carrying on, in my opinion, suspect is imbibing.

Andy: What?

Barney: Getting himself gassed!

- Episode #115, "Hot Rod Otis"

Barney thinks that Otis has had a "snoot full" and is sound asleep in "Sheriff Barney," but that does not stop Fearless Fife. He is determined to "probe the subconscious," and his psychologism is classic Barney. "O-tis. O-tis Campbell. You picked up some bootleg liquor. Where did you GE-ET the liquor? Where did you GE-ET the liquor?"

There was no question where one of my audiences GOT the liquor. The elderberry wine had flowed freely at the banquet in Las Vegas, and when FREEly is involved, people tend to go overboard. It was a "happy" group, and I was there to speak to them. Yeah boy. The main dish was something like "chicken paprikash." It had been removed and baked Alaska was being served, so I slipped out to freshen up before my speech. It was one of those rare nights when I briefly wondered if I could sneak away.

I was gone no more than ten minutes, but when I returned, the sounds of group singing filled the hall. Nearing the ballroom, I realized that it was MY AUDIENCE that had erupted into song, a little surprising for a group of franchise owners. They were discovering voice muscles that they did not know existed.

I stood at the back of the room near waiters who had gathered to watch the emcee. He waved his arms with the extremely exaggerated movements of a choral leader, and I was surprised he did not twirl off the riser. Mayberry choir director John Masters would have been horrified because somebody was way off-key. A couple of them were practically off their chairs.

After a few more bars of "When The Saints Go Marching In," the leader saw me in the back of the room and immediately SLICED his arms through the air to stop the singing. A couple of guys kept going until their wives elbowed them.

When quiet was restored, Mr. Director spoke to me through the microphone. "We were just practicing what we could do for entertainment if you did not come back. "Row, Row, Row Your Boat" was coming up next. I was just getting ready to divide everybody into groups."

A waiter muttered to me, "Wherever you were, go back. I'm laying odds this group cannot sing in rounds."

Chirp, Chirp, Chirp

Rafe: Barney. Barney! I hate to butt in, but that ain't the way it goes.
Barney: . . . Well, yeah, that's just another way of doing it. It's the same song.

- Episode #83, "Rafe Hollister Sings"

Old-timer Luther does not understand when Andy stops the band from playing in "The Sermon for Today." He thinks they had it going "real good," but then, he cannot hear. Andy thinks that they have the spirit, but ought to get together on the tune. I saw the same problem when I spoke at the DuPont 25-Year-Club annual event in Asheville, North Carolina.

The tone for this banquet is set the year before. At the end of the night, officers are announced for the next year, and I do mean "announced." The current committee just selects some folks, from flag bearer to president and an odd assortment of titles in between. The new slate of officers is totally surprised, pushed to the stage by people who are relieved they were not on the list, and sworn in before they can get out of the room. Their only assignment is to plan next year's banquet, after which they get the thrill of surprising another group of friends. The only rule? They cannot reappoint those who appointed them.

Two people are tapped for the prestigious positions of song leaders. They do not have to have musical backgrounds or possess barbershop quartet talents. They do not even have to be the same height so that their voices will blend better. In fact, being able to carry a tune is not a prerequisite. It is not even given a minute's consideration. The only criteria for the honor is having someone on the previous committee think it would be funny if you were named song leader.

Early in the evening the night I spoke, the two songsters of the year, holding up DuPont signs, led the group in "You Are My DuPont" to the tune of "You Are My Sunshine." They said it was "You Are My Sunshine" so I guess that is what it was. The guy next to me had one of the worst voices I had ever heard. He had a knack of hitting a note just enough off to make my skin crawl. I am sure he was probably a wonderful person, but he could not sing. Of course, not everybody can sing, so I try to be tolerant.

But "You Are My Sunshine" sounded like the Mormon Tabernacle Choir compared to what followed. When that song was over, they announced it was time to sing the "25-Year-Club Alma Mater." The humorous words were printed in our programs. After five hundred people located their programs and fumbled to the correct page, one of the song leaders announced, "It's sung to the tune of the Cornell Alma Mater. We have no idea what that is, so just sing it to the tune of your high school fight song."

Five hundred people, at the top of their lungs, singing the same words to the tunes of five hundred DIFFERENT school songs. It gave heightened meaning to the word "caterwauling."

A Lovely Choice of Colors

Opie: Pa, did you get all them instructions?
Andy: If I didn't, I was the only one in town that missed them.
                                  - Episode #65, "Andy and Opie—Bachelors"

One of the scenes in *TAGS* that hits home the most with me is when Aunt Bee leaves town amidst a flurry of instructions at the beginning of "Andy and Opie—Bachelors." Oh, how I have been in the same situation as I hurried out the door to catch my means of transportation, the whole-time shouting instructions on what to do with a chicken or pot roast, and uttering Aunt Bee's exact words, "The list! I forget to tell you about the list!" We do count on good instructions. When they are correct, it is like Andy says, "We couldn't go wrong if we was blind-folded." And when the instructions are wrong? Total confusion.

Red Birds. Blue Birds. Yellow Birds. Yes, it was an education con-ference. At the conclusion of my speech, a committee member rose to explain logistics for the remainder of the meeting, and single-hand-edly threw five hundred people into confusion. "Everything is set up according to colors, and the dot on your name badge indicates your assigned group," she instructed. A few people frantically reached for registration packets that contained their badges. Most tucked their chins to see the information pinned in place on their shoulders. Because the badges were generally pinned out of the sight of the wearer, they were soon helping one another. "You're blue." "Red." "Did you say I am green?"

The order-giver proceeded. Looking at a sheet of paper with the dots in a row and explanations to the side of each, she instructed, "Brown dots go to Room C . . . or that may be red dots." People stopped writing. Heads leaned toward one another. "Did she say red dots to room C?" "I think it was brown."

"Green dots start out in room D," she continued, and then almost to herself, "Or is that blue dots?" Folks buzzed, "What dots to room D?" "I do not know. I am still back on the brown dots."

Clearly, the attendees needed it run by them one more time so they could get it, but the woman stared at her paper as though all of this was sinking in, then plunged ahead. "Yellow dots—yes, I think that's yellow—begin in room A."

At that point, she looked up and said, "I am not positive about these. I am color-blind."

Five hundred people sitting there, and the one giving instructions according to colors—was COLOR-BLIND!

Stomach Clock

Barney: Well, I happen to have this low-sugar blood content, and if I don't get my lunch by noon, then I get a headache, and I'm no good to anybody.

Andy: A few minutes one way or the other shouldn't make any difference.

Barney: Well, it does to me. I got a clock in my stomach.

            - Episode #124, "The Return of Malcolm Merriweather"

Barney swears it is so. He has a clock in his stomach and he goes by it. Tick, tick, it's time for lunch. Tick, tick, it's time for dinner. Hey, I believe him. I spoke to some folks who had the same thing.

My one-hour speech was scheduled to start at 11:00 a.m. At 10:45, I sat down on the front row of the ballroom and began to search through my purse, eventually pulling out my tape recorder and little clock. The people seated down the row watched this process with concern, perhaps fearful I might ramble on without realizing it was getting late. As I wound the clock and put it on the floor facing the stage, I commented, "It is always nice to know the speaker knows what time it is."

A man replied, "It does not matter, not one little bit. You can talk as long as you want to, but all of us are leaving here at high noon."

Go Feed Your Hungry Buzzard!

Andy: Now wait a minute. I had no idea what she was up to. Now, we're going to have to sit down and discuss this thing intelligently.

            - Episode #121, "Divorce, Mountain Style"

The door prizes at a September meeting in Atlanta were two sets of tickets to a Braves baseball game and one set of tickets to a local theater production. Winners' choice. The Braves were in a pennant race, so the room buzzed in anticipation of game tickets.

The first winner leaped to his feet at the sound of his name and shot both arms straight into the air. Victory! People glanced at one another in disgust. Well, he did not have to scream so loudly. They watched as he knocked over two chairs while running to the front to grab the baseball tickets from the emcee's hand. "Give you two hundred dollars for them," a voice shouted as the winner returned to his seat, shaking his head to indicate they were not for sale. The masses settled. There was still the chance at the remaining set of game tickets.

The next name drawn was a fellow who had left the room. Without even checking in the hall, the emcee—a real prince of a fellow— immediately declared, "You have to be present to win. He is not here. Draw again." The audience applauded. Friendly bunch of buzzards.

A moan spread through the room when the second name was announced. With no fanfare, a woman walked slowly toward the head table, her brow wrinkled in thought. Although every other individual in the room would have done questionable deeds for the remaining set of baseball tickets, it was not a clear-cut choice for her. People sat up and took notice when she looked back at her friends, shrugged, and mouthed, "The baseball tickets or the theater tickets?" Sensing this slight indecision, the vultures around the room rose from their chairs and shouted, "Theater tickets! Take the theater tickets!"

She bit her lip and looked from one set of tickets to the other, and then lifted her head back toward the audience. The chants grew louder. "THEATER TICKETS! THEATER TICKETS!"

But the winner was a pretty conniving female. Spinning abruptly, she snatched the baseball tickets from the emcee's hand, thrust them into the air, and screamed, "I have a child in college! Make me an offer!"

One of the vultures shouted back, "I will give you five dollars for your child and two hundred and fifty for the tickets!"

Trick or Treat Outfits

Andy: You're a fine public servant, you know that?
              - **Episode #133, "The Education of Ernest T. Bass."**

The Kansas School Foods Service employees met in Wichita, and the mayor was on hand to welcome them to the city. He was the only one in the room wearing normal clothes.

It was a costume event, and we all sat there in front of the mayor, hundreds of California grapes, M&M's, and "creatsters." Even the chicken on my plate was wrapped in something, but I still knew it was chicken. One couple dressed as Jack and Jill because they wanted to be different. I had lugged an old ringmaster outfit—top hat, tails, and whip—from North Carolina to wear during my speech. The whip was not one of those fancy Australian bullwhips, but the people at airport security certainly had asked about it.

But the mayor, dressed in a traditional suit, played it straight. He never alluded to the comical atmosphere in the banquet hall. In a very serious tone, he said all the right things about what to do while visiting his city. At the conclusion of his brief remarks, he turned from the lectern, and we all raised our hands to give the customary polite applause.

Before we could applaud, he quickly whirled back to the microphone and with a grin said, "One last piece of advice while you are visiting in Wichita. WHATEVER you do, DO NOT go out on the streets dressed like that.

As You Would Have Them Do . . .

Malcolm Merriweather: Aren't you kind? Aren't you kind?
                    - **Episode #89, "Andy's English Valet"**

Opie is disappointed when he seeks his father's philosophy of life, and Andy says, "I'm all for it." But when Andy realizes his son is writing a paper, he takes another stab at it. The ensuing short dialogue sums up the philosophy of the town. IT IS THE ESSENTIAL ELEMENT IN MAYBERRY HUMOR:

Andy: Uh, I've been thinking about that question you asked me.
Opie: Which one?
Andy: 'Bout my philosophy.
Opie: Oh.
Andy: Now, my philosophy is . . . Do unto others . . . as you would
           have them . . . do unto you.

                    - Episode #218, "Opie's Most Unforgettable Character"

I felt especially sad when I learned of race car driver Davey Allison's tragic death in a helicopter crash.[34] I did not know him personally but had followed his career with great interest because of something that had happened with his daddy and uncle at a speech years earlier. He came from good folks.

The time I met Bobby and Donnie Allison was at the Unocal-Darlington Record Club banquet before the Southern 500 race.[35] Past winners, their pit crews, other members of the "racing family" and media were in attendance. It was a swanky affair down to liqueurs and cigars after dessert for those who were feeling especially "sporty." At the time, it was a real macho event.

The meeting planner had already warned me that it might not be an easy speech, and I was quite apprehensive. Not only had the group of stock car drivers and their pit crews never had a woman speaker at this particular event, but a woman had never been permitted to EVEN ATTEND the banquet! "I am not telling them you're coming,"

---

34 David Carl Allison (February 25, 1961 – July 13, 1993) was an American NASCAR driver.

35 The Unocal-Darlington Record Club was a club in the NASCAR Grand National and Winston Cup Series from 1959-2001. The club ended permanently when Unocal left the sport in 2003. (https://en.wikipedia.org/wiki/Darlington_Record_Club).

my contact added. "They will probably get right quiet when you arrive at the reception."

Right quiet? Does Aunt Bee put a pinch of nutmeg in her apple pie?

A hush spread through the room when the fellows realized that for the first time, a woman—A WOMAN WHO WAS NOT SERVING HORS D'OEUVRES—was walking among the good ol' boys. I hoped my smile concealed my nervousness about the whole thing, but to be honest, it was one of the few times in my career that I was terrified. As a speaker, I felt like I might be in trouble, BIG trouble. Eyes squinted suspiciously every time I stuck out my hand and said, "I'm Jeanne Robertson. I am the speaker for the banquet." My nervousness made me say "SQUEAKER for the banquet" to one pit crew. They just stared at me until somebody finally questioned, "The squeaker?" When I walked away, I could hear the story spread throughout the room. "She said she was the squeaker." Of course, everyone was polite. Their mamas had taught 'em right, but even that did not prevent the awkward silence as I moved through the crowd.

Suddenly, there was a slap on my shoulder, and I turned to see two wide, mischievous smiles turned upward toward me. Donnie and Bobby Allison of "The Alabama Gang" from Hueytown, Alabama, had stepped forward to meet the speaker or the squeaker. Whatever. I have always read the sports page and recognized them immediately.

"You do not have to tell me who you are," I began, "I am an Auburn graduate, and I have followed your careers . . . "My sentence was interrupted in midair.

"An Auburn graduate? AN AUBURN GRADUATE!" they shouted for everyone in the room to hear. "Everybody, get over here! Oh, Lord have mercy, what is the world coming to? AN AUBURN graduate! Somebody has gone and let an Auburn graduate in the banquet!" They threw their heads back and filled the air with laughter.

"You couldn't get into the University of Alabama?" one of them asked. "Not smart enough? Not from good enough stock? What was the problem?" Again, they laughed uproariously, by now basking in the attention from the crowd that had gathered. I heard someone in the back mumble, "The Allison boys know the squeaker."

I was with "my kind" and opened my mouth to attempt to hold my own in traditional Auburn/Alabama banter. Before I could say a word, however, one of them turned to the onlooking crowd, thrust his head back, and proclaimed, "Listen up everybody. LISTEN UP! This lady is our speaker tonight, and she is a friend of ours. She went to Auburn, so I am sure she has not had a happy life. As a favor to the Allison boys, we want y'all to be REAL NICE to her."

In the speaking world, we call that "being home free." And this "squeaker" will never forget why she was. That night, I had two angels in my pocket.

Snowballing Out of Control

Barney: Gimme a C chord on that thing, will you? I want to check my pitch.

- Episode #83, "Rafe Hollister Sings"

A thousand sleepy conventioneers, reaching for coffee, sat straight up when the high school marching band burst through the ballroom doors. Trumpets, trombones, tubas, and drums were all passing close to the adults' ears. Sitting at the head table, I could see the teenagers' faces. They enjoyed causing a stir.

Heads reeling from the noise, people sighed in relief when the band halted in the front of the room and stopped playing. My attention was drawn to the tuba player. He fit every description of a stereotypical "tubist"—a big ol' massive boy with a round cherubic face and unmanageable hair. I liked him.

A song leader was introduced to lead us in "America, The Beautiful." When he arrived at the microphone, he pulled out a little gizmo that pitched a song and began to search for a note. "Hmmmm." When he thought he had it, he leaned to the microphone. "HMMMM." The young people cut their eyes in his direction, and I detected that for the slightest moment they found this to be humorous. Quickly, however, they straightened up, and we all started singing.

We sang where the fellow put us, which was way too low. Quickly, he said, "Wait, wait. That is not it." He tried again. "Hmmmm." Too high. My eyes were drawn toward the tuba player who was beginning to chuckle. He pursed his lips to hold back.

At the lectern, the searching continued. "Hmmmmmm. Hmmm. Hmm." Then, the man stopped and said, "I pitched it that low so the ladies could join in." A stale joke from a nervous song leader was the last straw for Mr. Tuba. The young man put his instrument on the floor and bit into his sleeve. His shoulders shook. The band director's stare only made it worse.

By then, the song leader searched for the key on his own. "Oh-Oh say." "OH-OH say." Ooooooh say." Finally, he said, "Just sing it anywhere."

Ol' "Tube" buried his red face into the wide, round end of his instrument. He was a trembler. We saw the back of his head and his body moving up and down in laughter. A trumpeter standing by his side patted him quietly on the shoulder.

All I could think about was what Andy said in "The Guitar Player" about the one-man band from Altoona. "Wadn't that the fella that got all mixed up, and come durn near poppin' his eyes out blowin' through the wrong end of a clarinet?"

With that thought, I started chuckling so hard and trying to hold it back that the lady to my right leaned over and PATTED ME on the shoulder!

It's a Miracle!

Goober: All I had to do was give her three dollars, and she looked right in that crystal ball and told me I'm gonna be a millionaire. It's definite.

- **Episode #183, "The Gypsies"**

My speech for a national convention of hair salon franchise owners was on developing a sense of humor. It had to be, for I know very little about styling or cutting hair. A reception was held after my speech, and in keeping with their theme, fortune tellers were sitting at small tables in each corner of the room. I decided to give it a whirl and lined up with the salon owners amid the sacred incense to find out what was in my future.

The lady with all the answers wore dangling earrings and a shawl that probably came from a gypsy-queen ancestor, or at best, a princess. (They could have also come from a rummage sale.) I heard one time that crystal balls only work for a few seconds, and then they cut off. Unfortunately, I caught one during downtime. It was just as well because Goober is probably right in "The Gypsies." "Just because they can look in a crystal ball and tell the future, don't mean they know the first thing about rain." What did she know about professional speaking?

This woman claimed she did not need a crystal ball to tell the future, and I suppose she was right. I am happy to report she gazed at my palm for a while and told me there was no question about it. It was definite. My hair salon would do quite well that year.

Are There Any Questions?

Clara: Professor, of all the wildlife you've ever encountered, which would you say was the most dangerous?

Professor Hubert St. John: Well, Miss Edwards, I would say that is a toss-up between a wounded leopard and a lovely girl.

- Episode #230, "Aunt Bee and the Lecturer"

Oh, you professors are too good. For example, take the one I heard before a speech in Puerto Rico. This professor knew mounds of facts, there was no doubt about it. For an hour, he recited extensive information about the history of the island and the state of government. A man with worldwide renown, he knew heaps more than he had time to share, which was nice. All too often, speakers (including myself) know much less than the time they take to tell it.

If the college professor had a weakness that day, it was that he used no humor in his convention presentation. He had a sense of humor as he later proved, but it was not a planned part of his program. For forty-five minutes, he delivered a wealth of information, and with five minutes remaining, he called for questions and answers. Hands flew up all over the room. Everyone wanted to pick the brain of the learned man. Even when he did not get mighty good questions, he had mighty good answers.

The lecturer looked through the sea of arms and nodded at a lady who rose and slowly drawled, "Ah've noticed this little frawg around all of yo' bushes heah on the island. Somebody told me y'all call them 'tree frawgs' and they're jus' darlin."

The professor nodded and interrupted her. "Yes, you are referring to the Puerto Rican tree frog, the coqui. They . . . "

She stopped him mid-sentence. "Yea'as, Puerto Rican tree frawgs. That's correct." Murmurs trickled through the crowd. How nice of her to tell him that he was correct. "Well, mah question is," the southern belle continued, "may ah take some of the Puerto Rican treefrawgs back ta Arkansas with me?" (She was not acting up. She was truly interested.)

Audience members chuckled and cut their eyes at one another. Tree frogs had not been mentioned in his prepared text. What a question to ask when there was such limited time, but the wise historian answered kindly. He deserved one of Andy's "mighty fine character medals." "You could," he said politely, "but they would die. The coqui will not live in the United States, and I am assuming that would include Arkansas."

The laughter was stifled by the hands that again quickly flew up, and he turned to call on someone else. Before he could do so, the first woman, still standing, kept talking. "Ah hope y'all don't mind mah askin', but why DO they all die?"

In unison, heads turned from the questioner back to the front of the room, where a very patient man smiled and replied, "Because, madam, they get homesick."

Trade Secrets

Goober: I'll pick my own words if you don't mind.

- Episode #232, "Suppose Andy Gets Sick"

North Carolina's longtime Commissioner of Agriculture, Jim Graham, strode to the front of the picnic area to address the members of the North Carolina LP Gas Association at their annual convention. There was no lectern for notes, but the Commissioner did not need one. He had a small piece of paper curled in his left hand, but without looking at it, he began his "few words" to the audience. A politician reminiscent of tent revival days, he was accustomed to being before an audience. It comes with being Commissioner of Agriculture for over thirty years. I wonder if he has to kiss babies every time he runs for re-election. Heaven only knows how many pickin' he has pulled off a pig, and chickens he has eaten with his fingers at Founders' Day picnics across the state.

The Commissioner grabbed the microphone in his right hand, planted his feet squarely on the ground, and slid his speech out of his mouth in good ol' boy, Tar-heel style. For the next few minutes, he worked his crowd, the rolled piece of paper always prominent in his free hand. He combined the right amount of homespun humor and information about his department. People liked him. He was our kind of folk.

I was at the convention as a spouse but was watching through the eyes of a professional speaker. And as a professional speaker, there was no doubt in my mind as to what was written on that little piece of rolled-up paper clutched in his fist. I waited to see how he pulled it off.

For a good twenty minutes, the Commissioner spoke without missing a beat. But as he drew to a close, he drawled, "Welllll," and at the same instant, slowly began unrolling the paper while continuing to look right in our eyes. "It's been my pleasure to be here," he continued. Then, RIGHT THEN, he sneaked a peek at the unrolled paper and read, "at the North Carolina LP Gas Association Convention."

He looked up, smiled as his hands rolled the paper back up, and said, "Thank y'all for invitin' me."

Dance 'Til Your Stockings are Hot and Ravelin'

Barney: Wind up your smile, Andy.

- Episode #62, "Cousin Virgil"

Choir director John Masters strips Barney of his solo part when he hears Gomer sing in "The Song Festers." Imagine! A man of Barney's musical talents. Gomer eventually fakes laryngitis so as not to hurt his friend's feelings, but Barney refuses to take back the part. After all, he is not a plaything. He has pride. Eleanora Poultice, Barney's voice teacher, has to set him straight. "And you call yourself a trooper? You get over to that hall and give them what-for!" It works, and who will forget Barney's declaration, "I'm going on. My music, Eleanora."

A tap dancer I saw would have brought a tear of pride to Eleanora.

The small auditorium for my 1993 speech in Wausau, Wisconsin, was luxurious, and I was fascinated by the computerized lectern. The top of it resembled the cockpit of a small plane. Words printed in small letters controlled the curtain, lights, and video equipment with the mere press of a fingertip. This lectern did everything for the speaker except pour a glass of water. How times have changed.

My Wisconsin audience had not arrived, so I eased into one of the plush, comfortable swivel seats. My mind wandered back to the sixties when I was emceeing local pageants almost every weekend in auditoriums that were a far cry from this one. I thought about the countless Jaycees who opened curtains by pulling heavy ropes—occasionally on cue—in auditoriums that had not been modernized "electronology," to use one of Barney's words. I remembered the guy who crawled on his belly on the backstage floor to connect eight drop cords for a tiny light on the lectern.[36] I chuckled recalling the spotlight fellow who taped dozens of flashlights together and directed the combined beam toward center stage. Suddenly, I remembered a particular pageant in a small town in Alabama, and I started laughing out loud. That story began when I asked one of the contestants a routine question. What was she going to do for her talent?

When she spoke, I knew she was not from the South. In a thick northern accent, she answered, "I'm gunnar tap dance."

I looked up from my notes and drawled what people always drawl in that situation. You're not frum 'round heuh, are ya?"

An easy guess. They were fresh arrivals from New Jersey, and her parents thought entering the local pageant might be a good way for her to meet people. Not a bad idea, but she was concerned. Realizing the stark contrast in accents, she feared the Alabamians would burst out laughing when she introduced herself in the opening production. "And when they see my tap dancing . . . "she added, shaking her head to indicate she was not yet Rockette quality.[37]

"Don't yu worry 'bout it the least lil' bit," I assured her, not realizing how southern I sounded. "Jest do tha bes you kan. These people are gonna LUVVV you." I put at least three syllables in the word "love" and sort of slid it under the door. "LUVVV YOU."

She was bewildered. Trying to figure out what the word was, she slowly repeated, "They're gonna . . . LUVVV me?

"Yes. LUVV. L-O-V-E," I explained.

She eyed me suspiciously, nodded her head, and walked away.

Her prediction about her accent was on target. The next night at the actual pageant, there was a slight ripple through the crowd when she introduced herself in the parade of contestants. The Alabamians exchanged silent looks that indicated, "Is she one of ours?" but she was smiling, and they were polite. Everything was fine. The pageant

---

36 Extension cords

37 The Radio City Rockettes dance company based in NYC.

progressed from the opening, through the evening gown competition, to the talent division.

The music the tap dancer had selected was "Baby Face." [38] All of us born before 1960 know the tune well. It has a good, steady, tap dance beat. "Baby face, dum, dum, dum, dum. You've got the cutest little baby face. Tap tap tap tap." Not too fast, not too slow. Just right for her level of tap dancing.

The Jaycee in charge of music—a guy I will call Elmo—was stationed in a five-foot-square crow's nest high above the backstage. He was as happy as a kid in a private treehouse. Before the pageant started on the big night, he slowly climbed the ladder which was nailed straight up the side of the wall. It took him to his sanctuary and location of the official pageant music system: a record player turned toward a microphone. He carried with him the contestants' records and a couple of six-packs of beer. Elmo was a good guy—not a genius and certainly not a high-tech sound technician—but how much ability did it take to put the arm of the record player down in the right place at the right time?

During rehearsal the previous night, pageant workers discovered it took a little more ability than previously thought. As a matter of fact, there was a hushed discussion about removing Elmo from his position. When the record was a 45 single, he had no problem, but several times during the rehearsal, he had to find the correct music in the middle of a longer-playing album. His hits and misses screeched through the auditorium sound system—urpp, ekkk, schkkk—and each time, the unexpected noise startled an old dog that slept next to the backstage door. He would howl at the top of his lungs—"Yowwwwllll"—and the director would shout at the top of his, "Get that dog outta here!" Then, "Elmo! Get it right or let somebody else do it!" Elmo would shout back,

---

38 "Baby Face" is a popular Tin Pan Alley jazz song. The music was written by Harry Akst, with lyrics by Benny Davis, and the song was published in 1926. It has been recorded by numerous artists, including Brenda Lee, Little Richard and Bobby Daren.

"Listen here, Mr. Cecil B. DeMille. You stick to directing and leave the records to me!" Elmo and the director were brothers.

During rehearsal, Elmo mastered the art of placing the needle correctly on cue. By the time he climbed to the crow's nest on pageant night, he was so confident he could handle the situation that he figured all the beer in the world would not hurt him. When I introduced the tap dancer on the big night, Elmo had the "Baby Face" record in place and ready to roll. This one was easy. No searching for the groove. It was a single 45.

The curtain opened and there she stood in some sort of a tap dance-ready position; arms extended straight out with her palms flared up toward the audience. Elmo put the needle in place, and when the record spun, he sat down and popped another top. Below, the nervous tap dancer stood in front of her new hometown and waited to hear the first familiar sounds. When the music came, it was unrecognizable. The record was not on 45 speed. The record player was still geared for the previous contestant's record 78 speed! So instead of the nice steady beat of "Baby Face, dum, dum, dum, dum," it screeched in a rapid high pitch, "Bbyfcedumdmdumdm. Ugothcutisltlebbyfce!"

Hairdos shot up on the people seated directly in front of the stage amplifiers. A startled judge jumped so quickly in his chair that he lost balance and fell over. And from behind the auditorium, the old dog let out a "Yowwwwwwllll."

If that had been me or most other people with a little experience on their side, we would have stopped and simply said, "The music is on the wrong speed. Please put it on 45 speed and start it over." But this was a young woman in front of new people who had already smiled at her accent. She made no such request. Instead, she started trying to tap dance . . . at 78 speed!

Jaws dropped. People stopped chewing whatever they were chewing. The contestant worked furiously in center stage to move her legs and feet fast enough to keep up with the music. Her arms circled by her sides so fast that she looked like a hummingbird. A man in the front row leaned toward his wife and said, "She's gonna rise up off that stage, mama. That's her talent. Watch this! SHE'S GOING UP!"

The director and I bumped into each other below the crow's-nest and started whispered screaming. "ELMO!" "ELLMO!!" Elmo's face appeared from nowhere and looked down, oblivious to what was happening below. He swallowed a mouthful and said, "Whut?"

"YOU'VE GOT IT ON THE WRONG SPEED! THE WRONNGGGG SPEEEED!" Elmo glanced toward the flurry of arms and legs. His expression changed to shock, and he and his beer immediately disappeared behind the wall of the plywood box. Nothing slowed on stage. By then, the veins on the tap dancer's neck were standing out and perspiration ran down her face as she desperately tried to keep up with her music.

But an interesting thing was also happening "out front." Through all of this, the contestant was smiling. SMILING! And the instant the audience saw her smile, they swung in behind her enthusiasm and started clapping and stomping in 78 speed with her. The more they did, the more she smiled, and the faster she moved her legs and arms. Just when I feared she would pass out, Elmo finally found the correct button and pushed it off 78 speed . . . past 45 . . . and down to 33 1/3!

The sluggish, deep voice on the record slurred out, "BAAABY-FAACCE. YOUUU GOTITITHUUUH CUUTUST LUTTLE BAAABY FAACE." People stopped clapping and stomping. Men swallowed chewing tobacco. Women too. But this contestant—who had earlier been so nervous about performing in front of her new hometown—gave them one of Eleanora Poultice's "what-fors." After a few seconds, she flashed her biggest smile and fell right in with the new speed. She just shifted gears with the music and started tapping in exaggerated, slow movements to 33 1/3. And the audience? Well, those who still had the energy to stand, slowly stood and shifted gears with her, clapping and rocking with each slow downbeat of the music. Others slid down in their seats in exhaustion from laughing. She smiled broader. The trooper had them in the palm of her hand, and she knew it.

But this was a talent competition. Something had to be done, and the emcee was the one to do it. I started out on stage—where the contestant was in the process of delivering a slow, greatly exaggerated shuffle-step-ball-change. She and her fans were having so much fun, she did not notice me until I was a few steps away. Her arms circling slowly and feet still tapping at Jello speed, she then whipped her head around in my direction and shouted through gritted teeth, "GET OFF THE STAGE! THEY LUVVVV ME!"

Small, but Wiry

Andy explaining to Opie why he needs Miss Peggy as a friend, in addition to Barney: I can't take Barney to a dance. He's too short.

- **Episode #64, Opie's Rival"**

The attendees at the conference were asked to indicate by return mail what they wanted for dinner. Figuring people would forget what they had selected, the organizers wrote the order under each person's name on their registration packet.

The emcee was a fellow I will call Tom White, who stood about 5'4" and could laugh at himself. He warmed up the group for me when he told them it was a good thing, he was not sensitive. Written in the top left-hand corner of his registration packet was "Tom White, shrimp." Then he turned to a buddy seated near the front and added, "Notice that Al has 'chicken' next to his name." (You'd better watch it, Al.)

I quickly pulled out my packet. Yep, there it finally was in black and white—"Jeanne Robertson, HAM."

Proud, Proud, Proud, Proud, Proud

Ernest T. Bass, when he receives his Special Award for Learning: I'm proud. I am so proud.

- **Episode #133, "The Education of Ernest T. Bass"**

When I had speeches several days apart for two different groups in Colorado Springs, Colorado, Jerry went with me for a vacation between events. We did the typical tourist activities including a crowded train ride to the top of Pike's Peak. It is a long way up there. We started off among trees that seemed nice and full and ended up at cold, white peaks.

The fact that I am an Auburn University graduate is mentioned in my standard introduction, and after the second speech, a man approached with a question. "Have you been in Colorado for several days?"

"Yes."

"And did you go to the top of Pike's Peak Sunday afternoon?" I had.

He shook his head back and forth. "So, it WAS you who was shouting 'War Eagle' toward the snow-covered mountains?"

I 'fessed up. "It could have been unless ANY OTHER AUBURN person happened to be there. Most people did not know what I was shouting. On the long train ride back, they let me sit by myself."

"Well, I knew," he said with faked ire. "It was like a bolt out of the blue. I went to the University of Alabama, and I could not believe that even at the top of Pike's Peak, I cannot get away from it."

I was proud. I was so proud.

Give 'til it Hurts

Andy, referring to charity: I was kinda explaining to Opie there's two kinds of people in the world. There's givers and there's takers. And Opie, he's somewhere in the middle. He's a squeezer.

- Episode #5, "Opie's Charity"

Andy tries to do a little squeezing of his own when the All Souls Church needs money in "The Church Organ." He tries to squeeze the financing the old-fashioned way: business leaders chipping in. Not very creative, but they need a lot of money. Cake sales, raffles, kissing booths, and charity bazaars will not do the trick. Who they need is the best money squeezer I have ever seen: Mr. Byron Leewright from Mineola, Texas.

I met Mr. Leewright at the annual Mineola Hay Show banquet, where it is a tradition to auction off the thirty-five top-graded bales of hay in the Hay Show competition.[39] The proceeds go toward scholarships for local youngsters, so people come ready to make contributions under the friendly guise of bidding against one another.

Byron Leewright, the emcee/auctioneer, reminded me of Mayberry's Mayor Pike. A short rotund fellow, he proudly told me that he had conducted the auction for all twenty-five years it had been held. At the banquet, he explained the process to me and added with a distinct east Texas twang, "Now see here, Janeen, I may need yo' help during the auctionin' so stay up here on the stage after your little talk."

I told him my name was "Jeanne" and that I would be happy to help any way I could. Seconds later, I overheard him tell someone, "Janeen's gonna help out if we need it."

Before the bidding started, Mr. Leewright was by my side again with more instructions. "Now look, Janeen, we're just a bunch of hay farmers down here, and sometimes folks are shy about shouting out. If the action slows down, I want you to throw in a bid to get things rollin'. They will jump in if somebody gets the ball going."

"You can count on me, Mr. Leewright," I assured him with a smile. "And by the way, that is 'Jeanne' as in the old TV show, *I Dream of Jeannie*." He thought about it a couple of seconds and said, "Whatever you want, but help me out when I need it."

The bidding started quickly with the top-graded bale selling for $900 and progressed rapidly at first. Then, suddenly, folks seemed to get frogs in their throats. Everything slowed down. Waaaaaaay down. Mr. Leewright was at the microphone, beads of perspiration gleaming on his forehead, cajoling the crowd to bid on the few remaining bales. "Come on boys, you can go higher than that. It's for a good cause."

---

39 Established in 1976, the Mineola, TX Hay Show is the longest consecutive running hay show in the United States.

I was seated near him at the head table. After one particularly long, drawn-out sale, he whispered, "They've gone quiet on us, Janeen. Throw in a bid on the next bale and get things started." With that said he turned back toward the audience. "What do I hear for this fine bale of hay?" he boomed, and cut his eyes in my direction.

I raised my hand and shouted, "A hundred and fifty dollars!" There was a distinct gasp as every head in the place turned toward the bidder.

But before they, or I, had a chance to think further, Mr. Byron Leewright slammed down his gavel on the lectern and shouted, "SOLD, TO JANEEN FOR A HUNDRED AND FIFTY DOLLARS!"

The crowd applauded wildly and laughed at my shocked expression. Mr. Leewright looked me straight in the eyes and almost dared me to say anything as he proudly threw back his shoulders and rested his hands on his stomach. I sat there a few seconds considering my options, and then slowly smiled back. When all the hay was sold, I wrote out a check and quietly calculated what I was NOT going to make for traveling all the way to Texas.

When I had the fountain pen in my hand, Mr. Leewright came up to tell me goodbye. I know a town character when I see one, and I was already trying to imagine how many years local folks would chuckle about the out-of-town speaker who got snookered at the Mineola Hay Show. He quietly but firmly took the check out of my hand, and said, "Thank you, Janeen, you're something else."

(And so are you, Mr. Leewright. So are you.)

Ain't Making It

Aunt Bee: I have to do a little rehearsing if I'm going to do a good job.
- **Episode #187, "The Foster Lady"**

Aunt Bee has a surprise for the director in "The Foster Lady." She has written a jingle to the tune of "Harvest Moon."[40] Most people in the room are taken aback when she sings a few lines of "You ain't had such shinin' since January, February, June, or July." Goober thinks it is "real catchy."

Sometimes even a high degree of preparation and clever wording will not do the trick. The plates of chicken casserole had been removed at the banquet, and the outgoing president was "saying a few words" when his mind went completely blank on him. He was in the middle of, "It has been a wonderful experience serving as your president because you represent . . ." and he just drew a blank. It showed all over his face and panic did too. Everyone in the audience knew his memorized remarks were gone into the dust bin of history if help did not arrive. Several times he repeated "because you represent . . . beeecause . . . BECAUSE you represent . . .

Finally, he turned toward his wife, and we saw her lean in his direction. "The heartbeat of America," she whispered loud enough for folks in the lobby to hear.

He broke into a wide smile. "Oh, that's right, the heartbeat of America. I KNEW it was something catchy."

Maintaining Our Position in the Community

Howard Sprague: Well, it's a little different when you go on TV with a statewide audience.

- **Episode #216, "Howard, the Comedian"**

I was winding up a speech at a banquet in Savannah, Georgia when a TV cameraman suddenly burst into the room. He put his bags down on the floor, slung a camera to his shoulder, and started going through the crowd. For the next few minutes, he took shots of the

---

40 "Harvest Moon" was written by Neil Young and was the first single released on his 1992 album, *Harvest Moon*.

audience laughing and close-ups of folks nervously toying with forks, very aware of his location at all times. People continued to look in my direction, but they sat a little straighter and smiled if they thought they were in the camera shot. I was aware that I was losing my audience's attention, but did not worry about it too much. I was too busy turning toward the camera as he came in my direction. Suddenly a waitress I will call Olive, coffee pot in hand, cut right in front of the head table. She blocked the photographer's view of me and glanced toward the camera. (Look toward the little red light . . . and smile!) I thought she was going to start singing.

When I sat down several minutes later, the president of the group noticed the visitor gathering his equipment to leave. He turned quickly toward the young man. "Excuse me. We appreciate your coming over. When will this be shown?" All eyes shifted toward the welcomed guest. Olive stopped pouring coffee and looked up.

As he walked toward the exit, the cameraman sang out, "I do not know, sir. They just sent me over here to get some footage. I am the crime reporter."

Olive turned to the audience and announced, "Oh, for Pete's sake. I have already been on THAT."

Putting Down Roots

Opie: What did you do to your hair, Goob?
Goober: Uh, that new barber in town is one of them hair stylists. He
           says everybody ought to have their own personal hairstyle.
                                    - Episode #249, "A Girl for Goober"

The company president's recent hair transplant had its own personal hairstyle. Mainly it was still "taking root." Like weeds on an infield, small clumps of hair sprouted on the top of his head, but he sat bravely in front of his sales force during the annual banquet. His situation was certainly the topic of conversation at each round table, but he smiled and reacted good-naturedly to the kidding. Not bad for a company president.

The sure sign that he was a secure individual with extremely good self-esteem and a sense of humor came later in the evening when the chicken with crust had been removed from the tables, and the emcee made introductions. "To my immediate right is our director of training, and I will ask him to stand so we can see his overlapping stomach," he announced with a grin. Laughter rippled through the hall while the gentleman smiled and rose to his feet.

The master of ceremonies continued. "To my far right is our vice-president, and I will ask him to stand so we can see how tall he isn't." The short vice-president rose and playfully pretended to snap his napkin like a locker room towel toward his introducer. (More laughter) The spunky group was having a good time.

Then the emcee slowly turned toward the only man remaining at the reserved table, the company president. "Next . . ." He hesitated and stared right down at the top of the president's head. Soft laughter percolated through the crowd as people anticipated the coming remarks. All eyes focused on the uncontrolled and unmanageable, transplanted growth. The president glanced upward to indicate he knew what was the center of attention. The laughter erupted.

"And next," the emcee repeated slowly, lifting his hand for quiet, "I will introduce our company president and ask him to stand . . . just because I want to!"

Beautiful "Perserved"

Rafe Hollister: My daddy lived to be a hundred, and I don't aim to break the tradition.

- Episode #56, "The County Nurse"

The good thing about living a long time is that most people pick up some "smarts" along the way. For example, let me tell you about a matriarch I saw who had attended a long string of conventions through the years, and was introduced to say a few words at a sorority national meeting. As her impressive accolades and credentials were listed, the college-age women were polite, but their body language and glances showed they were not interested in hearing their much older "sister." (When DID the party start?) But the older alumna had not worked with young people all those years for nothing and she was a bird in this world.

With a precisely-timed Groucho Marx imitation and a sly smile, she opened her comments, and within seconds had them eating out of her palm.[41] We could practically see her flicking the famous cigar in her hand. "At this point in my life, I may not have much of a future," she began with faked sadness, "but oh, Oh, OH (move those eyebrows up and down, Groucho) what ah#*% of a past."

Officious

Howard: Well, somebody's got to keep track of all the city's official documents. Like this bike license of yours. Now if twenty years from now someone would want to know the exact day that you got it, I'd have it.

Opie: Well, who'd want to know that?

Howard: Just in case somebody wants to know.

- **Episode #235, "Howard's New Life"**

At the conclusion of my speech, the emcee wrapped up the three-day conference and gave final instructions to the attendees. "Be on the bus in fifteen minutes. Pick up your box lunch of cold chicken and potato salad as you leave the auditorium. Leave your keys in your room. Pick up your T-shirts with the conference logo." Just when he thought he

---

41 Julius Henry "Groucho" Marx (1890-1977) is considered one of America's greatest comedians. He was a well-known vaudeville performer, starred in numerous radio, film and TV productions and was known for his bushy eyebrows and his ever-present cigar.

had completed his announcements, his co-chair, who was a detail-oriented, by-the-book, serious woman sitting in the front row, passed him a note. She could have been Howard Sprague's business partner.

"Oh yes," the emcee sighed, folding the piece of paper after he read it. "Do not forget to fill out the conference evaluation sheet and . . ." He stopped, looked at the woman, and asked, "What do they do with the evaluations?"

Before she could respond he added, almost in a plea, "We do not read them. Should we even bother to take them up?" The people in the audience roared with laughter. They were ready to go home.

The officious woman managed a slight smile as she spoke. "YES, we need to take them up. People should put the evaluations in the box at the back of the room," she instructed in a slightly impatient, deliberate tone that indicated they had previously discussed that information.

The emcee repeated just as deliberately to the group, "Put—them—in—the—box—at—the—back—of—the—room." Then he added, pounding his fist on the lectern, "This conference is adjourned. Last one out, BRING THE BOX!"

***

From these past pages, one thing should be clear. The workplace is chockfull of Mayberry humor. While my occupation puts me in different places and situations daily, this is not a requirement to experience this delightful side of life. Mayberry humor is found in all lines of work and is always available for those who choose to look for it and live it.

Now for the last chapter in Part II, "Looking for Mayberry Humor in Bizarre Situations." You will need some sandwiches for this trip because you will not be home for supper. While you are getting those, make sure you turn off the gas stove and the radio because you do not want the house to go BOOM! What to bring? That is up to you. But if there is not enough room, leave your suit behind.

We will leave the squad car behind now, and go by private car. Maybe we will take Aunt Bee's slick convertible that she buys from Goober in "Aunt Bee Learns to Drive," Yeah, that will be fun! That car is a beauty and is in top-notch condition. The seats are soft because the previous owner, 290-pound Jed Koontz, broke them in. The motor purrs like a kitten. It does have just the one crankcase, but the horn blows. Of course, we do not know how many miles it has on it, because as Aunt Bee believes, what the previous owner did is none of her business.

Anyway, it is time to head out and take a look at some bizarre situations. Quoting our favorite deputy in "Barney's First Car," "Now, I'll drive, so I'll sit in the front seat." (If you get carsick, sit by a window.) Barney's advice in "Cyrano Andy" may be also appropriate in these bizarre situations.[42] "You'd better set back, pal. This could be a jolt."

---

42 Cyrano is a reference to the play, *Cyrano de Bergerac,* written in 1897 by Edmond Rostand.

In Bizarre Situations

Andy: Barney, I know that we've not always understood one another, but so far as I can recall, this is the first time we've ever been on two different planets.

- Episode #142, "Three Wishes for Opie"

One doubter at the often-mentioned Orlando banquet said, "REAL people would not get themselves into situations like the people do on *The Andy Griffith Show*." Of all the nerve!

My highly scientific, observational research tells me that the bizarre situations and predicaments that often provide the basis for thirty minutes of entertainment on *TAGS* are "pret-tee" similar to what I see happening "out there" today. And none of us want to fly in the face of scientific fact, do we?

Surely readers will question me on this one, even those who have agreed with me up to this point. Come on now, Jeanne, they may be thinking. This is all beginning to get to you because some of the situations on *TAGS* are outrageous. A goat swallowing dynamite? A fellow riding a cow down the main street of town? An automobile dismantled inside the courthouse? Do you think I will believe that? What do you take me for? A jerk?

I promise it is so, and it is enough to make your hair stand on end. Traveling around the country and in my experiences at home, I encounter situations that are so similar to some in Mayberry that I stop right in my tracks and think that maybe Barney is right in "Three Wishes for Opie." Maybe it is "entirely possible that there are forces in the atmosphere that are able to control our fate."

True, a goat swallowing dynamite might seem slightly farfetched, but right in my own county just a few years ago, we had a goat named Lulu that predicted bad snowstorms with such accuracy that the school superintendent put more faith in her predictions than in the Weather Bureau. Lulu got it right nine straight storms! She was written about in the newspaper and appeared on several talk shows, and would still be predicting storms today if she had been half as good at predicting dog attacks.

No, the situations in Mayberry are not so farfetched. Some of them may be pushed out on the branch a bit, but they are not hanging off the end of the limb, not according to what I see. So, I will ask the skeptics to reserve judgment. Just this one time, PLEASE reserve judgment while I supply true stories for evidence. Then Judge Cranston's instructions in "Aunt Bee the Juror" can be your guide. It will be your duty to "bring in the verdict based on that evidence."

Loose Scalp

Andy and Barney gossiping after Dick Rinnecker walks by:

Andy: He's got his hat on.

Barney: Yeah, I noticed that.

Andy: He musta heard on the radio where the wind might be coming up today.

Barney: I wouldn't wear one of them wigs for all the money in the world. I'd live in terror I'd get caught in a sudden wind.

- Episode #117, "The Shoplifters"

I did not ask the American Airlines flight attendant for Mayberry humor because that always leads to an explanation of my project, and I was very busy that day, I just asked if she could pinpoint something funny that happened to her while working. "Just think about it during the flight," I had said, "and let me know if anything comes to mind."

She immediately squatted in the aisle next to my seat. "I do not have to think about it at all. There is no question the funniest thing that has ever happened to me occurred on an all-nighter from New York to the West Coast." This is the story she related.

As the plane took off, most passengers turned off their lights and settled in for several hours of sleep. A few folks pulled out books, and the flight attendants prepared to offer drinks to those who were awake.

Before the plane left the ground, one of the passengers seated on the aisle had gone to sleep with his chin resting in his hand and his elbow on the armrest. When the plane was in the air, his head began to bob ever so slowly to his right. By the time the flight attendants served drinks, it was hanging over his armrest in the aisle.

Two flight attendants at the back of the plane prepared the drink cart for service. When it was ready, they began to maneuver it slowly up the aisle to the front of the plane. One attendant was facing the front, with an arm stretched behind her to pull the cart. My friend was pushing.

As they slowly progressed up the aisle, they passed the aforementioned gentleman. His head was now a tiny bit further into the narrow pathway separating the rows of seats. Neither woman realized it, but the corner of the beverage cart just barely caught the top of his head as they pushed by. It did not awaken him. He did not react at all, because instead of hitting his scalp, the corner of the cart had caught the back of his toupee and flipped it through the air! FLIPPED IT THROUGH THE AIR!

The toupee traveled a few feet, just far enough to land on the hand of the first attendant. To have something hairy come flying through the air and land on one's hand in a darkened airplane would startle even the most stoic person. This young woman was no exception. Apparently, this is not covered in flight attendant training.

The moment she thought some type of "animal" was on her hand, she reacted and slung the "creatster" away from her in a panic. The toupee soared through the cabin of the plane and landed flat out, about three rows up, on a passenger's neck. This fellow had been quietly reading, but when something hairy landed on him, it brought him to his feet, hollering, "Get it off! Get it off!"

The passengers sleeping in the immediate vicinity were awakened instantly, and general pandemonium swept through several rows. The flight attendants with the cart had gone in different directions soon after the "thing" began traveling through the plane. One headed toward the first-class section; the one telling me the story retreated to the rear. Within seconds, they regained their composure and hurried back to the center of attention.

The passenger who thought he had been attacked calmed down and held the toupee in his hand. The look on his face said, "Was there a body with this when it came on board?" Almost everybody in a five-row area was wide awake. Almost everybody.

It cannot be explained, but the then-bald gentleman who owned the toupee was still sound asleep. He had not moved a muscle. His mouth gaped open a little, and his head—looking very different than it had a few minutes earlier—was still bobbing out into the aisle like a buoy on water.

Oh, they tried. They really did. The passengers did their best to stifle their laughter, but it was tough. The flight attendants had the toupee in hand and stood by the sleeping, hairless passenger trying to decide what to do. They were also trying to hold back tears of laughter and do their best to keep things glued together. Every time their eyes met the eyes of a passenger who knew what had happened, all parties involved broke up again.

But the flight attendants knew what had to be done. After a few minutes, they began ever so carefully to place the toupee back on the man's head, making every effort not to disturb him. Placing it on the top of his head was no problem. Positioning it was the challenge. Picking up several hairs at a time, they tried to turn it into place. After a few maneuvers, they decided to leave well enough alone. And the man slept on.

Passengers in other parts of the plane also slept through the entire incident. Only a small group saw the whole thing, including the replacement procedure. They and the flight attendants were limp with exhaustion. It wears you out to try to hold back all-out, uproariously loud laughter. It wears you out!

About the time they gained control, the center of attention suddenly awakened and sat straight up. He stretched a couple of times, stood, and proceeded down the aisle toward the lavatory. It was more than people could take. The hairpiece was essentially hanging on his ear.

That was not the case, of course, when he emerged from the little room. Everything was perfectly straight and in order. He returned to his seat, walking by some of these same people who suddenly became interested in a variety of things: tying their shoes, looking out the windows into total darkness, reading old copies of something like *Aviation Journal*—anything that would keep them from meeting his gaze. Eye contact would have thrown someone into hysterical convulsions. And if one of them had "lost it," it would have started a chain reaction. He plopped back down, folded his arms, and slept the rest of the way to California.

When the plane landed, the passengers hurriedly gathered belongings and began the usual procedure of inching toward the exit door. The semi-famous passenger did not realize it, but the people around him did not look his way. They could not. They had worked for several hours to get themselves under control. A few more minutes and they would be safe. Most people just wanted to get off the plane without laughing again. No one said a word. Just a few more steps. A FEW MORE steps.

And then it happened. The ol' last straw on the camel; the solvent that let everything come unglued. With his toupee precisely in place, the gentleman who had unknowingly generated so much confusion passed the flight attendant at the door and sang out, "Don't know WHEN I have had a nicer flight."

People dived under nearby seats.

A-Ten'- Shun!

Mayor:	All right, Sheriff. You've convinced me. They can go to the capitol. But it's beyond me how you ever whipped that ragtag group into shape in such a short time.
Andy:	Oh, patriotism and perspiration, Mayor.

- Episode #72, "The Mayberry Band"

Gomer does his best to be "police worthy" when Barney swears him in as deputy in "Andy's Vacation." Among other things, Barney has a problem with his shoes and is blue on the knuckles from polishing them. He got the toes and sides but missed the backs. Barney tries to admonish him. "Now an old German soldier once told me, always polish the backs of your shoes 'cause that's the last people see of you and remember." Gomer does not see the importance of it because he is not marching off to war. In Wisconsin, I saw proof that the backs of shoes are not always what is remembered about people sworn in for duty.

"Please rise for the presentation of the colors and the pledge of allegiance to the flag."

The opening session of the convention in Green Bay, Wisconsin, started like thousands of others I have witnessed. We stood, and when the noise quieted from squeaking chairs and shuffling feet, the familiar "A-ten-shun!" sounded in the back of the room. The four-person color guard moved down the center aisle with dignity and perfect timing—right, left, right, left. The only sound was the commanding officer saying whatever it is they say. Hut? Hup? High-yup-pa-yah? People cut their eyes around the room to see if it was time to put hands over hearts. Some did. Some did not. Some wavered back and forth.

The color guard reached the front of the room, and they snapped their feet in place with their backs to the audience. On command, they turned abruptly to the right. The audience stood perfectly still. I noticed the diversity of the four people: different races, both genders, and various sizes.

Smoothly stepping in unison—right, left, right, left—the four glided to the right side of the high stage where the head dignitaries stood. Up eight steps without breaking stride, they "righted and lefted" until they reached the flag stands where they stationed their flags in synchronized motion.

At the microphone, someone began, "I pledge allegiance to the . . . . "The previously undecided people quickly placed hands over their hearts. We completed the pledge, half the hands dropped down, and the foursome turned to regroup and leave.

This time they marched to the left side of the stage and unknowingly headed straight for trouble. There were no steps. Yes, steps had been there when they rehearsed, but they were . . . GONE! The color guard crossed the wide stage until the first uniformed man arrived at the edge and learned of the dilemma. He stopped his forward momentum but kept marching in place while he surveyed the situation. He was a good eight feet from the floor.

The people in the audience began to stir because we could see the problem. The last three in the color guard were unaware of the exact situation but knew they were not making forward progress. It did not matter. They stayed in single file behind the leader and continued stepping in place, going nowhere. Right, left, right, left.

The lead man never broke his cadence while he contemplated his choices. A group decision? Not at that point. Turn back? Probably not. Lose the dignity of the presentation of the colors? Out of the question!

After just a few thought-searching seconds while marching in place, the first man moved to the edge—right, left, right, left—and then JUMPED to the floor! His knees buckled slightly when he landed and the audience automatically flinched in sympathy. He regained his composure and glided away from the stage to make room for the next person. Right, left.

Behind him, the woman followed suit. Right, left, right, left, JUMP! Her knees also buckled, the audience buckled with her, and she started walking again. The third person? Same thing. Right, left, right, left, JUMP! Throughout the room, people bent their knees to absorb his landing shock. And finally, the fourth and by far the largest of the group arrived at the ledge. Eyes around the room widened. He was a BIG guy. Right, left, right, left, BOOM! Everybody buckled waaaay down. People exhaled as he smoothly regained his balance and caught up with the first three who were waiting for him, still stepping in unison.

All in place, the four moved to and then up the center aisle with as much pride and dignity as I have ever seen. They never cracked a smile.

NOT SO for the people in the audience who fought for self-control. Faces were red. Eyes were teary. People who still had their hands over their hearts were squeezing clothing. The instant the four uniforms disappeared through the back doors, the audience broke into applause of appreciation while howling with laughter. Yep, patriotism and perspiration. Plenty of it.

Rolling Stock

Barney: You know, Ange, it's a great feeling when you get out on that cycle and go racing down the highway. You know, it's just me and the wind and the wheel.

- Episode #112, "Barney's Sidecar"

Barney is so proud of the "mechanically perfect" motorcycle he purchases at the War Surplus Auction in "Barney's Sidecar." Andy has his own idea about the whole thing. He figures if they take the motorcycle away from Barney and fill the sidecar up with sand, it will make a great place for his childish-acting deputy to play on weekends. Of course, he will need a bucket and shovel.

I saw a couple of other guys who needed to have their rolling stock taken away from them. They did not have jackets, helmets, or goggles, but they painted a similar picture at a banquet in Greensboro, North Carolina.

The theme of the big party after the banquet and my speech was "Fantasy Island."[43] The company planners had come up with an idea that was to be the icing on the cake, the perfect touch. They had found the ideal way to lead their employees from the banquet room atop a hotel into the larger, decorated room down the hall. At the conclusion of dinner, two regional managers of opposite physical sizes suddenly burst into the banquet room riding in a golf cart. By any standard, it was a show-stopper.

The fellows wore white tuxedos and bore amazing resemblances to the characters they were impersonating, Tattoo and Mr. Roarke of the old television show. They drove in and out of the tables, waving at their friends and giving autographs, and stopped in the front of the room to do a little routine.

After a couple of quips, they invited everyone to follow them down the hall to "Fantasy Island." They got back into the golf cart, put it in reverse, and CRASHED it into the wall behind them! Not bumped, CRASHED!

People bent double with laughter. The men were uninjured, but the golf cart was out of kilter and would not run. The wallpaper was ripped and the wall was dented. The more they maneuvered the gears and tried unsuccessfully to get the cart to move forward, the more people howled. When Tattoo ad-libbed, "We got a little problem here, Boss" folks went bonkers.

The hotel personnel did not share the enthusiasm. Waiters and waitresses ran from the kitchen and halted when confronted with Tattoo and Mr. Roarke, who had climbed out of the cart. A furious maitre d' rushed in and surveyed the damaged wall. We could tell he did not want to kill them, but we suspected he wanted to hurt them a little. It did not help the situation when Tattoo waved his cigar at him, shrugged, and said, "We should have taken 'de plane."

A few seconds later, the guy impersonating Mr. Roarke gestured toward the broken golf cart, looked down at Tattoo, and said, "I have always told you, 'Don't worry about the SMALL stuff."

---

43 *Fantasy Island* is a fantasy drama TV series that aired on ABC from 1977-1984.

That was too much. One guy laughed so hard I thought he would fall over in his plate. The maitre d' even smiled slightly when Tattoo answered, "OK, Boss."

But they did not forget their mission. When the crowd quieted, Mr. Roarke put his arm around Tattoo's shoulder and became the wise character from the television show. "Do not worry about this, Tattoo," he advised. "For you see, it is only a fantasy." And out of the room they walked, leading the guests and leaving the broken rolling stock behind them. . .. Expensive little "icing on the cake."

Squirt Attack!

Barney's landlady, Mrs. Mendelbright: Nobody leaves a washbasin the
way you do.

- Episode #104, "Up in Barney's Room"

The "body of a judo fighter." "A deadly weapon." "A walking time bomb just waiting to go off." These are ways Barney describes his body to Andy in "Barney's Uniform." Fred Plummer is big and slow and heavy and wants to beat Barney to a pulp. But "Fearless Fife" hates to get in a fight because goodness knows what damage he might do. (Barney's judo instructor says Fred will kill the deputy.)

I thought about skinny Barney and big ol' Fred (the *TAGS* characters, not the Bedrock citizens) when I asked another flight attendant to tell me a funny occurrence.[44] She remembered a good one.

She was working in first class where a bulky, slovenly-looking man sat directly in front of a smaller, neatly dressed guy. As soon as the plane left the ground, the larger gentleman pushed his recline button and mashed his seat as far back as it would go. The passenger behind him said nothing but squirmed around trying to find room for his legs. He ordered a glass of wine.

---

44 Bedrock's citizen, ol' Fred, is a reference to Fred Flintstone of animated TV series *The Flintstones* that aired on ABC from 1960-1966.

When the meal was served, the larger passenger in the front seat declined a tray. He just wanted to sleep. The second man wanted to eat. But when he put his tray down, it was flush up against his chest due to the seat in front being reclined to its fullest extent. The diner, with several drinks in his system by that time, tapped the man in front of him and asked if he would put his seat up a little. "No," the annoyed larger guy boomed. He folded his arms and shifted his weight for a better snoozing position. "I paid for this seat, and I can do anything I want to with it." He had a lot of nasty in him.

The response irritated the smaller man, but he shifted his weight around again and said nothing. He did have another glass of wine. He was dead sober when he got on the plane, but he was getting over it. During the meal, however, he decided he was just too crowded, and again offered up a plea to the man in front of him. He woke up the big fellow when he tapped him on the elbow, which was well-extended into view, hanging over the armrest.

"Look, this tray is practically in my chest. I can barely eat, and I would appreciate it if you would bring your seat up just a little." The first response was a shake of the head, back and forth. There was no movement of the seat. Suddenly, the immense man curled his lip and snarled backwards, "A squirt like you shouldn't need much room."

The smaller man was riled. Frosted! Like Barney, his skinny little veins were popping. He glared at the top of the head that was barely visible over the seat, fumed in silence, and eventually continued with his meal . . . and wine.

The flight attendant telling me the story was at the front of the plane when this all transpired, and happened to look down the aisle to see a rather bizarre sight. A hand—the body attached to it completely hidden from view—slowly lifted a full glass of wine over the head of the sleeping passenger in front of it. Reaching its peak, the hand tilted back and forth and circled gracefully over the head as a mother would do with a spoon, trying to trick an infant into opening its mouth. Back and forth and around we go.

The flight attendant watched helplessly as the hand completed its circling and positioned the glass squarely over the big man's head. It then methodically turned at the wrist and slowly poured its contents on the target below. No mere quick dumping of the wine. The hand made a statement!

The big man, sleepy and sputtering from the liquid running down his face, unbuckled his seat belt, stood up quickly, and crashed his head into the overhead bin. That is when his cursing began. While he tried to get his bearings and fumbled to wipe away the wine, the source of the liquid rose like a martyr and raised the empty glass in the air. "It was worth it!" he proclaimed, and then threw the glass down into his seat and ran up the aisle for the lavatory. Feisty little fellow.

Seconds later, the wine-soaked passenger pounded on the locked lavatory door, shouting obscenities and threatening death. He was ready to boil. All of the flight attendants converged on this scene, but it took the co-pilot to finally get the injured party back to his seat, amid his screamed threats to the lavatory door of "I am gonna kill you!" "You gotta come outta there some time and when you do, I am gonna pulverize you!" "You're a dead squirt!"

It was quiet inside the lavatory. Outside, the senior flight attendant began negotiations. She had a situation on her hands—a REAL situation. "We know you are in there. It is all over now. Come on out. He has returned to his seat." Silence. "You will be all right. No one is going to hurt you." More silence.

She tried to stay a step ahead of him. "Sir, there is no way out of there except through this door." Hearing this, the wine-soaked passenger shouted from his seat, "Tell the squirt to slide through the toilet!" With that, the co-pilot and several male passengers helped Mr. Obnoxious to the rear of the plane.

Finally, from behind the lavatory door, a wee voice spoke to explain, "It was worth it."

"I am sure it was, sir, but you have to come out now."

"No. I am not coming out. He will kill me. But tell him that I said it was worth it."

One by one, the attendants pleaded. "We cannot land with anyone in the lavatory. You will have to come out." When their pleas fell on unresponsive ears, the co-pilot and eventually the pilot took turns explaining the consequences. After each request, there was a long pause while he considered the alternatives, and each time he eventually answered quietly, "I am not coming out."

So it went, and true to his word, he stayed put until after the plane eventually had to land. The flight attendant smiled as she finished her story. "I guess, of all the experiences that have happened to me in flying," she said, "that is the funniest."

"Oh, no, that's not enough," I pleaded. "What happened?"

"Well, the last time we saw the little fellow, he was moving up the airport concourse with the FAA and airport police completely circling him. The protective ball of muscle and badges must have given him the same sense of security as the lavatory door. When the group passed the still furious winehead, who was giving his statement to authorities, the arrested man hurled one last taunt over the shoulder of a huge policeman, "IT WAS WORTH IT!"

Pounded Steak a la Henry

Opie: Gee, Pa, I'm so hungry I'd be glad to eat anything.

                                          - Episode #162, "The Bazaar"

Fellow speaker Robert Henry and I chanced to be on the same flight. The trouble with Robert is that he never got over his shyness. He was already seated when I boarded and quickly started hollering in his loud-but-lovable, good ol' boy style. "Lawd have mercy! Jeanne Robertson! THE FUNNIEST woman speaker in America has come on this plane!" Robert always calls me the funniest "woman" speaker. This gives him room to be the funniest speaker. Both of us have a long way to go.

It took only a few seconds for people to rearrange seating so we could sit together. With all of Robert's shouting, they would have switched planes for us to sit together.

We talked about the hassles of travel, and Robert told of his late arrival at a hotel the previous night. He was starving to death. "STARrrrrVIN'," he emphasized with his pronounced southern drawl. Room service was closed. The restaurant was locked up. There was no kid wandering the halls offering peanut butter and jelly sandwiches.

On the way back to his room from the empty vending machines, Robert spotted the answer to his prayers on the hall floor; someone had placed a room service tray outside a door. Whoa. In the middle of the tray was a plate, and on the left side of that plate were the remains of a great big ol' hamburger.

At the sight of this cold piece of meat peeking out from a seeded bun, Robert came to a complete stop. His mouth watered. Oh, it looked good. He rubbed his tongue between his lips. "It looked reeeeal good," he assured me.

"Nah," he said out loud, to an empty hallway. "Can't do it. I don't know how long it has been there." Of course, thinking about it further, it was probably only since the dinner hour. "Hmmmmmmmmmm."

He looked down again. It might hold him over until breakfast. "Nah," he said a second time. "Am I crazy? I don't even know who ate the other half."

Then he began to rationalize. "But this is a nice hotel. There's no riffraff here." He bent over to see if by some chance the hamburger was still a little warm, and suddenly snapped straight up. "I am not gonna do it," he told himself and walked up the hall.

Twenty feet later, he turned back for a glance. It was still there! "Let me just look at it one more time," he decided and circled back toward the tray. Stalking the leftover hamburger became his #1 job. When he got right above it, he looked back over his left shoulder down the hall. Not a soul in sight. He glanced over his right shoulder. Empty space. And in one quick swoop, he GRABBED what remained of the hamburger and STUFFED it in his mouth as fast as he could.

It is all right with me if Robert Henry is funnier.

Make Her a Star!

Andy: I'll be dogged. I'll just be flat dogged. Don't this beat any-
           thing you ever heard of?

- Episode #5, "Opie's Charity"

There is a variety of talent in Mayberry: Andy and Opie play the guitar; Barney plays the harmonica and cymbals; Gomer can sure sing; Goober does impersonations ("Judy, Judy, Judy, Judy, Judy").[45] Howard takes a stab at stand-up comedy; Aunt Bee and Clara cowrite songs; Burley Peters plays the chair, and the Darlings are terrific blue-grass musicians. But none of these diverse talents can be compared to a "dramatic reading" that I witnessed.

The talent competition at a small-town pageant I emceed seemed routine during rehearsal. There was a singer in town who sang "Trees," a pianist who played something like "Dance of the Bunnies," and then . . . "I am going to do a dramatic, interpretive soliloquy of death, with dance," the bright-eyed young woman told me. I will call her Violet Rose.

Why not, I thought. A dramatic, interpretive soliloquy of death, topped off with dance. There should be one in every pageant. I started making notes. "So, you are a dancer?"

"Not really, but there is a bit of dance in my interpretation, so please mention it in the introduction."

"Consider it done," I said, scribbling notes.

She pointed toward the tablet to indicate "add this." "I choreo-graphed it myself."

"OK, you chor-e-o-graphed it yourself." My pen was flying.

"And wrote the interpretive soliloquy," she chimed in.

---

45 "Judy, Judy, Judy, Judy, Judy" is attributed to the actor Cary Grant but was most likely the invention of celebrity impersonator Larry Storch. He was doing a Cary Grant impersonation when Judy Garland walked into the club, and that is how Storch greeted her. (https://www.carygrant.net/articles/judy.htm)

"Now, let me get this straight," I said respectfully. One who played four chords on the ukulele and "rendered" an original song in the Miss America Pageant does not poke too much fun at another's talent. "You are doing an original, dramatic, interpretive soliloquy of death that features a dance that you choreographed? Is that correct?"

"Well, it's just a little dance, but I will appreciate it if you would mention it."

I wanted to say, "Did you make your costume?" but I held back. She was nice, and frankly, I had been there.

The nervous pageant director joined us, booming directions at Violet Rose. "Do not forget that you will be penalized if you go over three minutes. Do not go under that time by much or the judges will think it was all you can do. THREE minutes. That fellow over there will be timing you."

He pointed to a Jaycee holding a stopwatch attached to a cord around his neck. We all exchanged smiles. The director continued, "He will raise his arm to signal when your time is running out." From across the way, the man lifted his arm to show us he knew how to do it. The old coach in me emerged. "Does he shoot off a gun to start each number?" I asked. The director ignored me.

Through the years, I have seen many unusual things happen at local pageants, but what unfurled that night at dress rehearsal was something one tells her grandchildren. I knew the audience would be equally spellbound twenty-four hours later.

The next night, people packed like olives in a jar into the local college auditorium. I introduced the pianist, who was several years away from performance level, and then the singer, whose odds of winning were around 34,000 to 1. Her odds improved when it was Violet Rose's turn.

"And now, ladies and gentlemen, let's watch number three, who will present an original, dramatic, interpretative soliloquy of death, featuring a dance that she choreographed. All right, three . . . Miss Violet Rose Coal!"

There was polite applause as the curtain slowly rose. I stayed at the lectern to watch the reactions.

The "dramatic interpretation" portion came quickly. For the first fifteen seconds, Violet Rose mumbled something about death being inevitable. This was not news to the audience, but they listened respectfully. Then, for the remaining two minutes and forty-five seconds . . . she died. And the town watched. Captivated.

Violet Rose had one of those pretend knives with the rubber blade that bends back and forth. The blade also slips into the handle which means if the "stabbing" is performed just right, the blade disappears. It was obvious Violet Rose held a toy in her hand during the fifteen-second soliloquy as she peered down at it contemplating hara-kiri. When the "fatal blow" came, it brought a laugh rather than a gasp from the audience because she did not hit herself just right. In full view, the blade bent to the side on her stomach.

Holding a tormented and somewhat shocked expression on her face, Violet Rose frantically wiggled the knife to get the blade to disappear. It never did, but because she took her routine seriously, people fought back snickers. Women fixed "jinxing rays" on their husbands and children, daring them to laugh. But even the women were not prepared for what followed.

Having completed the "soliloquy" and the "stabbing," Violet Rose went into the "death" portion of her program. Doubled over, she moaned loudly—"ugggghh"—and "died" on the left of the stage. Then she drew herself up, changed her location, and "died" on the right. Just when we thought it was all over, she looked up gasping for air, moaned again, and staggered toward the back curtain. The audience shifted eyes and heads as if following a slow-motion badminton match.

At the rear of the stage, Violet Rose slumped over and fell toward the floor; but at the last instant, she GRASPED the curtains and pulled herself back to a standing position. As she leaned forward, the weight of her body forced her toward the audience with a series of rapid, little bitty steps. We had just seen the "with dance" part.

She moved so quickly to the front that all five judges, thinking she was going to "dance" herself off the stage and on to their tables, winced backwards and threw their hands up for protection. Right at the lip of the stage, however, Violet Rose looked out with a pained expression, reversed directions, and staggered away. She zigzagged by me at the lectern, and when she moved on, the Jaycee behind me with the stopwatch mumbled, "Ain't she got talent?" I could not respond.

The director of the pageant, who made a career out of teaching drama to those high school students who did not want to take "shop," shouted instructions into his headset to the Jaycee on the spotlight. "Keep that feather spot on her! Staaaaay with her. There she goes. STAY WITH HER! Fade to blue." The Jaycee drawled back through the walkie-talkie, "Forget blue. Shoot her, and put her out of her misery."

People sat stunned. They were not sure what they were seeing, but they knew they had never seen it before. Two minutes later, Violet Rose hit the floor on all fours and began what was later referred to as the "help me" segment. She reached toward the ceiling with one hand, while she clutched the bent blade at her stomach with the other. The audience glanced upward to see if anyone was going to throw down a rope. Then she stretched her free arm toward me. With her arms and legs extending in different directions, she looked like a wandering spider. I shook my head. I could not help her.

At two minutes and forty-five seconds, Violet Rose stopped moaning. The Jaycee slowly raised his hand to indicate that her time was running out. He was correct in more ways than one. Ten seconds later, she drew to a standing position, and the spotlight widened to pick up her entire body. At EXACTLY three minutes, Violet Rose let out another moan that rocked the light fixtures, twirled around, and collapsed—toes up—in the center of the stage.

The hush that fell over the auditorium after Violet Rose began her talent now shifted into eerie silence. The Jaycee slowly lowered his arm. No one moved or spoke. People were wrung out.

The Jaycee tapped me on the back and moved the stopwatch toward my eyes. "Three minutes on the dot," he whispered. "Ain't she got talent?"

The director spat into his headset, "Curtain. Lower the curtain!" Backstage, a Jaycee began the squeaky task of lowering the heavy, dark-red velveteen from the rafters. "Faster!" the director whispered. Unfortunately, the curtain, like many of the Jaycees, ran on one speed. The audience sat quietly, stretching their necks to see the contestant who lay on her back in the center of the stage with her eyes shut, toes still aimed straight toward the ceiling, and the spotlight beaming down on her. The curtain continued its descent toward its resting place.

It was then we realized something important. At the conclusion of that stunning, precisely timed event, amidst all the moaning, twirling, clutching, and reaching, Violet Rose somehow missed her final mark and died too far to the front. The curtain would cut her smack-dab in half. From the waist down, she would still be out front!

Squeeaaaaak. Velveteen was on the way. I froze. The stopwatch man dropped the small clock on the cord to rest atop his large stomach. The director tried to instruct someone to "kill the lights," but when he moved his lips, nothing came out. He looked like a fish trying to eat. Rounded lips out. Lips in. Soon, he gave up and lowered the walkie-talkie to his side. He could see his directing career coming to an end. Crumbling! Smashed! Shot!

It may be the only time in history the "wave" has been performed at a local pageant, and it was in slow motion. People in the front rows saw what was happening and sat up in their seats for a better view. This caused the people behind them to move forward and glance alternately from the lowering curtain to the contestant on the floor. The next people had to stand in crouched positions to see, and so it went. The wave spread to the rear of the auditorium until people in the very back were standing on their tiptoes.

Squeeaaaak. I knew Violet Rose's mind was racing. Where was the applause? At least her mother and father could clap? How about her sister? When the curtain was about halfway down, her curiosity got the best of her, and I saw her take a peek upward and quickly pinch her eyes shut. She had grasped the situation.

This bizarre example of Mayberry humor should be a reminder never to underestimate people, especially a person who has thrown herself around a stage for almost three minutes like a fish flopping in slow motion on a rowboat floor. The entire audience watched as the velveteen finally brushed the top of Violet Rose's body. That was when she gave one last, loud, "UGGGGHH" and suddenly FLIPPED OVER BEHIND THE CURTAIN!

The red material landed in a heap on the stage floor as people jumped up and down and exchanged high fives.

The Jaycee with the stopwatch looked in my direction and broke into a broad smile. Our eyes met and we shouted in unison, "AIN'T SHE GOT TALENT?"

***

In searching for current examples of Mayberry humor, one only has to keep her ears open to hear what I call "Gooberisms." In general, these are any mispronounced or unusual words and phrases, and any strange conversations that are reminiscent of the humor on *The Andy Griffith Show*. For my purposes, they are comments that are made not only by Goober, but also characters such as Barney, Gomer, Floyd, Briscoe Darling, Warren, and Ernest T. Bass. I find these comments to be very representative of what I hear today. You might be thinking that surely, I do not run into people saying stuff like "sheik," "kleptomenerac," "shazam," "suavity," "nave," "aPATHy," "inarculated," "schizofreeniac," and "Sigmund Prude." Well, of course, I do, because *TAGS* made these words part of our vocabulary.

But if Mayberry humor is still abundant—THE POINT!—then people of the nineties must have their own strange concoctions of words and phrases, and must participate in conversations that shoot off in different directions like "Gooberisms." Well, we do. It is back to that "human factor" again. Human nature stays the same. Even when our words may be incorrectly used or pronounced, or our conversations adrift, folks around us generally know what we mean. And it's funny. Here are a few of my favorites.

Barney: Floyd, let me explain something to you once and for all. Now, a peace officer's got an image to protect in this community and that means he can't be giving in to any silly superstition. Now you got that?

Floyd: Sure, sure. I understand that. But what's that got to do with the chain letter?

- Episode #146, "The Lucky Letter"

✳✳✳

Andy: Barney's been bit by the green-eyed monster.

Gomer: They got some stuff down the drugstore that'll keep 'em off ya!

- Episode #126, "Barney and Thelma Lou, Phfftt"

✳✳✳

Goober: Yeah, the special's great.

Gloria: What is it?

Goober: A dollar seventy-five.

- Episode #151, "Guest in the House"

✳✳✳

Barney: Well, I take it in stride. You know, when you're a big city cop, you just look at things from day to day. Eat, drink and be merry, because tomorrow, it's for whom the bell tolls.

- Episode #212, "Barney Comes to Mayberry"

***

If you do not find the above quotes at least mildly amusing, go back to the front of the book and start over. Or, better yet, put the book down and go mow the lawn. It may be that you are one of those for whom the Mayberry humor bell will never toll.

I will share a few of the ones I have accumulated by just listening and taking notes. They are short, quick, and to MY point, if not their own. And in keeping with my promise, these "Gooberisms" are true. You have only one requirement. As you read these quips, try to imagine Gomer, Goober, Barney, or Floyd, et al., saying the lines. Enjoy!

***

He had a way with words. A passenger behind me remarked to his buddy, "I can't go Wednesday night. That's the night my wife has her ARABIC dancing."

***

It had been a beautiful drive to the resort outside of Blaine, Washington, but I gasped when I rounded a curve that gave me my first view of the water. It was mud! Yards and yards of murky, globby mud stretched from the shore to . . . way out there. I thought I had just encountered "The Blob."[46]

When I checked into the hotel overlooking the ocean, I asked the young desk clerk about it. "I noticed the waterline and have a question. Is the tide low right now, or is it always this way?"

Not the brain center of the resort, she said, "I do not know. I have only worked here two weeks."

---

46 *The Blob* is a 1958 American science fiction horror film. It was directed by Irvin Yeaworth and written by Kay Linaker and Theodore Simonson.

***

She was stirring up a hornet's nest, and he could not unstir it. At a school yearbook convention, a publisher told our table about a call he received from a frenzied mother who claimed her son's life had been ruined. His last name was spelled incorrectly in his senior annual. His name was D-A-V-I-S and it was spelled D-A-V-I-E-S. She interrupted the publisher's apology to add, "What is really bad is that he has called several of his friends, and it is spelled wrong in their books, too!"

***

Policemen do it. Firemen do it. And on this day, somebody had to do it. The emcee at a luncheon during an insurance claims conference in Chicago made the following announcement, "The afternoon session on infertility has been canceled. The doctor has been called to the hospital for an emergency delivery."

***

How do you do that? A distinguished-looking man dressed in a business suit passed near me, and my client offered information about him. "See that man? He's one of the leading architects in Birmingham, and do you know what he loves to do?" I did not even try to guess. "He likes to crush beer cans on his head. Just puts them up there, and smashes them flat with his hand."

Well, a person has to do what he wants to do to be happy.

***

I just did not go far enough in my thinking. It was 11:50 a.m. when I ran up to the Delta counter in Salt Lake City. "Can I get on the 12:01 flight to Cincinnati or the 12:05 flight to Atlanta? I am booked for later this afternoon, but I can go now." The agent grabbed my ticket and started punching her computer. I kept talking. "Both flights connect with service into Raleigh-Durham." I was in luck. She switched my flight, handed me the ticket and I took off. Several feet away, I turned back to shout, "Which way am I going?" She replied, "Up the escalator and straight ahead."

"No, I mean Cincinnati or Atlanta?"

"It does not matter. Either way, you have to go up the escalator and straight ahead."

***

He might be what they call "accident-prone." A man at a banquet, "We have three children. A daughter 21, a son 19, and a three-month-old baby called 'Oops.'"

***

Maybe he needed a bottle of pop to cool off. There was a Ross Perot sticker on the bumper of my cab in Mobile, Alabama, about a year after the '92 election and a week after the Perot/Gore NAFTA debate, so I brought up the subject.[47] The driver said, "I don't know what was wrong with Ross in that debate. He sure had his DANDRUFF up."

***

In October 1990, the Crisis in the Gulf captured our attention. Briscoe Darling might have said that the "proceedings were in the ground" because President Bush had, indeed, drawn a line in the sand. For three months we had heard that pounding, pounding, pounding promo on TV, while the world waited to see what Saddam Hussein

---

47 On November 8, 1996, Vice President Al Gore and former presidential candidate Ross Perot debated the merits of the North American Free Trade Agreement (NAFTA).

would do.[48] At a luncheon, a woman commented to me, "My husband is in the Reserves and might get called up." She hesitated several seconds and then said in a quiet tone, "I guess you've heard about the trouble in the Gulf?"

***

He was a desperate, determined hunter! A man in the next airline seat told me he was a "Skip Searcher." He hunted people who had "skipped town" or had been abducted. He enjoyed his work AND talking about it. According to him, hunting animals is not difficult, but hunting humans is something else. He even said, "It's more of a challenge because humans leave no written records." And animals DO?

***

Talk about being misunderstood! The emcee at a national conference was reading to the audience about the next year's convention site. "The hotel has a health room, a swimming pool, and a very nice hair SALOON."

***

Some people sure are odd. In line at a car rental counter, I could hear the traveler at the counter saying, "That won't do! That won't do at all!" The agent had told the woman the price of the car per day, and added "that includes seventy-five miles of travel." The woman

---

48 ". . on August 2, 1990, a force of one hundred thousand Iraqi troops invaded Kuwait and overran the country in a matter of hours. The invasion of Kuwait led to a United Nations Security Council embargo and sanctions on Iraq and a U.S.-led coalition air and ground war, which began on January 16, 1991, and ended with an Iraqi defeat and retreat from Kuwait on February 28, 1991." (https://history.state.gov/milestones/1989-1992/gulf-war)

retorted, "Well, how is THAT going to help me? I have to drive almost a hundred miles. What am I supposed to do at seventy-five? Get out and walk?"

***

My client took me to lunch at Anthony Bryan's, one of the most famous barbecue restaurants in Kansas City, and forewarned me about the "d-core." The place would look like a dive, and they would probably serve my food with their hands. It did, and they did. On the way out, the local fellow told me, "One time this place closed two months for remodeling, and when it opened, nothing had been changed."

***

That might work. When I checked into the Disneyland Hotel in Anaheim, I asked the bellman if there was an exercise room in the hotel. He seemed surprised and responded, **"No.** People who bring their children to Disneyland do not generally need any more exercise."

***

The renowned insurance consultant's remarks were over, and it was time for questions from the good ol' boys in the company. After a few awkward seconds of silence, a fellow rose. He looked like a man with a couple of thoughts. "Some companies are getting into personal lines, and some companies are getting out. Is it that some companies are dumber than others? If so, are the dumb ones getting in or out?"

The consultant answered, "Yes."

***

Of all the rotten luck! On a day with very little Mayberry humor, I called the hotel operator and asked her to tell me something funny that had happened in her work. She said that a hotel guest, sounding sleepy, asked for a 4:15 a.m. wake-up call. She informed him it was 4:30 a.m. right then. He said, "4:30! Dadburn it! Dadburn it! I have overslept again!"

***

Maybe it was a bad phone connection. (Maybe it was my accent.) I called my client before a speech in Arkansas to go over particulars such as transportation and what to wear. "Now let's see," I started. "I am going to fly into Jackson, Mississippi, and drive up to Eudora in a rental car."

"If that's not too much trouble."

"No problem," I answered, and switched gears to the dress for the banquet. "Now, what about attire?"

He paused before answering. "Well, they usually have a tire in the trunk of those cars. You can check when you get it."

Well, it's just not the same thing, but I did let it ride. "Um, OK. What is everybody wearing to the banquet?" I asked, altering my approach. "Is it dressy?"

His answer let me know I would be speaking to folks who spoke my—and Mayberry's—language. "Just wear Sunday-go-to-meeting clothes."

***

His "corporation" had really grown, so a friend was not surprised at the question on an annual beach trip. "Put on a few pounds, Ralph?"

Ralph kept dealing the cards. "Yeah, I guess I have. I'm up to two hundred and forty-two, but it's no problem."

People around the table exchanged glances. "No problem? Why not?"

"Cause my scales only go up to two-fifty."

Ralph went on to explain that he had tried to diet. "Bought some of that special stuff, Cambridge, but it didn't work."[49]

"It didn't?"

"Naw, and I tried it with everything. Peanuts, chocolate, potato chips."

***

Bless her heart. She had on a blue suit, pearls, and a little hat. I wondered if white gloves were in her purse. During a flight out of Greensboro, I offered to share a newspaper I had found with the sweet little lady next to me. "Would you like to see a copy of the *New York Times?*"

She said, "No, darling, I don't believe so. I do not know A SOUL in New York City."

***

What in the world would Calvin Coolidge say? The morning after one of the 1992 Presidential Debates, I was staying at the North River Yacht Club in Tuscaloosa, Alabama, and went to the lobby for free coffee. Several members sat gazing at the morning news of the debate. One man said to no one in particular, "Does anyone remember Harold Stassen?"[50] Silence. He continued, "He ran for President several times." More silence, so I spoke up, "Isn't he Nancy Kassebaum's

---

49 Cambridge diet was initially developed by Dr. Alan Howard of Cambridge University in 1970 and was later introduced as a commercial product in the US and the UK.

50 Republican Harold Stassen ran for president nine times between 1948 and 1992.

father?"[51] And I cross my heart and hope to die if one of the women did not say, "Is she a member of this club?"

***

The woman was not a featherbrain. I prefer to believe she just lost her head for a second or two. Staying at an airport hotel, I called the operator and asked if they had twenty-four-hour shuttle service to the airport?

She said, "We certainly do. It starts at 6 a.m."

***

He had a green thumb when it came to raising money. The auctioneer at the banquet held up one of the potatoes from the bushel basket for the audience to see. Profits benefited a worthy cause and bidding began at five dollars and went up. Finally, the auctioneer proclaimed, "Sold! To the fellow in the third row for twenty-five dollars!"

"And now," he said reaching into the basket, "for the second potato."

***

Well, they cannot throw a real big barbecue while in the air. A nearby passenger asked what was being served on a luncheon flight. "Chicken salad," the flight attendant informed her, and added casually, "I have not tried it, but I think it was the same salad we had on the flight last week."

The lady spun around in her seat and asked in horror, "Has it been in the refrigerator ALL THAT TIME?"

---

51 Nancy Kassebaum is an American politician who represented the State of Kansas in the US Senate from 1978-1997. She is the daughter of Al Landon who was Governor of Kansas and the 1936 Republican nominee for President.

***

I "double-dog dare" you. The flight attendant announced, "Ladies and gentlemen, please remain seated until the pilot turns off the seat belt sign. At that time, you may stand and take everything off."

***

Let's not raise our voices. It was a good thing someone was in charge who knew the score. A woman called into airline reservations, "I wanna book a flight to Europe."

"What city in Europe would you like to go to?"

There was a long pause, and then, "Well, just how many DARN CITIES can there be in Europe?"

***

It was not the most amazing thing I have ever read, but it was definitely Maryberryish. Right in the midst of my search for Mayberry humor, I picked up the newspaper and read that the Avon, Colorado Town Council voted 4-2 to name its new bridge "Bob." (It is a big bridge over a real river, not an oak tree over a narrow spot.)[52] They had other choices, but the majority thought "Bob" would be fun. Mayberry lives!

***

It might be worth a try. The head of a United Way Campaign drive for his company told me they had success by offering a chance at prizes to employees who increased their pledges over the year before. If they

---

52 In 1991 the town of Avon chose the name Bob for the bridge that spans the Eagle River and connects Avon with Beaver Creek Ski Resort.

did NOT increase their pledges, they won a chance on a dinner with a company vice-president.

***

Socializing during business hours? Even Otis Campbell does not come up with this way to camouflage a nip or two. Listed as the evening program at a computer convention, "7-10 p.m. SCIDS. Social Communication Internal Discussion Session." It was a three-hour cocktail party.

***

It takes newfangled ideas to attract young folks. In Ohio to speak at a large Ruritan meeting, I noticed that everyone in the audience was old.[53] Friendly? Outgoing? Enthusiastic? Yes, to all three. But old. I was almost fifty myself, and they looked old to me! (Those whom I could see.)

I asked the man seated next to me if they were doing anything to attract younger people into the organization. "As a matter of fact," he whispered, "we have started a club at the local high school."

"No, I am not talking THAT young. I mean forty-year-olds. New blood."

He understood. "We have made a concentrated effort along those lines. We are doing everything we can to make the club appealing to that particular age group."

Five minutes later, the song leader got everyone to stand and join him in singing, "Wait 'Til The Sun Shines Nellie"![54]

Yeah, boy. Pull in those younger people. That will do the trick!

---

53 Ruritan is a community services organization that began in 1928. It has some 25,000 members serving more than 900 communities.

54 "Wait 'Til the Sun Shines, Nellie" is a 1905 popular song written by Henry Von Tilzer and Andrew B. Sterling.

✳✳✳

He must have been "ept," not inept. CEO, presenting a beautiful, inscribed gift to the outgoing Chairman of the Board, "I left my glasses at home, so I cannot read this plaque. But whatever it says, we REALLY mean it."

✳✳✳

Well, you ARE the clever one. During a banquet in Mississippi, I asked my contact what else was on the program. He said, "Not much. I will introduce the officers and then you. The man giving the invocation came in here this afternoon and got that out of the way."

✳✳✳

It was just a matter of terms. A teacher friend passed the school custodian and said, "Are you all right today?" He said, "Nope, I'm half left" and kept walking. She said she did not "get it" until she got down the hall.

✳✳✳

Makes you think. Double-checking with the man who had been assigned to take me to the airport the next morning, I said, "So, I will meet you in the lobby at 7:30 a.m.?" He answered, "I will be there." We were both from out of town, so I asked, "And you know the way?" He said, "To the lobby? Oh sure, I've been going there all week."

✳✳✳

I believe Goober puts it well in "Emmett's Brother-in-Law" when he said, "A lot of married men think they got a mind of their own, but they really ain't." In Pittsburgh during a snow delay, I heard the following announcement over the entire airport system: Mr. So-and-so, please check with the airlines for revised information from your wife. This is REVISED INFORMATION that will negate her other NINE calls.

***

Maybe they were slow in getting their federal aid. I told a friend about speaking at The Homestead, a glorious old hotel and resort in Hot Springs, Virginia. In referring to the mineral springs on which the hotel is built, I added, "It has everything: a library, tea in the afternoon, hot baths." She said, "My word! Don't most of the hotels where you speak have hot baths?"

***

A sadder but wiser Sherlock Holmes. That is how we could describe the person in charge of the cagey detective work done at a small college several miles from my house. A cash drawer on campus was robbed several times, not of monumental amounts, but steadily over a period of time. Finally, the person in charge of such things took on the investigation with Barney Fife gusto, planning to use high-speed, photographic, surveillance equipment to nab the criminal.

Our investigator planted cash in the drawer to entice the crook. Then, to ensure solving the mystery, he also set up school video equipment and left it recording overnight.

You guessed it. The thief got the money AND the expensive equipment and has never been heard from again. (I bet Sherlock would rather not talk about it.)

***

And last, but not least, let's remember Mayberry visitor Briscoe Darling. I thought I had met ol' Briscoe himself when Comish hens were placed in front of us at a banquet in Mississippi. The man next to me looked down and said, "I don't like to eat nothing that's served with its rear end looking me in the face."

***

So, there you have it. A few "Gooberisms" that I deem to be a bit bizarre and reminiscent of what happens on *TAGS*. More evidence that Mayberry humor is alive and well! Most of what I just shared with you happened recently in my Mayberry world, not on TV in the sixties. It is another reminder that while we cannot always explain human nature, we can always enjoy watching it function. I urge you to do the same because you never know when the next bizarre thing—large or small—is going to "bust" loose.

Part II—Looking for Mayberry humor that is real nearby—ends with these bizarre incidents. Now it is time to turn Aunt Bee's car toward home for a breather.

We have got a final long trip ahead when I will have my last opportunity to illustrate that Mayberry humor is EVERYWHERE! In Part III, we will see as many charming little towns as possible, and a few "embryonic megalopolises." (Big cities to you non-*TAGS*aholics.) Pack all the clothes you have AND the "chester" drawers. We are going clear around the country, and you will not have a chance to go by home except when we pass near your state.

And good news! On this last trip, we are flying. On a jet! Who gets the window seat? We leave on flight #17, and we are going first class because anytime we keep ourselves in a humorous state of mind, we go first class. This is history we are dealing with, folks. You will be a part of it, and you will not even need a travel voucher. Your ticket came with the purchase of *Mayberry Humor Across the USA*.

PART III.
FINDING MAYBERRY HUMOR
ACROSS THE USA

Before the Trip

Englishman Malcolm Merriweather, a visitor to Mayberry: Well, just
  think, I might have traveled the length and breadth of
  America without ever finding out what Americans were
  really like. I used to think you were quite different, you
  know. And then I came into your home and saw how you
  lived, and you're not different at all, really.

  - Episode #89, "Andy's English Valet"

I am a North Carolinian, so when I am in other regions of the country, it is not unusual to be asked, "Have you ever been to Mayberry?"
or "Do you live near Mayberry?" I am always amazed at the number
of people who believe it to be a real, honest-to-goodness place. But
then, I understand. *The Andy Griffith Show* was so well-done that it is
painful to visualize the town as a set on a studio lot. The thought of it
makes me feel funny inside. I do not like it, not one little bit.

Sometimes I wish I did not have to tell questioners the truth about
Mayberry. After all, some people think there is no Santa Claus, and
look at the joy believing in him can bring. But the inquirers are usually all "growed-up" people who should be able to face reality; folks
who usually cover quickly as Barney often does by saying, "I knew
that!" It is just that they did not know it, not for sure. When I tell them
that there is no real town of Mayberry, there is always that tiny little
hint of disappointment. As I mentioned, I DO understand.

Wouldn't it be a nice place to visit? To drive around a curve on a North Carolina road and suddenly be in Mayberry? We could tool by Wally's Fillin' Station on the outskirts of town and see Goober's beanie or hear Gomer say "Hey." Blocks later, Aunt Bee might be hemming one of Clara's dresses—probably the one where she lost all that weight and the thing hangs eight inches too long. If we rolled down the car windows, perhaps we could hear Opie calling football signals to his buddies in the vacant lot or practicing with his band.

Downtown, Floyd would be sitting on the bench outside the barbershop, quoting Calvin Coolidge or his Latin teacher in barber school. Emmett might be working on a toaster in his Fix-It Shop, and discussing the topic of the day as Howard Sprague stands nearby telling what his mother said about it. We could see Ellie coming out of the drugstore to make sure she has parked in the right place. Helen Crump and Thelma Lou would be walking down the sidewalk, school papers or grocery sacks in their arms, discussing their next double date.

At the courthouse, there would be a strong probability that Otis would be "resting" in his jail cell, the key hanging on the wall within easy reach. Barney would be sweeping out the back room, putting up wanted posters, or polishing his bullet. And all the other characters we love so much would be going about their familiar routines, miraculously in town together on the day of our visit, even though they pass through the series at different times. Best of all, though, Sheriff Andy Taylor would be at his desk. Everything would be OK in Mayberry. But do not jump in your car just yet.

Of course, the truth is that Mayberry is a "pretend" town set in North Carolina for *The Andy Griffith Show*. Many think the town is supposed to be Mt. Airy, Andy Griffith's hometown. Andy says that it is not, and if Andy says it, it has got to be true. Andy would not lie. But whether or not the show is modeled after one specific place, Andy Griffith's small-town, North Carolina upbringing is evident throughout the series.

Because our state is so intricately connected with *The Andy Griffith Show*, North Carolinians have the tendency to think of ourselves as the chosen few as far as Mayberry is concerned. We love it when the characters talk about friends and relatives scattered throughout the state. OUR state. It seems very real to us that something is always happening down in Raleigh, the state capital. OUR state capital. We smile when Andy mentions the sheriff's convention in Siler City. OUR Siler City.

While we are certainly pleased with all the easily recognized references, we North Carolinians are further thrilled at all the coincidental tidbits from our state that seem to pop up throughout the series, tidbits we think other people might miss. I cannot help but smile when the Taylors check into the Piedmont Hotel in Los Angeles. After all, I grew up in Graham, which is smack-dab in the middle of the Piedmont area of North Carolina. Andy Griffith's alma mater, The University of North Carolina, is mentioned several times. Since I am a Duke University fan, I definitely notice that Andy manages to work in "it's a great school" when referring to UNC, Duke's arch-rival, and adds that students' grades have to be "above average" to get in there. I also notice a quick reference to "Hillside University" which Andy calls a "fine school." Any North Carolinian worth having tar stuck to her heels knows that the original campus of UNC is located in Chapel Hill.

These names and phrases were not skillfully interwoven to test us. The people involved were putting out a weekly television show, not planning trivia contests for future generations. The reason that *TAGS* has the flavor of North Carolina is because Andy Griffith had such a hand in the finished product that his own low-key, Tarheel style and upbringing flowed over to the writers. The other members of the creative team, in turn, were smart enough to play off of his strengths. Some of the trivia we natives notice on the show today might surprise even the people connected with the series. I am sure some of it gets stretched far beyond what was intended or even possible. For example, in "Andy's Investment," Andy mentions Encyclopedia Europa. "Ah-hah," a North Carolinian might say to herself. "That is Andy's way of sneaking in another reference to his UNC-Chapel Hill background. Surely he is referring to the Hotel Europa located there today." In reality, the Hotel Europa opened long after that episode first aired. But, hey, maybe the hotel was named after the encyclopedia reference? See what I mean about getting carried away? I am sure those connected with the project could not have predicted that years later we would delight so in finding familiar little traces—legitimate and otherwise—of North Carolina throughout *TAGS*. They might even be amused by it all, but it serves to emphasize my point. There is no doubt about it. *The Andy Griffith Show* may be enjoyed by all, but it is special to us, the anointed few who live in The Old North State.[55]

It is not my intention to in any way take away from that pride North Carolinians have in *The Andy Griffith Show*. In fact, I will lead the parade in bragging rights. But as much as we Tarheels would like to claim Mayberry, its attitude and special brand of humor as exclusively ours, the truth is that it does not belong solely to any area. It transcends our North Carolina boundaries and reaches lovingly to all who love it in return.

Go with me now, past the boundaries of North Carolina on a state-by-state trip through Mayberry, USA, and enjoy some of the stories I have seen, been a part of, or heard during speaking trips. For you see, Mayberry is not a particular place. It belongs to no state or region. The delightful humor of Mayberry is everywhere, and we will find it as we go from state to state.

So, to answer the question, "Have you ever been to Mayberry?" Oh, for goodness gracious sakes alive. Sure. I go there all the time. I am ready to go again.

Everybody to the airport!

---

55 The Old North State is a nickname for North Carolina, and is also the title of the state song and the state toast. The moniker dates back to 1710.

Mayberry USA
State-by-State Examples

--- Alabama ---

A Jinx-

Barney:	You ain't planning on a game of cards or checkers this evening, are you?
Andy:	Why?
Barney:	Well, if you get close enough to Henry, you're going to be somebody's pigeon.

- Episode #49, "The Jinx"

Barney and about everybody else hanging around the barbershop, except Andy, decide Henry Bennett is bad luck in "The Jinx." They do not want him looking over their left shoulders during card games, patting them on the back in horseshoes, or fishing in their boat. Floyd even remembers that his son had once been jinxed by Henry touching a baseball. It had nothing to do with his boy being a poor baseball player. No, there is no doubt about it. Henry can put a hex on folks. Unfortunately, there is probably a doctor in Alabama who feels the same way about me.

At a hospital Christmas banquet in Anniston, Alabama, I was seated with staff members and spouses. The emcee announced it was time for the door prize drawings, and everyone started fumbling through their pockets for stubs. A doctor seated beside me, a reserved man who had said very little up to that point, reached in his coat and pulled out a square ticket with the number 678 written in large, bold, black print. I could read his ticket, and I did not even have in my one blue contact. They were BIG NUMBERS. He placed his ticket on the table in front of us just as the emcee announced, "The first winning number is 6-7-8."

I turned in his direction. "You won! That's your number! 6-7-8!"

The physician studied his ticket while eyes at our table shifted in his direction. He did not move a muscle or comment.

"Well, get excited," I whispered. "This may be something you will never forget." I did not think the prize was a portable television, but it had to be better than a beer can opener with an umbrella on it or a ceramic pelican.

Still, the winner said nothing. "Don't you think he should shout BINGO?" I asked the others. They agreed as the emcee slowly repeated, "6-7-8." The doctor's wife nudged him with her elbow, and from somewhere deep inside, this gentleman suddenly pulled up a faint "Bingo."

"Oh, come on," I urged. "Give us something to remember. Give us a bingo with some enthusiasm!"

It worked. "BINGO!" he suddenly bellowed at the top of his lungs. People quickly turned in our direction as he rose and walked toward the lectern, taking the big square ticket with him.

It was at that precise moment that I noticed everyone else at my table had standard, smaller door prize tickets that were half the size of his. It was too late. He was at the lectern in front of all his friends, trying to collect the prize with his wife's coat check ticket.

"No, Don, that is a coat-claim stub," the emcee announced with a big grin. (Wouldn't you know his name would be Don?) People roared. Don quietly put the ticket back in his inside pocket and returned to his seat, never saying a word.

He waited about a minute before he leaned in my direction and said out of the side of his mouth, "I want to THANK YOU for encouraging me to shout BINGO! You certainly were correct. It was something I will NEVER forget."

--- Alaska ---

Save Room for Dessert!

Andy: I don't believe I've ever heard of it.

Barney: Sure you have, Andy, you just forgot. That's baked Alaska. It's that new dessert that come out since it become a state.

- Episode #42, "The Clubmen"

When I began to lay out my evidence of the existence of Mayberry humor, I promised to go light on the jam and basically stick to the truth. And the plain, unvarnished truth is . . . here I am ready to tell you about Mayberry humor in Alaska, and I have never been there. I beat everything, don't I? Nobody in Alaska has ever booked me to speak, but my feelings are not hurt because I do not take it "personal." Several invitations have come my way, but scheduling has never worked. It is a lonnnng way to Alaska from North Carolina. Not only that, there is the matter of the price of the ticket to consider. (As Andy Taylor drawls in "Off to Hollywood" when Aunt Bee and Helen suggest splurging on a family trip to California . . . "and the mon'ney!" He wants to think about that. He wants to think about that a lot.) However, I know there IS an Alaska because I have spoken to so many of their desserts. It is often a part of banquet fare: chicken, potatoes, baked "Alaska." Cannot wait to meet them on their own turf! [56]

---

56 Jeanne finally spoke in Anchorage, Alaska on September 27, 2001 for the NAWIC (National Association Women in Construction) conference.

--- Arizona ---

Morning, Honey. (Goodbye, Dear)

Tom Silby: I don't drink no more, Andy.

Andy: You don't?

Tom Silby: Without Annabelle to answer to, I found I didn't need to
             drink.

- Episode #5, "Opie's Charity"

Henpecked Tom Silby thought the solution to the problem of a nagging wife was for him to disappear. Of course, when he reappears in "Opie's Charity" several years after his funeral—the finest Mayberry has ever seen—it is a surprise. I heard about a man whom I believe also contemplated a "scram-a-voo" from an overbearing wife.

A cab driver in Phoenix, Arizona, told me about picking up a couple at the airport. The woman had been bossy to him when he attempted to put the luggage into the trunk. Finally, she just took over the operation. The cabby recalled, "I put luggage in and out of my trunk all day long, but I did what she said. Sure enough, we had to do it over, and her husband let her rule! He just stood there and shook his head. I think he was scared to speak."

One of the pieces of luggage had a broken handle, but when she eventually got it all situated, the woman asked if she had time to go to the airport gift shop. The husband just shrugged his shoulders, so the cabby assured her she had the time, and back inside she went. The driver returned to the front seat, and the husband climbed in the back.

Soon after, the back door slammed shut, so the driver started the cab and pulled away. TWENTY-FIVE MINUTES LATER, the husband meekly spoke for the first time. "My wife's still at the airport." When the cab had been at the curb, he had noticed the back door was partially open and had slammed it shut.

It is interesting to me that this fellow noticed a little thing like a slightly open door, but overlooked that his wife was not on board when the cab drove away. Or maybe he did not overlook it? And how about the fact that he failed to mention it through twenty-five minutes of traffic? Well, opportunities do not come along every day. Tom Silby took his. The man in Phoenix just thought about it awhile.

--- Arkansas ---

Oh Boy, the Governor

Governor: Yes, I thought it was important enough to come here and tell you myself.

Andy: Well, it was mighty nice of you, Governor. We shore do appreciate it.

Governor: Yes, I'd like to stay here and visit with you some more, but I have to start back to the Capital.

- Episode #76, "Barney and the Governor"

The Governor is scheduled to make remarks during Founders' Day in "The Cannon." Andy worries that the dignitary will not make it on time because of state business. Aunt Bee is concerned too because she gave instructions to take the shrimp out at one o'clock. They have no cause for concern. When the three-block parade starts, the Governor is present and accounted for. However, one never knows with politicians.

My speech in Little Rock, Arkansas, happened to be when the legislature was in session. This meant that Governor Tucker was busy with first one thing and then another. It was explained to the audience that the head of the state regretted he could not attend but had sent his prepared remarks which the emcee would read word for word. Unfortunately, the emcee did. The opening lines included, "As I look out at you," which brought a few chuckles. Several minutes later those chuckles rose to all-out laughter when the substitute read, "And that is why it was SO IMPORTANT that I slip out for a few minutes to be with you today."

--- California ---

Get Your Nerves Tucked In

Andy: Are you awake?

Barney: Yeah, all you got to do is just (finger snap) and I'm up.

- Episode #94, "Mountain Wedding"

It is four o'clock in the morning, and Andy and Barney have a long drive ahead of them in "Mountain Wedding," but the sheriff cannot get his deputy to wake up. He tries shouting, ringing an alarm clock, shaking him, shouting in his face, and blowing a whistle. Finally, Andy just snaps his fingers, and that is all it takes.

The snap of a finger will not wake me up, but the radio alarm in the next room at the Hyatt in Monterey, California, did the trick at 2:45 a.m. It began with a steady beep, beep, beep. My natural reaction was to put a pillow over my head until my neighbor next door turned off the alarm. Ten minutes later, it was still beeping, and I was wide awake. Surely it was broken. Beep, beep, beep, beep. Our beds must have backed up to each other. The noise was just . . . right . . . there, and so continuous. Beep, beep, beep, beep.

I pounded on the headboard wall and got no response. There was enough noise in there to wake the dead, and someone was sleeping through the whole thing. Of course, someone might actually be dead or the room empty. I suspected the latter and called the front desk to please send someone to turn off the noise. It was driving me up the wall.

Beep, beep, beep, ... Twenty minutes later, I was walleyed. BEEP, BEEP, BEEP. Why didn't someone do something? BEEP! BEEP! BEEP! I had never realized that alarms get louder the longer they sound. Was there a ledge connecting our rooms? It would be worth a try. After a few more minutes, I called the front desk again.

"This is Jeanne Robertson. I called thirty minutes ago to report an out-of-control, runaway alarm clock in the next room."

"Yes, Mrs. Robertson, I remember. I am sorry we have not turned it off yet. We are looking for hotel security." (I guess the guy was busy checking doorknobs.)

"Why will you need security? Just send a bellman or the night audit person up here with the key to get inside and smash the clock. Bring me the key and I will do it. I would LOVE to do it."

She said, "We cannot just unlock a room door and go inside. We have to have a security guard."

Her explanation might have appeased the rare individual who has never stayed in a hotel. I did not buy it.

I practically cried into the phone. "YES, YOU CAN go into a room without a security guard. Have someone pretend to be a maid. Just stand outside the door, unlock it, shout HOUSEKEEPING! . . . and walk right in!"

Five minutes later I heard someone open the door to the next room, and immediately afterwards there was silence. When it seemed safe, I eased the pillows off my head and slid one under the side of my face. Finally. Peace and quiet. It was 3:30 a.m. I still had time to get some sleep before my speech at 10:00 a.m. Like Barney, if I get a headache, I am not going to be any good for anybody. As Andy says in "Family Visit" when he has to sleep with Ollie, "All in all, I'd say it's one of the most active nights I ever spent," but the confusion was finally over . . . I thought.

Just when I returned to a deep sleep, the telephone rang. RING! RINNNG! My hand hit it in the dark and the heavy part of the equipment crashed to the floor, but I managed to get the receiver to my ear. A cheery voice on the other end said, "Just checking. Is everything all right now?"

--- Colorado ---

How Are Things With the Government?

Goober and Floyd, reading an out-of-town license plate:
Goober: That's a United States Government license plate!
Floyd: Looks like trouble.

- Episode #165, "Aunt Bee on TV"

It IS trouble when a government car pulls into Mayberry in "Aunt Bee on TV." An agent from the IRS has arrived to tell how much tax is due on Aunt Bee's game show prizes. He loves his work, but I am not so sure people love him. Maybe that just goes with the territory when one works for "Big Brother."

It was late when I arrived in Denver, and the cab ride to the downtown Radisson was a long one. Near the hotel, we passed a small park in the center of a number of white buildings. Early the next day, I asked the desk clerk about walking in that area. "Oh, that is Civic Plaza," he told me. "It is a small park, surrounded by government buildings. It's not far."

Being a small-town person, I asked if it were safe to walk in the Plaza that early in the morning. The bellman glanced at his watch and said, "Yes, it is safe now, but you had better be gone by nine o'clock. That's when the politicians start coming in."

--- Connecticut ---

Peekaboo

Andy: I believe I'll clean the mirror.
Opie: Aunt Bee just cleaned it yesterday, Pa.
Andy: You can't have a mirror too clean.

- Episode #194, "Aunt Bee's Crowning Glory"

A woman I met may claim that she was not a snoop—Aunt Bee maintains the same thing—but she will NEVER convince me.

The sales clerk at a hotel in Connecticut, which will have to remain nameless, told me that she had recently started working in the gift shop and had yet to see anything funny. "But before THIS job," she said, opening her eyes further for emphasis, "I worked in housekeeping and something REALLY FUNNY happened there."

At that hotel, the bathroom doors are covered with full-length mirrors. In addition, the closet doors, which open and shut like accordions, are mirrors. "When the door in the bathroom is shut and the closet door is open, a chain reaction is set up," she explained. "I worked wake-up, which meant I took coffee and a newspaper up to the rooms early in the morning. Many times the guest had just gotten out of the shower, and would hide behind the door and reach a hand through for the tray." She raised her eyebrows and smiled. "But with the mirrors set up that way, we often saw people in all their rearview glory." (I believe she had 'em if they didn't jump.)

I smiled at the thought of folks crouching behind slightly opened doors with their backsides in full view of the person on the other side. It was slightly amusing if it were not you. The sales clerk laughed, but several seconds later, gave away that she had a wild streak in her when she said, "It was a HORRIBLE thing, but I was always careful not to look TOO long."

(SNOOP!)

--- Delaware ---

Clipper Happy

Floyd: He cuts his own hair.
Barney: Did he tell you that?
Floyd: Didn't have to. I can spot an amateur head a mile off.

- Episode #29, "Quiet Sam"

I had fallen into the hands of a strange barber who gave me a scalping—a REAL scalping. Any naturalness to my contour was gone. Trust me, a poodle trimmer would have left more hair on my head. However, I had asked for it that way because we were going on vacation, and my curling iron was not. I had one more speech before we left. It was for the Delaware Agricultural Industry Dinner and only one day after my scalping.

A chicken farmer approached me at the reception. "So, you are the former Miss North Carolina who is speaking to us tonight?"

"Yes sir, I guess I am."

He shook his head. "Well, I will be honest with you. I am surprised."

"Oh," I chided. "You heard 'Miss North Carolina' and thought she would be much younger?"

"No," he replied. "I thought she would have hair."

--- Florida ---

Checkpoint Chickie

Barney: Mayberry unit No. 1. Uh, all units. Uh, Roger and over. Over and out. Over and under. Ten-four. Four-ten. Ten-four. Bye.

- Episode #19, "Mayberry on Record"

The driver of the resort van in Panama City, Florida, was a young man named Mike. I was his only passenger. When we crossed over a long four-lane bridge, we passed a car stalled on the opposite side. He clicked on his two-way radio.

"Fifty-two to base."

After a short pause, a woman's voice responded. "Come in, 52."

"We have just passed a car in trouble on the bridge. Please call the Highway Patrol and tell them."

She was hesitant. "Call the Highway Patrol?"

"Yes, the people in the car need help. The Highway Patrol will take care of it," he responded matter-of-factly and put down his radio.

"Ten-four," the woman suddenly said through the little box. Mike shook his head and caught my eye in the rearview mirror. "She's new. I have told her a hundred times not to say 'ten-four,' but she has seen too much television." He went on to explain, "We always call for help in this type of situation. A stalled car on that bridge will back up traffic for miles." I nodded. Seemed reasonable to me.

A few minutes passed and she returned. "Base to 52. Come in, 52." He attempted to respond, but she interrupted him. "Are you there, 52?"

Mike sighed, "I'm here." He bounced the heavy receiver in his hand and waited.

"The Highway Patrol wants to know which side of the bridge the stalled car is on."

"The side from the beaches, toward the airport."

"Ten-four." Click. She was gone. Mike shook his head.

We rode on. In a few minutes, "Base" was back. "Fifty-two? Come in, 52."

More head shaking. Mike reached toward the dashboard. "I am in."

"The Highway Patrol says it is not their responsibility. It is the city police's."

Mike rolled his eyes at me. "Then—call—the—city—police," he said slowly, his extraordinary patience beginning to waver. "And do not say 'ten-four'! Just say 'OK, Mike.'

A few seconds passed and then her meek voice said, "Sorry."

Before long, the sound of the two-way system again filled the air. Mike mumbled "unbelievable."

"I hate to bother you, fifty-two, but the city police want to know what kind of car it is."

Mike's shoulders drooped and he rolled his head toward his window for a split second before snapping the handheld transmitter back toward his mouth. "Tell them," he said very deliberately, "that on the bridge, there will be a line of cars that is not moving. The one in trouble will be at the front!"

There was no response, and Mike said to me, "She's thinking." Seconds later, the woman said, "ten-four."

--- Georgia ---

Two Can Play That Game

Barney: Play the game! Play the game! I hate it when you get "obtuse."
- Episode #117, "The Shoplifters"

Most of us understand Barney's dislike for people who get "obtuse." We probably do not like it when they are "obtrusive" either. But even when Barney has the wrong word for the wrong word, we understand what he means, and it elicits laughter.

In Atlanta, I sat at my assigned table with a friendly bunch of good ol' boys who enjoyed kidding. These company managers began teasing in the buffet line. One of them watched me make my selections and announced for the benefit of all within earshot, "A bell goes off when the plate reaches a certain weight."

"And when they saw you," one drawled in my direction, "they went to get the Liberty Bell."

During the meal, we discussed something dear to all of our hearts. What it was . . . was football. My Auburn Tigers had beaten Georgia that year, and I was up on the latest jokes. As I recall, I told most of them. (Boy, when I get "obtuse" . . ..) When the football talk subsided, the conversation turned to basketball, and the Georgia Tech fans lit up. For several minutes they discussed their Yellow Jackets and the upcoming Atlantic Coast Conference Tournament. When one of them took a long breath, I mentioned that my husband was a former Duke basketball player and that Duke was seeded No. 1 in that particular tournament. (There is that "obtuse" thing again.) One of them muttered, "If we did not like you, we would ask you to move to another table." Another said, "The vote would be mighty close."

The conversation switched to past speakers at that event and to whom they could book in the future. I suggested several folks, and suddenly remembering I was in Georgia, said, "Oh, I know another good speaker your group might enjoy. Have you ever heard Barbara Dooley, the wife of former Georgia coach, Vince Dooley? [57]She is great!"

One of the University of Georgia fans answered immediately. "Yep, she's one of the speakers we tried to get for tonight, but she was already booked."

When their laughter subsided, a Tech fellow mumbled, "Most of the GOOD speakers were."

I hate it when people get "obtuse."

--- Hawaii ---

Fashion Plate

Barney: Well, that's just about the silliest looking thing I believe I ever saw.

                    - Episode #131, "Barney's Physical"

There Opie stands in the Taylors' living room, dressed in the wild shirt and short pants Aunt Bee has bought for him. She is convinced the outfit is perfect for his upcoming trip in "Off to Hollywood." Andy

---

57 Vince Dooley was the head football coach (1964-1988) and the athletic director (1979-2004) at the University of Georgia. Barbara Dooley was a real estate agent and had her own radio show at WRFC in Athens, Georgia that broadcast five days a week. She was also the author of two books, and a speaker.

tries to support Aunt Bee, not knowing that she has bought matching father and son outfits. Before he knows what is happening, Andy is also clad in a typical tourist outfit, short pants and all. At least she has not purchased flimsy swimsuits.

The shop in the Hyatt Regency in Hawaii was crowded with conventioneers. In the middle of the shoppers was a couple whose name tags indicated they were from Kansas. The wife had persuaded her middle-aged husband to try on a bikini swimsuit made of elastic, stretch material—the teeniest bit of material. The man was in the small dressing room and his wife hovered outside the door, inches away.

"Do you have it on?" she shouted over the top of the door, loud enough to be heard at the lobby registration desk.

His response was hushed. "I think so."

"Well, come out and let me see it."

There was a long pause. Buyers exchanged little smiles, pretending disinterest.

"I do not want to come out there," was the muffled response. "It is just about the silliest thing I have ever seen. I feel like a fool."

She ignored his comment. "You cannot tell in there whether you like it or not. Come out here and let me see it on you."

There was no movement. She lowered her voice to a more persuasive level and leaned toward the door. "Just let me see what it looks like on you. NOBODY ELSE is looking. NOBODY cares."

I resisted an urge to walk over and say, "Ma'am, if you have to coax him out of the dressing room, you will never get him down to the beach." Because he was her husband to do with as she pleased, I let it ride.

Suddenly, like a jailer's key turning in a hollow dungeon, we heard the sound of the cornered man fiddling with the latch. Chitchat around the small shop subsided. I found myself nonchalantly pricing a ship in a bottle that I did not want to buy. Did not want to miss this.

The door opened just wide enough for the mother hen to peer inside the little cubicle. "Oh, for crying out loud," she said quickly. "You do not want that! They would laugh you right out of Kansas!"

--- Idaho ---

Isn't That Clever?

Barney: You know something I found out?

Andy: Hum.

Barney: If you ride into the wind with your mouth open and you put your tongue up on the roof of your mouth, it's impossible to pronounce a word that starts with the letter S.
                          - Episode #112, "Barney's Side Car"

In my line of work, I entertain some extremely large groups with my little humorous speeches. However, I often have the opportunity to bring laughter to very small groups, even when I do not mean to. This peculiar characteristic is best illustrated by what happened during a trip to Idaho.

I had heard about the famous floating green on the 14th hole of the Coeur d'Alene Resort Golf Course in Idaho before I went there for a speech. The green floats way out there in Lake Coeur d'Alene with the distance from the tee varying each day. It would take a tornado to blow the green close enough for my ball to hit it from the tee. Fortunately, the golf balls also float because most of the drives splash in the vicinity of the grassy "barge." The golfers then boat over to the green and continue with a second ball, or third, or fourth. (The day I was there, I watched some of them try a long time to land a ball on that green.)

The very exclusive resort also features a driving range where duffers hit floating balls toward targets marked by buoys in the lake. I looked like somebody's hobo friend, dressed in ragged walking clothes and tennis shoes. But clutching the wood and iron I had brought all the way from North Carolina, I boated over with the best of them to the clubhouse. I barely play the game—and certainly do not dress for it—but I had a card that proved I was staying at the hotel, and I was determined to at least take advantage of the driving range and hit a few balls into the water. That is what I did. I hit a "few" balls into the water. Unfortunately, I had a large bucket of balls, which meant most of mine trickled down toward the water's edge.

After a while, I gave up and boated back to find a bicycle, One of the guys on staff seemed especially sorry to see me go. Well, the exact way he put it was, "We SURE DO HATE to see YOU go." I believe I brought joy to his day.

The only bicycle available that afternoon was one with a child's seat on the back, so I rented it for an hour and took off. It did not have foxtails on the handlebars or anything else fancy, but it was pretty new. The coaster brake held, and I was having a ball breezing along trying to pronounce words that start with the letter s'. That is when I had the opportunity to bring joy and laughter to a second small group of people.

Toward the end of my hour, I peddled my bike—empty child's seat and all—near a bunch of ten-year-old local kids. Just to show off a little, I rode with no hands when I passed them. They fell on the ground laughing when one of them shouted, "HEY, LADY! You lost your baby!"

Wonder what they did for entertainment when I flew home?

--- Illinois ---

Too Much "Smart"

Investigator Upchurch: That sounds like a reasonable hypothesis of the modus operandi.
Barney: Well, yeah, that's another way to put it.

- Episode #70, "The Cow Thief"

Some things cannot be explained. Like the time I checked into the wrong hotel, and they had my reservation. I was supposed to stay at the Holiday Inn in Carbondale, Illinois. That information was written in three places in my speaking packet: a letter from my contact, handwritten notes made during a conversation with my client, and the speaker's travel checklist sent from my office. All three indicated in black and white: Holiday Inn, Carbondale. So, I drove straight to Carbondale and checked into the Ramada Inn. It must have been one of Barney's "psychic phenomena." There is no other explanation as to why I do these things.

At the desk, I said, "I am Jeanne Robertson. Do you have a reservation for me, made by the school system?" The college student/clerk stepped away from the counter and fumbled through a few papers. Then he made me feel like a guest of honor. "Yes, we have, Mrs. Robertson. We have been expecting you. Just fill out this information." Minutes later, I was in the room.

Late that evening, I pulled out my paperwork to double-check the time my client was to meet me in the lobby the next morning. I was at the WRONG HOTEL! Thoroughly confused, I grabbed papers out of every folder, expecting the Twilight Zone music to kick in at any moment.[58] This Ramada Inn HAD a reservation for me. They were expecting me!

Some things CAN be explained, however. The same young man was still on duty when I rang the front desk. "You will not believe this," I began, "but I have just discovered I am in the wrong hotel. When I checked in, do you remember me saying, 'I am Jeanne Robertson'? Do you have a reservation for me, made by the school system?'"

I could sense his chest sticking out with pride. "Yes. I covered very well, didn't I?"

---

58 *The Twilight Zone* is an American science fiction horror anthology series. It was created and presented by Rod Serling and ran for five seasons on CBS from 1959 to 1964.

--- Indiana ---

Adult Education

Barney: It's a planned curriculum, Aunt Bee. I mean, the school
board works out a proper balance between mind and body.
                    - Episode #157, "Opie Flunks Arithmetic"

It was a beautiful day in South Bend, Indiana, so I walked from my
hotel to the campus of Notre Dame. I found the student union and
got a slice of mozzarella pizza, but when I left the building, I exited
through a different door. After thirty minutes of wandering, it became
apparent I needed help just getting off the campus.

Several male students were approaching me on the sidewalk. They
wore shorts and tennis shoes, and one tried over and over to twirl a
basketball on his index finger. Well, that was fine. There is more to an
education than two times two.

They noticed my southern accent immediately when I stopped them.
"'Scuse me, this is my first time on y'all' s campus, and I have gotten
all turned around." The expressions on their faces gave their thoughts
away. Who was this very southern woman the age of their mothers?
Since there's no business like show business, I turned the accent up a
notch. "Could y'all puh'lease point me in the direction of town?"

Immediately, one of the guys said, "Town? There's a TOWN? Did
you hear that fellows? There's a TOWN!" One of his buddies shook
his head and chimed in, "No, I do not think so. I've been here almost
a month, and I've never been to a town. No ma'am, never heard of
a town."

Remembering my experiences with Beaver in college I smiled
and said, "That's what happens when you spend so much time in the
library." We all laughed, and they gave me directions, but as I walked
away, my motherly instinct kicked in. About twenty feet down the
sidewalk, I turned and screamed, "AND STOP CUTTING CLASS!"

***

OK, As long as we are in Indiana, and just to play fair with the rivals, let me tell you the Mayberry humor that happened to me on the Purdue campus. It reminded me of Floyd's question in "Look Paw, I'm Dancing" after a youngster says that his mother will be by later to pay for the haircut. Floyd asks Goober, "What happened to the days when it was cash on the barrelhead? Credit! Eh!"

I went to Lafayette to speak at the Chamber of Commerce banquet and stayed at the Purdue student union. It had been almost thirty years since my college days, so it was fun to stay right in there "amongst 'em." When I saw a long-winding line of young people on the main floor, thoughts surfaced of fall registration. Oh, how we used to wait in line for hours to get the classes and professors we wanted!"

Times change, however, and this was made vividly clear as I rounded the corner. The students were lined up at an automatic teller machine.[59]

--- Iowa ---

Haven't You Heard? I'm Innocent!

Howard Sprague, writing about Andy umpiring the big baseball game against Mt. Pilot: Once a man is asked to handle a job like that, any decisions he makes should be accepted in the spirit of good sportsmanship—right or wrong.

- Episode #195, "The Ball Game"

After a speech for the Iowa School Boards Association, a shorter, slightly balding gentleman stepped forward and gazed up at me. "Hearing you tonight brought back a memory," he said, and then unknowingly related an excellent example of Iowa-style Mayberry humor.

---

59 An ATM.

He officiated high school girls basketball in Iowa. At the state play-offs one year, a team had a player about my height, 6'2". In the third quarter of a close game, he called a foul on her, and when he blew the whistle and signaled in her direction, the teenager spun around and glared at him. People in the stands froze and awaited her reaction. The referee sensed that she was going to do the wrong thing, but he was incorrect. She slowly smiled and said, "OK, you got me. Good call." She even handed the official the ball, but when she passed him, she reached down and patted him on the top of his head. The fans roared approval. He let it go.

The game got closer in the last minutes, and at a crucial point, the referee called another foul on the tall, young star. He saw it with his own two eyes. It was interference, a clear blocking foul. This time, however, she disagreed, and there was no hint of a smile. As a matter of fact, when she wheeled around, there was fire in her eyes as she looked at him as if he were a pestilence. A pestilence! For an instant, the man in charge thought she was going to blow up. But no, with an inner strength, perhaps fueled by the desire to stay in the game, the athlete mustered restraint. With the crowd watching every move, she smiled through gritted teeth, but mumbled, "I do not agree, but it's your whistle." The referee moved toward the scorer's table and seconds later, this young player again played to the fans when she walked by and patted him on the head a second time. He definitely was not thrilled, but with seconds left in the competition, chose to ignore it again.

The moment the final horn sounded, the officials headed to the referees' locker room, where the man telling me the story eventually looked in the mirror and had his pride punctured. There on the top of his head . . . were two wads of chewing gum.

--- Kansas ---

Hoot! Hoot! Yuk! Yuk!

Barney: Oh, come on, Andy. Boy, you're funny, you are. You ought to go on the radio and be an all-night disc jockey. At least, then I could turn you off!

- Episode #37, "The Perfect Female"

The thing about rain is that we either get too much of it or not enough. After a three-hour storm delay, our flight headed off into the wild blue yonder aiming for Wichita, Kansas. Once airborne the pilot announced, "Ladies and gentlemen, we are past the bad weather. I have spoken with the Wizard of Oz, and it looks like smooth sailing into Kansas." Disgruntled passengers groaned, not in the mood to hear about the Wizard. There is a time . . . for that type of commentary, but it was not that day. A pilot with the same airline was seated across the aisle from me. He looked out the window.

The Captain persisted with chit-chatty comments throughout the trip. Every time I fell asleep, his chatter made me fall awake. When we landed in Wichita, he concluded his show with, "Ladies and gentlemen, after you leave the plane, just follow the yellow brick road to the baggage claim, click your heels twice, and your luggage will be there."

I cut my eyes toward the pilot near me. This time he avoided eye contact by looking down, but that did not stop me from speaking. "Do they teach you this in pilot school?" I asked. He shook his head slowly. "No, he dreamed this up on his own."

A man seated behind us joined in the conversation. "And if he thinks we can click our heels twice and have our luggage, he is STILL dreaming."

--- Kentucky ---

It's Free!

Goober: Well, who's gon'a believe we stayed here if we don't have evidence?

- Episode #242, "Goober Goes to the Auto Show"

The health conference in Paducah, Kentucky was well organized. My client had checked me into the hotel before I arrived, and gave me the room key when I stepped off the flight. "There is no need to check out tomorrow," she instructed. "Just give the key back to me when we return to the airport. I will handle everything." When I saw the long line at registration, I was thankful for her efforts.

The next day, the same hostess drove me back to my flight, but I forgot to give her the key and still had it in my purse when I boarded the plane. Minutes later, the gate agent came through the door and announced over the public address system, "Will passenger Robertson please identify herself. Jeanne Robertson."

From the back of the plane, I raised my hand. "I'm Jeanne Robertson."

The gate agent spoke right into the microphone a second time for all to hear placing special emphasis on my name. "MRS. ROBERTSON, will you PLEASE send your hotel room key to the front of the plane." (What was this guy? Some kind of a "wisenheimer?") [60]

The passengers looked at one another for a few seconds and then started chuckling. Seconds later, an interloper across the aisle leaned in my direction and lectured, "MRS. ROBERTSON, they want their towels back, too!"

---

60 According to the *Merriam-Webster Dictionary*, a wisenheimer is a smart aleck.

--- Louisiana ---

Throw a Dragnet Over the Whole Town

Opie: I'm going home. This place is a bad influence.

- Episode #32, "Bringing Up Opie"

The ladies are upset—UPSET!—when they descend on the courthouse to complain about the performance going on over at the carnival in "Banjo-Playing Deputy." Clara says, "It's called the Sultan's Favorite. It's a sort of 'gucci-hucci' dance." The women think it is disgraceful, but Floyd does not see it that way, and he has seen it six times. But then, as Floyd asks, "Can a person EVER get too much culture?"

Jerry and I were checking into the Marriott near the French Quarter in New Orleans, and there were teenagers everywhere. Over twenty thousand were in town for the National Lutheran Youth Convention. A national meeting? The Lutheran YOUTH group? NEW ORLEANS? Not my first choice to take young people on a church trip. Let me tell you, New Orleans can be pretty risqué. Barney would take one look at it and advise throwing a dragnet over parts of the French Quarter.

While we waited in line, I struck up a conversation with one of the chaperons and asked why New Orleans was selected. Obviously tired and unhappy, she snapped briskly, "I'm from South Dakota. I DID NOT select it!" She was in for a long week.

She soon spoke again to establish credibility. "But the kids have strict rules about where they can go in the French Quarter. They are NOT permitted to go on Bourbon Street." I muttered, "Well, I am SURE they won't."

Later that night, Jerry and I walked down the famous Bourbon Street. I do not think they had toned down anything because the young people were in town, but I am not sure. We could not peek into a single one of the joints. Teenagers were crowded around every door.

Hadn't noticed it before that night, but Lutheran young people all have such BIG EYES. Must be hereditary.

--- Maine ---

Elbow and Rule Bending

Andy: You see, son, rules are very important things. But some-
           times they seem to get in the way when we're trying to
           help somebody. So, what we do in a case like that, we don't
           exactly break 'em. We just bend 'em a little bit.

                                          - Episode #4, "Runaway Kid"

It may be one of the big secrets of getting along in life: knowing when
to bend the rules and when not to. In Mayberry, Andy Taylor always
seems to sense which way to play it. Fortunately, many others in this
world do too.

When I arrived at the Bangor, Maine airport in May 1991, it looked
like a riot of color because of the impressive display of red, white,
and blue ribbons around the facility. This was not unusual a couple of
months after Desert Storm; most airports were proudly displaying the
national colors along with the popular yellow ribbons.[61] But Bangor
was decorated to the hilt, and later I found out why.

Every plane returning from the Gulf made its first stop on U.S. soil
at the Bangor airport. Here the personnel deplaned for a few minutes
while the aircraft was refueled. The military man meeting me proudly
pointed out that the people living in the area turned out to greet
EVERY SINGLE PLANE. Perhaps they thought they had some sort
of rendezvous with destiny. They waved flags, cheered, and applauded
as the soldiers deplaned. Local radio and newspapers spread the word
of arrivals. How wonderful! How Mayberryish! (Gee, in Mayberry, a
gold shipment passing through town draws a crowd.)

---

61 Yellow ribbons began to appear in the US in support of our troops during the
Gulf War (2 Aug., 1990-28 Feb. 1991.) Desert Storm, was the second phase of the
war and marked the first US major conflict with Iraq.

Knowing the non-drinking policy in the Gulf, I asked if beer was the first thing they wanted?

"Well," the officer said, "it is illegal to have beer at the airport. But amazingly," he added with a grin, "there are always a few cases around. Unauthorized, of course."

Of course. Go for it! Rule bending at its best!

--- Maryland ---

The Special

Barney: Now here at the Rock, we have two basic rules. Memorize them so that you can say them in your sleep. The first rule is: OBEY ALL RULES! Secondly, do not write on the walls as it takes a lot of work to erase writing off of walls. [62]

- Episode #95, "The Big House"

I did not think I would be able to get an eighty-cent special through room service at a small hotel on Maryland's Eastern Shore, but without a menu, I had no idea. There was not one in the room, so I called the restaurant to inquire. The woman on the other end was silent a few moments, then said, "There ought to be a menu on the dresser, but I hear most rooms do not have them."

She WOULD BE THE ONE to hear about it.

"Well, let me look again," I said. "I will call back."

"Naw, it does not matter," she explained. "Just let me tell you the dishes we prepare for room service." My choices reminded me of one of my favorite episodes on *TAGS*, "Convicts-at-Large," when the radio announcer gives the aliases of escapee Big Maude Tyler, also known as "Clarisse Tyler, Maude Clarisse Tyler, Annabelle Tyler, and Ralph Henderson." That is a laugh-out-loud line, and so were the options the room service woman reeled off for me. She said, "You can have

---

62 The Rock is a nickname for the Mayberry jail.

a shrimp boat, fried shrimp, boiled shrimp, shrimp salad, or a hamburger." (No shrimp enchiladas?)

Thinking she would laugh, I asked, "Can I have shrimp on my hamburger?"

After a few seconds, a very serious, OBEY-ALL-RULES voice said, "We DO NOT vary the menu!"

--- Massachusetts ---

Back Bay Boston

Andy and Opie walking home after seeing a movie:

Opie: Did you notice that Gregory Peck has an accent?

Andy: An accent?

Opie: Well, he don't talk like you do.

Andy: Well, that's 'cause he's a northern person. Someday we'll take a trip up there, and you can hear it in the flesh.

- Episode #104, "Up in Barney's Room"

According to most information sources, English is the main language in Boston and North Carolina. I might need more proof.

"Would you like to stop at ahraba?"

It seemed like a casual question when my contact asked it during the ride from the airport to the hotel in Boston.

"Ahraba?"

"Yes, we have time."

I wondered what in the world she was talking about? Ahraba? I knew I was a long way from hominy grits, and she knew I was not Back Bay Boston.

We rode on. "I do not know what an 'ahraba' is," I admitted a block or so later.

With a puzzled expression, she looked several times from me back to the traffic in front of her. Finally, "Ah-ra-ba," she repeated, enunciating each syllable. She could repeat it five more times if she wanted to; I had never heard of an "Ahraba." I did remember a small Caribbean island.

"Aruba?"

"No, AHRABA. A place where you go to eat oystas."

It hit me. "Oh, a RAW BAR?" Oysters! (I did not tell her that my friends and I usually eat oysters in chili sauce.)

"That is what I said. Ahraba."

It is not always the accent, however. "Ahraba" was fresh on my mind early the next day when I returned to the Boston airport and headed for the ticket counter. Every frequent traveler has certain idiosyncrasies that become extremely important for reasons known only to them. For example, I want an aisle seat. Window seats are tolerable, but trips seem so much longer when you are the man in the middle. See, three's a crowd. Of course, the worst thing is to have someone sit next to you with their darling baby. When I am seated in the smaller first-class section, I will take any aisle seat in that section. When flying coach, my preference is an aisle seat halfway back in the plane. My upgrade coupons were running low, so this trip, I was flying coach.

The agent glanced in my direction as her fingers flew across her computer keyboard. "Ah'd like an aisle seat in the cenuh of the plane," I said.

She rested her wrists on the keyboard and looked up at me. In a thick Boston accent, she asked, "Where would you like that seat?"

Uh-oh, here we go again, I thought. She is a Bostonian, and I sure do not sound like I come from around here. I bet she cannot understand my southern accent. To be mischievous, I started to drawl my best "Youwannapieceahpie?" but I did not. Speaking very slowly, I enunciated every word. "Ah'd—like—an—aisle—seat—in—the—cenuh—of—the—plane."

She tilted her head and stared at me a few seconds, and said, just as deliberately, "ALL—OF—THE—AISLE—SEATS—ARE—IN—THE—CENTER—OF—THE—PLANE."

--- Michigan ---

You Tell Me and I'll Tell You

Andy: You know what I think, Barn? I think that was real demo-
           cratic of you. Real democratic.
Barney: How I vote, brother, is my business!

- Episode #103, "Opie's Ill-Gotten Gain"

Holland, Michigan, is one of the most Republican counties in the United States, and President Bush had campaigned there the day before my Chamber of Commerce speech in '92. The town was still abuzz when I arrived. During the reception before the banquet—which was jokingly called a "Republican caucus"—all the talk was about the election, President Bush, and Republican politics. Everyone made it a point to say, "You may not be aware of it, but this is the strongest Republican county in the country."

When I moved away from one small clump of people at the reception, a woman tugged on my sleeve. Feeling compelled to let the out-of-towner know a little more, she whispered, "Everybody here is NOT Republican." She had the courage of her convictions but liked to whisper them. I whispered back, "They told me there was one of you."

I might as well have thrown a jar of kerosene cucumbers in her face.[63] Horrified, she asked, "Did someone say something about me?" I teased, "Sure. They see your vote every time. There is always one, and they KNOW whose it is."

During table conversation later, I related the incident which I thought was humorous, but was met with blank stares for several seconds. Finally, one man broke the silence when he squinted his eyes and asked, "EXACTLY what did the woman look like?"

---

63 In TAGS Aunt Bee makes terrible pickles, that Andy has labeled "kerosene cucumbers."

--- Minnesota ---

Work It Off! Work It Off!

Barney: You know what I'm gonna get? Two chili-sized burgers with chopped onions, ketchup, piccalilli, and mustard, a side of french fries, a slab of rhubarb pie, and a chocolate malt. How does that hit you?

Andy: That'll lay on your chest.

Barney: You work it off, man, you work it off!

- Episode #123, "Fun Girls"

Andy lies on the courthouse floor pretending to be unconscious in "Andy Saves Gomer." The plan is for Gomer to come in and save him; but instead, Opie appears. Being a quick thinker, Andy immediately flips over and starts doing push-ups. He claims he likes to do at least fifteen a day.

Agreeing with Andy that one needs exercise, I put on my warm-up outfit on the afternoon of a banquet in Minneapolis and went to check the meeting room before heading out to walk. No one was in the huge facility, and I had a question about the setup. A waiter in the kitchen told me to wait in the ballroom while he contacted the person in charge.

Back in the large hall, I passed the time counting tables, checking silverware, and straightening centerpieces. Not in a speaker's normal contract, but what the heck? It seemed like the neighborly thing.

Unbeknown to me, I had a couple of companions. Two guys working on the spotlights were behind a one-way glass up in the audiovisual room at the back of the hall and had me under constant surveillance.

Minutes ticked away, and I was getting antsy because my exercise time was dwindling. I started stretching a little, reaching for my toes if not actually touching them every time. (Darn that pan of cashew fudge!) Still, no one came.

In a few minutes, I moved out of sight of the main doors, got on the floor, and started doing sit-ups. Up, down, up, down. I hit my limit quickly, struggling on the last ones—thirty-eeeeight, thirt-tee-ninn-nne, FORTY—and fell back onto the floor in exhaustion.

Suddenly, a spotlight turned into the monster that ate Minnesota, with its full beam right on me as I sprawled on the floor.[64] A mysterious voice boomed through the sound system, "Come on, ma'am. You can do five more."

--- Mississippi ---

Ain't He Wonderful?

Ernest T. Bass: You can afford to be mighty proud of yourself.
                              - Episode #113, "My Fair Ernest T. Bass"

A member of the group I was to address in nearby Biloxi met me at the Gulfport airport, and he did not want to mess up on his manners. He was a cultured, southern gentleman from Mississippi, and he fell all over himself trying to help from the minute I unfolded from the tiny plane. He tried to take the purse off my shoulder and even reached for the newspaper in my hand. I flipped up the handle on my rolling cart, and he was so accommodating that he almost snapped it back down in an attempt to help.

When I mentioned I had checked my hanging bag, he rushed to the conveyer belt to retrieve it. I followed, thinking he might want to know which bag it was.

We made pleasant conversation until the pieces of luggage began to bobble by. "That's it," I said, pointing to my beautiful orange and blue Auburn University hanging bag. He recoiled. "I, I cannot carry that."

"I beg your pardon."

---

64   *The Monster that ate Minnesota* is the title of a fake movie that appears on the marque of the theater in Mayberry.

He shook his head slowly. "Ma'am, I cannot carry an Auburn bag. My friends might see me, and I am not willing to hear about it for the rest of my life. You get your bag, and I will pull my car up to the door."

I started to tell him the orange and blue were not for Auburn, but for Mayberry Union High. After all, both schools have the same colors, a coincidence that would later make it easy to select the colors for the jacket of this book. He knew it was an Auburn bag, though, so I did not mention Mayberry.

The man was serious, and since I know about friendly college rivalries, I understood his actions. He was an Ole Miss fan. An AVID one. Aren't they all? "Quite frankly," I told him when I found that out, "I do not want an Ole Miss fan to touch my Auburn bag."

That night I related the experience to my Mississippi audience. They applauded him, and he basked in the attention.

I offered to take a cab back to the airport the next morning. However, a "southern gentleman" as he referred to himself, would not let a lady do that. Even an Auburn lady. (What an admirable quality.)

Early the next day, the "southern gentleman" pulled his car up to the front of the hotel and pushed the button to pop open the trunk. Before he could get out, I shouted, "I have it," put my rolling cart in, and quickly slid into the front seat.

When we arrived at the airport, I said, "Pull up behind that cab over there and get out your billfold."

He was perplexed but had been married for years, so did as he was told.

I opened my door and glanced back at him. "I did not want to offend you, so I sent the 'old orange-and-blue' in that cab. 'Preciate it if you will pay the driver, while I get it."

He did. After all, he WAS a "southern gentleman."

--- Missouri ---

Age Before Beauty

Andy: Wasn't it you that said there is nothing to fear but fear itself?"
Barney: Well, that's exactly what I got! FEAR ITSELF!

                        - Episode #98, "The Haunted House"

As soon as I said a few words on the way to the airport in St. Louis, the cab driver noticed my southern accent. I knew what was coming. "You're not from around here, are you?" He was right. "Well, I sure hope you had a chance to go up in the arch," he added proudly.

I had not gone up in the arch that is the landmark of the Midwest and told him so. (Just looking up at it gives me the "squidgets.") He shook his head. "Too bad. You ought not come to St. Louis without going up in the arch." We rode on a few moments in silence before I asked, "Have you ever gone to the top of it?"

"Well," he answered slowly. "Not yet, but I'm thinking about it."

After several more miles, the friendly driver initiated more conversation. "I went down to the South once. People kept trying to get me to eat something called 'chitlins.'"

"Oh, sure, that is one of our big dishes in the South. Chitlins and grits."

He raised his eyebrows. "Do you eat them?"

"No, not yet," I said with a smile. "But I'm thinking about it."

"I bet you are," he chided. "You are going to eat chitlins right after I go up in that arch."

As Barney might say, "Exactilioso."

--- Montana—

Try To Control Yourself

Barney: They were kissing, Andy! Hugging and kissing! You couldn't
            have gotten a piece of tissue paper between them; they
            were that close. They were kissing!
                    - Episode #126, "Barney and Thelma Lou, Phfftt"

People in Mayberry do not think there is anything wrong with kissing. No siree. In "The County Nurse," Andy even says it feels "better
than a mule's nose." In Mayberry, though, people do not kiss so much
right out on the street unless they are hit by a "transport of emotion."
When this happens, others generally look away. I guess they agree
with Briscoe Darling in "Divorce, Mountain Style" when he says, "It
ain't proper to look at a betrothed couple when they are communing
with one another."

I was one of many passengers lined up to board a flight out of
Billings, Montana. At the front of the line next to the ticket agent, a
young couple was wrapped in a tight embrace and passionately kissing. Every passenger had to maneuver around them.

"Excuse me." "Pardon us." People were polite but cut their eyes at
one another in disbelief and amusement. Clearly many grew up in
towns like Mayberry where people courted a long time before even
holding hands in public. The happy twosome broke their embrace
with each interruption but continued to gaze longingly into each other's eyes. As soon as possible, they fell into a tight embrace where they
remained until the next passenger needed to get by.

After multiple repetitions of this sequence, the airline agent tapped
the young man on the shoulder and said, "Why don't you go to the
back of the line and stay together as long as possible. You can board
in a few minutes."

"Oh, neither of us is boarding," the youth responded. "We just put
her mother on the plane."

--- Nebraska ---

Well, I'll Be Doggone

Otis: Do you expect a man to go to bed when he's got the (hic) . . . hiccups.

Andy: Stand right there, and I'll get you some water.

Otis: Um, water. Oh, I don't know. I'll get sick if I mix my drinks.

        - Episode #145, "The Rehabilitation of Otis"

Does a four-legged "canine Otis" have to walk two chalk lines during a sobriety test? They might be able to answer the question in Nebraska.

A waitress in Omaha told me about a guy who came in early one morning and asked for Diet Pepsi in a plastic cup. He wanted to take it to his dog in his room. Apparently, the animal was not a morning dog. She told him they did not have Diet Pepsi. Would a Diet Coke be OK?

No, his dog wanted Diet Pepsi.

"How about tea?" she asked.

"No, he ONLY DRINKS Diet Pepsi, or . . . "He looked down at his watch, "Miller Beer. He likes Miller Beer, but I hate for him to start drinking so early in the day."

--- Nevada ---

Quality Criminals

Barney, referring to the Hubacher brothers: You know, they're three of the nicest fellows we ever sent up.

        - Episode #26, "The Inspector"

In "Helen's Past," the facts as Andy gets them, seem clear. Helen Crump was arraigned on August 4, 1959, on three charges: (1) concealing a .38 revolver in her purse, (2) dealing cards in an illegal gaming house, and (3) being in the company of a known hoodlum—Harry Brown. Of course, as is so often illustrated on *TAGS*, there can be two sides to a situation . . ..

My good friend and fellow speaker, Patricia Fripp, frequently tells of an inmate she met during a speech at San Quentin Prison. The guy's name was Frogie, and I have heard the tale so often I feel as though I know him. Apparently, he was a very personable fellow and well-liked by the other prisoners, probably the kind who sent Christmas cards and leather crafts to the officers who captured him. That is something to write home about, I suppose. It is a terrific story that I will leave for Patricia to recount, for I have my own Frogie story.

On a speaking trip to Lake Tahoe, Nevada, the last portion of my travel was on a commuter plane, and the only other passenger was an older woman who was frantic about flying on that size aircraft. In trying to reassure her, I discovered that this was her first trip from her small town since her husband's death the previous year. She had never been to Nevada, and her only gambling experience was church bingo. (The prizes were donated, so it was not really gambling.) The anticipation of seeing an old college friend faded as she lamented, "I do not know why I let my friend talk me into this! My husband always took care of everything when we traveled. I don't know if I will even be able to get to the hotel."

"Oh, traveling is fun," I assured her. "Just wait until you tell your friends at the bingo game about it." She smiled slightly.

Her words about her husband popped into my mind when I saw her standing empty-handed at the baggage claim. Her luggage had not made it. It was reminiscent of Opie in the initial episode, "The New Housekeeper," when he figures Aunt Bee is helpless because she cannot fish, hit baseballs, or catch frogs. This woman needed me, so I stepped into the role of the deceased spouse. I helped her start a trace on her bags, hailed a cab, and before long we piled in the back seat of the taxi and headed for the hotel where we were both staying. She laid her purse between us and slowly exhaled. It had been a long day, and

I tried to influence her outlook by saying, "No bags" is just another story to tell at church bingo."

"Maybe so," she replied halfheartedly.

The cab driver was a big, rough-looking man with long hair, but he appeared friendly. My new friend gazed out the window at unfamiliar surroundings, so I turned my attention to the cabby, still looking for evidence of Mayberry humor.

"How long have you been driving this cab?" I asked.

"Oh, 'bout a year in Tahoe. I used to drive in San Francisco."

The woman continued to stare at buildings, content to let us rattle on.

"I love San Francisco. How long did you drive there?" I asked.

"Not long. To tell the truth, I was in San Quentin before that."

At the mention of San Quentin, the lady snapped her head around so fast that I am surprised she did not crack her neck. Her eyes were like two frisbees as she mouthed, "San Quentin?" But I was leaning forward, resting my arms on the back of the front seat and saying, "San Quentin? I have a friend who was in San Quentin. Did you by any chance know a guy named Frogie?"

The woman's jaw dropped three inches!

The cab driver banged the palm of his hand on the steering wheel and turned his body in my direction. He was grinning from ear to ear. "Know him? KNOW HIM? Everybody knew Frogie. He was a terrific guy!"

Out of the corner of my eye, I saw the woman next to me slowly pick up her purse and then quickly clutch it to her chest. She then wedged herself into the corner of the seat, and she did not speak again for the remainder of the ride. Quite possibly, she never exhaled.

All the way to the hotel the driver and I exchanged Frogie information. What was he doing? Had he stayed out of trouble? Was he still married? Apparently, like Otis down at the jail, Frogie was one of the family.

The motor was still running in front of the hotel when the woman slapped a ten-dollar bill on the seat and bolted for safety. When she slammed the cab door, her skirt caught in it, but she did not open it again. She just frantically YANKED at the material until it broke loose, and then she disappeared into the crowd. I could not help but shout after her, "What's your hurry?"

I have thought about her often. There she was on her first solo trip to a gambling mecca, miles away from the sanctity of her familiar surroundings, riding in a cab with two people who were discussing a mutual acquaintance in San Quentin prison.

Wish I could have heard her tell it down at the church bingo game.

--- New Hampshire ---

An Arm and a Leg

Ernest T. Bass: I need twelve dollars for the honeymoon. Tents cost money, something fierce, you know. Gonna get a lantern, too.

- Episode #164, "Malcolm at the Crossroads"

Ernest T. sure chews his cabbage right the first time on this one.[65] The price of tents—and rooms—do cost "something fierce" and Andy notices it too in "Andy and Barney in the Big City" and tells his deputy, "The robbery I've noticed so far is what they're asking for rooms." That is yet another reason that I have always liked so many of the Mayberry folks. They tell it like it is. So did a teenager I met in New England.

Checking into the posh, expensive Bretton Woods resort in New Hampshire around 7:00 p.m., I asked the young woman at the desk about my client. "Are the Independent Insurance Agents currently in an event, or do they have a free night?"

Her eyes seem to enlarge as she looked up from her paperwork and slowly shook her head. "Well, I have only worked here this summer," she said, "but so far, I have not seen ANYTHING around here that is free."

---

65 The reference is to the phrase "to chew your cabbage twice" which means you are not going to repeat yourself.

--- New Jersey ---

A Fix on the North Star

Barney: The fact is I've got a rendezvous with destiny.

- **Episode #44, "Sheriff Barney"**

Professor Hubert St. John, *TAGS* visitor in "Aunt Bee and the Lecturer," does not expect to see Clara Edwards at the Taylors for dinner. It is a pleasant surprise because he thought they were "just ships that passed in the night." Clara gives him her best alluring smile and responds, "But apparently on the same course."

Like those ships at night, these were briefcases that passed in the morning. The three professional women in business suits boarded the shuttle van in the wee hours of the morning going from Atlantic City, New Jersey, back to the Philadelphia airport. They did not know one another and sat in separate rows as they positioned briefcases by their sides and nodded politely. Within minutes, however, they turned out to be the most talkative, funny women anyone would ever hope to meet. Aw, shucks, y'all, I was one of 'em.

It was one of those magical travel moments when strangers on a short trip hit it off instantly. Searching for Mayberry humor, I asked the other two women for humorous travel stories at the beginning of the ride. The levee broke, and the stories gushed forth. The instant one of us slowed down to breathe, another jumped in. Like teenage girls at a slumber party, we suddenly decided to compare briefcase contents. We opened our leather cases to reveal pantyhose, hairdryers, and travel irons among the files. There were no bobby pins, but two of us had orange sticks.[66] The sight of similar items made us laugh to the point of tears. One had something like a Mr. Cookie Bar next to her curling iron, and we split it three ways.

---

66 A sweet snack with an orange jelly center and covered in chocolate or other coatings. They are made by the Sweet Candy Company.

The briefcase comparisons were so hysterical that we were just about to dump out the contents of our purses when we saw the airport signs. The woman on the second row said, "Let's pay the driver extra to ride around the block." The other shouted from the back of the van, "At least slow down while I repack this briefcase."

The magic moment came to an end as we summoned the strength to climb out of the van. Someone managed to ask about the fare. The driver slowly shook his head back and forth and said, "Twice as much as usual for listening to the three of you."

We FELL back limp onto the seats for one more laugh!

Minutes later, three businesswomen with briefcases by our sides walked matter-of-factly down the concourse and waved goodbye as we veered toward different flights. None of us asked for names and addresses, and we have never seen one another again. It was a gift, a travel experience that could not be duplicated. Without saying so, we all knew it.

But every time I take the shuttle to or from Atlantic City, I buy something like a Mr. Cookie Bar to put next to my curling iron, just in case . . .

--- New Mexico ---

Another Satisfied Customer

Malcolm Merriweather: Could I do it on the never-never? Pay a bit now and more later.

> - **Episode #89, "Andy's English Valet"**

On a speaking trip to New Mexico, I spent time with my young cousin, Katherine, who was working there. She suggested we drive out to the Acoma Indian Reservation, about an hour from Albuquerque. It turned out to be our privilege to see people living as their ancestors had, with no running water, no electricity, and no automobiles. These Native Americans stay away from the big towns like Raleigh where everything is go, go, go, go.

As we walked past the old pueblos, women came out to show what they had made and to offer items for sale. The price was a little steep for the recent college graduate, but Katherine was considering one piece in particular. Turning the beautiful pottery over in her hands, she could sense the history of the place and was touched by the commitment of the people to the primitive lifestyle.

The silence was broken when the weather-beaten woman smiled up at her and said, "I take Visa."

--- New York ---

Out Of The Way, Sunday Driver!

Ernest T. Bass: I don't care, sheriff. I don't care. Like I just told you, I
          do not care!

- Episode #164 "Malcolm at the Crossroads"

The shuttle bus driver to my commuter flight was personable and outgoing and was driving lickety-split. As soon as we pulled away from the main terminal at La Guardia, with the vehicle weaving from side to side, he announced to the riders that he had just returned from a trip to Ireland. The tired travelers looked toward the front of the van in silence. They just did not care.

Remember, silence makes southerners from small towns very nervous. We consider it impolite to leave a person's casual comment dangling. A few long seconds later, I spoke up and asked him if he were visiting relatives in Ireland or there on business. I had not heard of any shuttle-driver conventions in Ireland, but sometimes news slips by me.

"No, I went for a bowling tournament," he answered, and suddenly swung the van between crowded vehicles creeping toward various airlines. People stared out of the windows at how close we came to sideswiping several cars.

"Oh, that sounds like fun. Did you win?" I asked, grabbing my rolling cart before it slid into another bag like a 4-pin in a 4-10 split.

"Didn't go to win," he sang out as he HIT THE BRAKE inches from a rental car. "I went to drink, and I guess you could say I won the gold medal."

A passenger with a thick New Yark accent threw both hands in the air and pleaded, "LAY'DEE! WILL YA JUST' LET DIS GUY DRIVE DA MACHINE!"

--- North Carolina ---

A Deal Is a Deal

Andy: What do you mean you got them off the New Orleans bus?

Floyd: It made a rest stop. All I did was ask if they wanted to see a famous landmark and a couple of legendary characters.

Andy: Floyd, you drug those folks in there for nothing.

Floyd: I did not! I charged them two bits apiece.

- **Episode #41, "Crime-free Mayberry"**

No wonder Andy is upset. Without prior warning, Floyd ushers the first tour group into the courthouse in "Crime-free Mayberry." The tour has been approved by the Greater Mayberry Historical Society and Tourist Bureau Ltd., which Aunt Bee chairs. Andy heads straight for their meeting where the mayor boasts that Mayberry will get "a lot of business from the tourists." Andy calls it like it is. "Well, right now, the tourists are getting the business from us."

In Mayberry and most everywhere else, tourists are attracted to the local economy. We certainly think so where I live in Burlington, North Carolina. Once called "The Outlet Capital of The South," we had over a hundred and eighty outlets on an eight-mile stretch of Interstate 85 when we were in our heyday. There was even talk of building a Six Flags Over Outlets, but the decision was turned over to the local city council. Last heard, they were still discussing it. (A little inside humor there.)

Now outlet centers have sprung up everywhere, and today Waccamaw Pottery is located across the South almost as frequently as Waffle Houses and Wal-Marts.[67] Well, not Wal-Marts. Still, the invitation is always there to COME ON DOWN and bring your money. We will sell everything we have at bargain prices. You better know we will. Be like Aunt Bee, who certainly does not want to throw away good money. She talks about shopping at an outlet store in Mt. Pilot in "Bargain Day." That is where she has found discontinued shoes for Opie that Andy thinks should have been discontinued about a half an inch sooner. His exact comment is, "At the rate he goes through shoes, he'll be through the soles before he gets anywhere near the toes." Welllll, the man said Opie would grow into them.

Most of our outlet shoppers, however, are not residents of North Carolina. They are our friends from the North. ("Friends from the North" is so much nicer sounding than "Yankees.") The local code name for them is "two-one-twos." Confusing? Well, that is the telephone area code for New York City. (As in "Here comes another carload of 'two-one-twos.' Put out those Going-Out-Of-Business signs!")

The "two-one-twos" come through North Carolina by the busloads, run into our outlets with money in their little outstretched hands, and plead, "Take it." We do our best to oblige. We want to get those funds before the travelers see the velveteen bullfighter pictures on the highways in South Carolina or the roadside orange stands in Florida.

When Aunt Bee chickens out of telling Andy she has dented the car in "Aunt Bee Learns to Drive," she stares off into space and says, "There is a sale of black socks somewhere if you need any." She is right! The sale is in Burlington! We sit there in our outlets and watch the "two-one-twos" pulllll at towels and hose and socks. They act like they have never seen a pair of socks, and we know they have. They wear them with sandals.

---

67 Waccamaw Pottery was started in 1977 in Myrtle Beach, SC. In 1982 it began to expand into other states. In the 1990s it became a home furnishing business as well, operating stores in the South and Midwest. The company ceased operations in 2001.

And we sit there and laugh and laugh and laugh. See, we know most of that stuff just came down on a truck from New York . . . the week before.

Sometimes the merchandise comes down on the same bus with the tourists. Local people have to rush it off the bus and through the back doors while others welcome the "two-one-twos" through the front. Rumor also has it that someone once sold a woman her own umbrella because she wanted one like the one she had.

(She got it.)

--- North Dakota ---

Deep Pink Ecstasy

Barney: Professor Matsumata wrote that.
Andy: He don't come from around here, does he?
                   - Episode #18, "Andy the Marriage Counselor"

Did you talk like that when you were Miss North Carolina? It is the question I am often asked. What do people think I will say? "No, that year I spoke Chinese." So many people in North Carolina DO SPEAK Chinese.

Of course, I really know what they mean. It is my distinctly North Carolina accent. Notice I did not say "southern accent." We have our own, although it is a first cousin to those in other southern states. And yes, I did talk like this when I went to the Miss 'Merica Pageant. (That's the way we say it 'round where I live—"The Miss 'Merica Pageant." My friends said, "I can't believe you're going up to the Miss 'Merica Pageant.") When I tell people that I did speak when I competed as I do now, they nod and smile. Their facial expressions say, "That explains a whole lot."

Whatever unique way of talking we Tarheels have, I have a double dose of it, and so does someone else we all know. I wish I had a buffalo nickel for every time during the past thirty years someone has said,

"You sound like that guy on the . . . uh . . . uh . . . you know, that TV show." "Andy Griffith?" "Yeah, you sound like he does." I know it. Although I have never had the pleasure of meeting Andy Griffith, his Mt. Airy and my Graham are just a whiff and a whisker away from each other. That also explains a whole lot.

Remember Lola Gillebaard from earlier in the book ("Part II: Looking for Mayberry Humor in the Mirror" to be exact)? Lola is the speaker from California who is allergic to sesame seeds and came to my house for Chinese food. Although she has lived "out there" for years, she grew up in eastern North Carolina, a hotbed for our kind of talking. We have become good friends, and one day she called. "Jean-neee," she drawled all the way from Laguna Beach. "Mah feelin's could have been hurt this moarning if ah hadn't ah kep my sense of humah." It turned out that another speaker (a definite busybody type) told Lola that she needed to develop her own style and stop trying to copy Jeanne Robertson. Lola could not believe it, but as we are prone to do, started worrying about it. She called me to see if I thought that too. I started laughing as she recounted the incident. It was so apparent that the nosey biddy did not understand. Lola was not trying to sound like me. Lola is from North Carolina. We ALL sound like this unless we have gone through elocution surgery and had a diction transplant. If you do not believe me, take a trip down here sometime so you can hear it in the flesh. (Bring some money for the outlets.)

During the first episodes of *The Andy Griffith Show*, when the cast was settling in, they attempted to "put on" very southern, country accents and overdid it a little. Soon they relaxed, and rather than try to imitate what they thought was our accent, they let the writers put them in North Carolina through the use of our colloquialisms and speaking patterns. Of all the main cast members on the show, Andy Griffith was the only North Carolina native. Jim Nabors and George Lindsey were from Alabama, and the rest were from "somewheres else." But when all involved arrived in Mayberry, they seemed right at home. (It is called talent.)

For the sanity of all English teachers everywhere, do let me say that I know there is a great deal of incorrect grammar on *TAGS*, but I am willing to overlook it for the entertainment value. In today's high-tech world, if one talks in Mayberry colloquialisms, people will look at you strange. I will vouch for it.

This book, though, is a study of humor, not accents. All I know is that much of whatever kind of talking they do in Mayberry—a source of humor to many including myself—sounds right to me. But in North Dakota? Now that is a different story. During a speaking trip to Fargo, I went into a large department store and I took my 6'2" body over to a saleslady to ask if they had a "tall department."

"Oh, yes," the lady said and pointed me toward a corner of the store.

I walked eagerly in the direction she had indicated and looked and looked, but could not find any clothes for taller women. So, I went back to locate the same clerk. "'Scuse me, ma'am. Ah must have gotten turned around," I drawled. "Ah could not find the talls."

She was most pleasant. "Well, follow me. I will show you."

We went right back to the same corner and stopped at a table stacked high with merchandise. She picked up something and turned in my direction. "See, here is a face towel, there is a hand towel, and over there are the large bath towels. Are you looking for a particular color?"

I stared at the "face TOWEL" in her hand. We call it a "washrag." (Talls? Towels? Well, yeah, they do sound alike.)

"Yes ma'am. I believe I want pink towels. Deep pink."

Back in North Carolina the next day—the home of the textile industry where towels are sold at discount rates even in some restaurants—my husband had a question as he watched me unpack. "Why in the world did you buy towels in North Dakota?"

"Oh, men do not understand something like this," I explained and headed for the linen closet. "I found the EXACT COLOR I wanted."

--- Ohio ---

The Big Freeze

Ramona: It rained last week, you know?
Ernest T. Bass: Yeah, I was right there in it.

- Episode #113, "My Fair Ernest T. Bass"

At the end of a week of terrible weather which hit the eastern part of the nation, I spoke at a Chamber of Commerce banquet in Dayton, Ohio. People who braved conditions to attend did not need a shortwave radio to get weather information from Greenland. They were right there in it. Two days earlier, the temperature had been 26 degrees BELOW zero.

The emcee had trouble getting people seated, especially the politicians, until he said, "Ladies and gentlemen if you do not find your seats, I am going to announce the school closings again."

The chicken was served within minutes.

--- Oklahoma ---

Higher Mathematics

Goober: How much is fourteen times five?
Opie: Seventy.
Goober: I's kinda sure of it, but two heads is always better than one when you're dealing with higher arithmetic.

- Episode #219, "Goober's Contest"

If you put me with someone else, you still will not have two heads in math because I do not do numbers well. Long division is OK, and "toting" up low figures works, but much past that has never appealed to me. I especially hated those thinking problems about how fast trains were traveling and when they would get somewhere. I stared at those so long I could have ridden the train and learned the arrival time firsthand. Nope, I did not step up in class at math time. My mind just seemed to wander then. Thinking funny stuff, I guess.

Knowing my math ability, it is easy to understand how perplexed I was while riding from the hotel to a high school in Norman, OK. I was there to speak at the state student council convention (on developing a sense of humor, not math), and my driver was a local teacher. Three teenage boys sat in the back seat, saying nothing while the adults chatted on. I inquired, "What direction is Oklahoma City?" I was making conversation and just wanted to get my general bearings.

The teacher said, "Well if you think of where we are right now as a quadrant, downtown Oklahoma City would be at about 200 degrees."

A quadrant? Two hundred degrees? What in the world . . .?

We rode on a few seconds, and I took a stab at something. "Do you teach math?" The students burst out laughing. I had hit the nail on the head and her expression showed it. It was like, "How did you know?"

As she nodded, I explained, "I never knew what time the train got there or how many miles it traveled. I am a humorist. An old basketball coach. A vague gesture in the direction of town is all I want."

One of the young men tapped me on the shoulder, pointed, and said, "Ma'am, it's over thataway."

Thank you. No need in making something complicated out of something that is not.

--- Oregon ---

That's What I Thought You'd Say!

Andy: Well, you know, in any good western, you never give away the ending. So, I guess you're just gonna have to wait 'til high noon to find out.

                    - Episode #179, "Wyatt Earp Rides Again"

My brother-in-law in Portland, Oregon, is a golf fanatic. Perhaps that should be written FANatic. Bob plays the game at a secret, questionable level, but like many hackers, he enjoys watching the professionals on TV. Golf moves a little slow for me on TV, so I am amazed at how he actually sits for hours watching a tournament.

"Yes," the commentator whispers. "They are walking up the fairway now. You should be able to see them on your screen at any moment. Oh, we just missed a terrific shot straight down the number four hole right to the pin." (Now we will switch to sixteen and watch them take their clubs out of their bags!)

When Bob and my sister Andrea cannot be at home during a big tournament, they record it, and later watch the entire last round from start to finish. Naturally, they do not want to know the outcome in advance. They want to see it unfold. This has often presented a problem.

The scenario is familiar, and it is irritating, isn't it? One person tapes a movie or sporting event; another person calls and tells the outcome. So much for suspense. In this case, Bob's mother, Phoebe, who is past eighty years old, is often the guilty culprit.

"What are you doing?"

"Watching the golf match on TV."

"Oh, so-and-so came from behind on the seventeenth and won. It was a thrilling finish."

@!?#

This scenario happened so often with Phoebe and others that Bob and Andrea started answering the phone with a threat disguised as a plea. "Whoever you are, if you know who won the golf tournament on television this afternoon, please do not tell me the name. We are watching the replay now."

And that is similar to what Andrea said when the phone rang in the middle of a big PGA tournament. The city of Portland had been closely watching the tournament all week because an outstanding local golfer, Peter Jacobson, had been doing extremely well. He was among the leaders when the final round began. Andrea and Bob were particularly interested because he played out of their club. They had to attend another event that afternoon, but they hurried home after the function. They were glued to their tape replay when the phone rang. Andrea picked up the receiver and quickly said, "Whoever this is, DO NOT TELL US if you know the winner of the golf tournament."

There was one of those pregnant pauses, and then Bob's mother said, "Well, I am certainly not going to tell you who won. All I will say is . . . Portland is VERY PROUD."

--- Pennsylvania ---

Just Me and My Luggage

Floyd: I'm so tired I can hardly keep my mouth open.
                          - Episode #216, "Howard, the Comedian"

The door-to-door peddler, Bert Miller, arrives in "The Merchant of Mayberry" with all of his aches and pains. His feet have been troubling him, and he has bursitis in his shoulder from carrying his suitcase around. Not only that, he has gotten to where he cannot stand the sound of doorbells. Reminds me of myself, traveling around the country.

My suitcase on wheels acted like a young child pulling against me when I arrived at the Philadelphia airport. The plane was late and my clothes were so wrinkled that I looked like I had just spent five days in jail. I was tired. My feet hurt and I wished I had some orthopedic loafers. My bursitis shoulder ached, and my bags seemed to have doubled in size. That day, I could not stand the steady drum of airport announcements.

There were few passengers in the halls as I trudged toward the escalator. "Oh, great," I thought in disgust when I arrived at the top of what should have been moving steps. The small sign said, "Turned Off." My shoulders sagged. I was going to have to pick up that rolling cart and carry it all the way down the steps. When you are dog, dog, dog tired, something like this takes on tremendous significance.

Then I remembered an important detail. I did not have to pick up a thing, nary a thing. Near every escalator, there is an elevator. Yo!

Almost tripping myself when I rearranged the wheels, I walked around the corner dragging everything behind me. Yep, there was the elevator, complete with a sign that reported, "Out of order."

Was the world called off for the day, or what?

My attention was diverted to a man who was leaning against the wall of the hall, watching me make these discoveries. The words on his shirt told me he worked at the airport, and he suddenly became the one to hear my opinion.

"Well," I began. "I have arrived in the City of Brotherly Love, and your escalator is turned off and your elevator is out of order."

He did not alter his position against the wall, but snapped his fingers, pointed in my direction, and said, "The Liberty Bell is cracked, too."

--- South Carolina ---

Hair-brained Idea

Andy: Pretty sight. A pretty, pretty, pretty, pretty sight.
                            - Episode #103, "Opie's Ill-Gotten Gain"

Prisoner Elizabeth Crowley needs to butter up Floyd, one of the witnesses against her, in "Andy and the Woman Speeder." She does so by flattering Floyd's professional abilities and asking him to comb out her hair. The lovable Mayberry barber is flabbergasted and explains, "Well, I'm a man barber. I've never combed out a woman's hair in all my life." This all occurs before she convinces him that he is an artist with "the touch." Too bad a pageant contestant I saw did not have it.

The local Jaycees in a small South Carolina town were excited because one of the contestants in their annual pageant was a knockout. After years of sponsoring the event and sending to the state pageant many young women they knew did not have a chance, they believed they had a winner. This made it all more fun. Malcolm Merriweather would have said she was "a regular bobby-dazzler." We will pretend the striking young woman's name was Bernice. She is now a serious businesswoman, so I will respect her privacy.

After several nights of rehearsal, the time arrived for the first talent practice. People around the little auditorium stopped what they were doing to watch as Bernice's turn approached. Her props called for a single chair and a little table in the center of the stage. "That's a good sign," a Jaycee mumbled through his walkie-talkie to his buddies. "The talented ones don't need a bunch of props."

No, the talented ones do not. Agnes Jean, the baton twirler who had just practiced, certainly did not need props.

Bernice's main "prop" was a friend who walked out on stage and sat down in the chair. Her hair was rolled tight in wire curlers. Bernice took her place behind the chair and in the allotted three minutes— JUST THREE MINUTES!—she ripped the coils from her friend's head, combed out her long flowing hair, and styled it in a flamboyant style of the day. Songs from the musical *Hair* played in the background. Bernice's talent was . . . styling hair. Floyd would have been so proud . . . no telling what Calvin Coolidge would have said.[68]

When Bernice pulled out the first roller that rehearsal night, Jaycees stopped building whatever it is they always build at rehearsals, and stood motionless at their various stations. As the combing progressed, one finally managed to drawl an expletive into his walkie-talkie, "S*#!*T@!" That pretty much summed it up, even though he should have watched his language because there were ladies present. One of the wire rollers dropped from Bernice's hand and rolled off the stage. Someone later said the state title rolled away with it.

---

68 In the episode "Aunt Bee's Romance" Andy says, "Well, as Mark Twain said, everybody complains about the weather but nobody does anything about it." Floyd responds, "I thought Calvin Coolidge said that? Andy, "No, no Floyd, Calvin Coolidge didn't say that." Floyd responds" What'd Calvin Coolidge say?" Apparently, no one on the show knows what Coolidge said, or would have said.

The next night the gorgeous Bernice waltzed through the opening number and created a buzz in the swimsuit and evening gown competitions. The townspeople were excited and the murmur grew each time she left the stage. They sensed a state winner. Maybe even Miss America! As Jaycees watched the momentum build, they exchanged glances because they knew talent was coming up.

Bernice was introduced by an emcee who barely had the nerve to make eye contact with his friends. "Our next contestant will display the talent of . . . styling hair."

An older man in the center of the audience leaned toward family members. "What did he say?"

"Sounded like styling hair, Grandpa."

"Whut?"

"STYLING HAIR!

"Oh? She's gonna FIX HAIR?" The elderly fellow thought a second and started chuckling. People in surrounding rows bit their lips to keep from following suit.

On stage, the contestant's friend—hair wound so tightly for the BIG SHOW that her eyebrows stretched upward—took her place in the chair. At the sight of the curlers, people wrinkled their brows and leaned forward for better views. What in the world . . .? The gorgeous, smiling Bernice walked out on stage, nodded to the judges, and got ready to do the best she could.

The music started, and so did Bernice. Her arms flew to remove the wire rollers and save as much time as possible for the important styling portion. But from the first tug, there was a problem, an uh-oh. You better know uh-oh.

"Show biz" nerves or hometown jitters? Stress because someone was timing the whole routine? Judges made her nervous? No such luck. In her eagerness to do well, Bernice had put a "double dollop" of Dippity Do gel on her friend's head during the rolling process. By the time she was introduced hours later, the stuff had dried and fused with the wire rollers. Bernice knew it the first time she tried to pull out a curler. So did everyone in the audience, because her friend sitting in the chair flinched instantly and mouthed, "Ouch!" The crowd laughed and that was all the "prop" needed to egg her on.

With the pull of each subsequent roller, the chaired prop widened her eyes, grimaced, and flinched her shoulders as she played to the attention that came her way. She pulled in opposition to Bernice's pull, her eyes rolling in a silent moan with the crowd. The spotlight shifted to her. People howled, and the gorgeous Bernice's smiling lips quivered. It was classic upstaging.

But a reminder. Never take "gorgeous" for dense . . . or for granted. When Bernice realized her talent routine was running amuck, she wound up her smile and suddenly YANKED a roller with all her might. The force pulled a large clump of hair out with the wire. Pain shot across the scene stealer's face. Her shoulders scrunched up around her ears as she glanced backward in horror and saw her hair hanging out of the round wire in Bernice's hand. Perhaps she also caught the fire in Bernice's eyes. She tried to stand, but before she could get all the way up, a hand from behind suddenly clamped on the top of her shoulder and firmly directed her back into the chair. WHOMP! The three minutes were up, and the gorgeous Bernice looked out at the audience and gave them her best—and biggest—pageant smile. Any wider and her teeth would have fallen out.

The old man in the center of the audience slapped his knee and shouted, "Git her, Bernice!" The rest of the crowd did not know whether to applaud or make an appointment.

--- South Dakota ---

I Want My Ukulele!

Jerry Miller: I think my future lies in the concert states.
- Episode #159, "Banjo-Playing Deputy"

Sgt. Carter puts a bucket on Gomer's head and tells him to sing in "Gomer Pyle, U.S.M.C." and that is what he does. Always positive,

Gomer later says, "You know, it does give your voice a nice ring." In "Andy and Opie—Bachelors," Opie relates Johnny Paul Jason's opinion that eating burnt food will give a person a good singing voice. WHERE WAS THIS VALUABLE INFORMATION WHEN I NEEDED IT?

Contestants in the Miss America Pageant have to display some kind of talent. They would not let me shoot hook shots, which was what I did fairly well. I wanted to play the guitar for talent, but I do not play the guitar, and blowing as hard as I could, I could not get guitar sounds out of an old jug. So, I finally decided to sing in the talent competition and accompany myself on the baritone ukulele. Before it was over, I rounded up almost every hog in the county. Of course, several smart- aleck media people called it a "comedy routine," but don't you believe it. I was singing the best I could. You better know I was. Unlike Burley Peters, the spoon player in Mayberry, I did not have a large repertoire. I knew four chords and three songs and could not sing a half-lick, but it was my small contribution to the world of music. (Warming up was my best thing—"Meeee, they, meee, they, meeee, they.") If I had just known about burnt food and buckets . . . or had been to South Dakota.

Checking in for a commuter flight out of Sioux Falls, South Dakota, I set my baritone ukulele case on the floor. The ticket agent looked at it for a few seconds and then gave it a little shove with his toe. "What's that?" I guess they are just accustomed to big guitars out west.

"My ukulele case. I am a ukulelist." (Hey, if a violin player is a violinist, and a piano player is a pianist, then Jeanne Robertson is a ukulelist!)

He put his pencil down and walked slowly around the case as though he were stalking something. "Well, what do you have in mind for us to do with it?"

"When I flew in yesterday," I explained, "they put it in that little compartment in the nose of the plane."

He stared at the case while he gave my comment some heavy thought, then asked, "Didn't that make it sound funny?"

"No more than usual," I assured him. "As a matter of fact, it might have made it sound better. The way I sing, I need all the help I can get."

"Well," he suggested with a grin, "if it will help, we could strap the ukulele in a seat and squeeze you into the nose of the plane."

--- Tennessee ---

Hard Stuff

Barney: Oh, come on, Thelma Lou, put two and two together. Read the handwriting on the wall. Blow away the smoke and look at the fire.

Thelma Lou: Barney, you're always throwing your education in my face.

- Episode #125, "The Rumor"

In Nashville to speak at an education banquet, I was seated beside the only student in attendance. She was to make brief comments representing the students of her state. When I asked where she planned to attend college, the gentleman seated to my right interrupted and indicated it should not be a problem. She made 1390 on the SAT. Since I would have to take it three times to add up to 1390, I was impressed and told her so. She said, "Did they have the Scholastic Aptitude Test BACK THEN? (A high IQ can be such a mixed blessing.)

Before her speech, this smart-as-a-whip young lady commented that she had just had a big exam that day and had studied all weekend. "I am so nervous," she confided. "I am afraid I will get up there and start reciting the fundamental theorem of calculus."

I nodded my physical education-major head in agreement. "I know what you mean. I am always afraid that I will do the same thing."

My experience with the math teacher in Oklahoma sprang to mind and I started chuckling. After a while, "Miss Back Then" turned to "Miss 1390 on the SAT" and said, "Will you please pass the butter.

If you think of where we are as a quadrant, it's about 200 degrees." (Another deep one.)

In "Opie's Ill-Gotten Gain," Barney Fife put it well. "Some people want it and can't get it. I got it, and had to get rid of it."

--- Texas ---

Sirens Blasting

Barney: We agreed to an escort parade and that's what we're going to have.

                             - Episode #31, "The Guitar Player Returns"

The 100 Club of Houston, Texas honors its local police in a big annual banquet. The first time I spoke at that event, Mayor Kathy Whitmire was a popular guest seated at the head table, but politics can be like the theater—heartbreak alley. When I returned five years later, the officer who met me at the airport made sure I knew that the police force and the mayor were at odds over a bitter salary dispute.

The mayor was not there, which was probably best. Her presence might have turned it into a jittery supper. After we ate whatever kind of chicken it was, the 1500 attendees hooted when the emcee announced, "Mayor Whitmire was unable to attend tonight." His statement was met with roars of laughter mixed with applause, and after a few seconds he held up his hand for silence. "Now just wait a minute. She did indicate she wanted to come," he explained, "and we sent a police escort over to pick her up." He grinned widely. "The last we heard, they were crossing the border into Oklahoma."

--- Utah ---

Bargain Day

Aunt Bee: What did you pay for it? Not the list price, I hope!

Andy: It was one of the best.

Aunt Bee: Oh Andy, Clara knows a discount house 30% off. They have bankrupt stock. Everything. Washers, freezers. To go and buy this without asking . . . .

- Episode #120, "Bargain Day"

Well, it made sense to me.

A few years ago, the fall of the Berlin Wall and the breakup of the Soviet Union resulted in radical changes in long-held boundaries in those parts of the world. It was no surprise that the big sign in the gift shop at the Salt Lake City airport read, "Globes—30% Off!" But I wondered why 30%, and of course, went inside to ask.

The lady said, "The 30%? Well, we just figured about a third of the world had changed, so . . . why not?"

--- Vermont ---

Business Experience

Barney: Sorry I didn't get in on that. It sounded like fun.

- Episode #82, "Class Reunion"

A shuttle driver in Vermont told me his funniest Mayberry-type experience. He was taking the stretch limo to the airport with several VIPs in the back when he saw a very large turtle on the highway. He immediately lowered the divider window and told his riders he was going to pull over for just a couple of minutes. There was plenty of time. They would not be late. The driver got out, picked up the turtle from the highway, took it down an embankment, and let it go.

"And do you know what?" he added. "When we arrived at the airport, one of the passengers gave me a fifty-dollar tip for stopping."

A voice in my brain said that he could be "working the tip" with that story, but he was ahead of me. Seconds later he said, "My son spent the rest of the summer out on the freeway letting that turtle loose for me."

--- Virginia ---

A Hundred on the Laugh Meter

Funeral parlor owner Orville Monroe: There he is again, Sheriff, arrest him. He's disturbing the peace. Right in front of my place of business.

- Episode #3, "The Guitar Player"

Jerry and I drove from an evening speech at Atlantic Beach, North Carolina, to Richmond, Virginia, for a speech the next morning. We arrived at quarter 'til three in the morning and we were plumb tuckered out. Jerry and I are not what you would call "swingers." We had not been out that late in years! By then, they had rolled up the sidewalks and put away the swings, but one guy was pulling all-night duty at the registration desk and greeted us. Before we checked in, I double-checked to make sure I was at the right hotel. At the mention of the group's name, he raised his eyebrows and nodded his head. "Oh, they are here all right. They had a big cocktail party tonight, and they were partying ALL OVER the lobby. I could not get my work done for them hanging around the desk."

"OK," I said, beginning to fill in the form. "I am speaking to them in the morning. I hope they did not stay up too late."

His face registered a little interest. "What are you talking to them about?"

"Keeping a sense of humor."

The words were barely out of my mouth when he quipped, "They don't need it."

--- Washinton State ---

Your Fault! Your Fault!

Barney: What I started? You're not trying to say this is all my fault,
            are you?

           - Episode #152, "The Case of the Punch in the Nose"

Some people are born collectors, and I am one of them. There is an accu-
rate count of the number of things I collect, but I am not telling it. Old
clowns (toys, not retired humorists), old humor books, storyteller dolls,
antique baskets, and flow-blue plates are just a few of my collections.[69] I
accumulate about everything except tinfoil balls. My husband says I go
into junk shops and say, "Tell me what it is, and I'll give you a dollar for
it. "This is what happens when a born junk collector is on the road so
much. At the end of a long trip, I look like a traveling pawn shop.

My most treasured accumulation is my beaver collection. (With all
the height in our family, one might think I would collect giraffes, but
I have never liked giraffes. I heard a noted authority on the subject,
Barney Fife, say that giraffes are selfish.) The fact that I collect beavers
should not be a surprise. When one's son is nicknamed Beaver from
birth, common sense demands that the mother immediately start collecting every little beaver she sees. And I have them: stuffed beavers,
porcelain, pewter, and bronze beavers, carved beavers, pictures of
beavers, and seven sizes of beaver puppets. They are scattered all over
the house and can be found behind doors, sitting in chairs, or peeking
from behind table legs. A neighbor once eyed them suspiciously and
asked, "How will you know if you have rats?"

Husband Jerry is not involved in any of the collections, especially the beavers. I do not think he purchased a single one, and I
know he has never shown them to guests with pride. Occasionally,

---

69 Flow-Blue plates are known for a blurry blue transfer-printed decoration set
against a white background.

he mentions that I might have enough beavers, which he did again when I brought home the two-foot wooden carving of one I found in Canada. He mumbled something about me having every type of beaver in the world. However, a few weeks later I went on a speaking trip to Spokane, Washington, and learned that was not true.

In Spokane, I was leaving for a walk when I passed the hotel gift shop, and there in the window—right next to a tiger eye ring—was a beaver I did not have. "Oh, loook. It is so cute. Not like any of the 162 I have at home," I commented to a man walking past me in the lobby. He sped up his step.

Within a few minutes, I was in the shop holding my prize lovingly in my hands. It was large, but soft and floppy, and had brown hair and the customary flat tail. His hair was so long and stringy that his eyes were covered up. The lady behind the counter said, "It looks almost real, like a large rodent." I disagreed but did not argue as I handed her my money. What did she know about stuffed beavers?

I hurried back to my room and tossed the beaver toward the bed before finally leaving to walk. I did not realize my toss missed the target, and the beaver fell to the floor amidst some of the covers.

An hour later I returned. When I got off the elevator on my floor, I noticed a small group of people gathered down the hall. Walking toward them, I realized they were standing outside my room. Something was wrong.

Two women from housekeeping were backed into the wall hovering close to each other for safety. One of them had a plumber's friend raised in the air over her head. The second one clutched a water bottle, fat side up. Clearly, they were distressed.

Standing with them was a guy from hotel security who had apparently taken charge in Barney Fife style. "Break it up. The show is over," he said to other guests in the hall. "Move along. The show's over! This is hotel business." My steps slowed as I approached the group.

"This is my room. Is there a problem?"

The security guard put his hands on his belt and leaned back a little like Barney would have done. "Mrs. Robertson, it has come to our attention that you have some sort of a pet in your room." (He knew my name?)

"No, I do not have a pet in my room."

Both women started talking and nodding their heads. "Yes, she does," they told the guard in unison. He put up his hand to quiet them and then turned back to me. "Now, MRS. ROBERTSON," he repeated officiously, "we are not going to ask you to leave the hotel, but the animal has got to go. We can arrange somewhere for it to stay tonight at your expense." I had turned into the beast of the fifteenth floor.

My mind started racing, and it did not have to go far. I knew exactly what the problem was, the stuffed beaver. Sure. "I think I can explain," I began. I was getting ready to say, "What you ladies saw was a stuffed animal I bought in the hotel gift shop." Before I could get the words out of my mouth, the woman with the plumber's friend jumped in with, "I went in there to clean up, and your pet ran across the top of my foot and scooted under the bed!" Her friend quickly nodded in agreement. "I saw it too."

The security guard stood taller and assumed even more authority. "We are going to have to get this straightened out, Mrs. Robertson. We cannot have animals in the hotel. It is against regulation. If we let one stay, we will have to let two stay. And then . . . "

"Give 'em forty, they take forty-five?" I mumbled, smiling to myself and thinking about Deputy Fife's reference to speeders.

"Pardon me?"

"Never mind."

I protested again that there was no pet, and the guard said, "Well if there is no pet, there could be a marmot in there. Sometimes they come up from the river, make it across the parking lot, and get into the hotel." I was not sure what a marmot was, but I did not want to meet an animal that could take an elevator to the fifteenth floor. That explains why I crouched behind the guard when he opened the door.

Behind our fearless leader, the two women and I cautiously entered the room. He crept along the wall, checked the closet, and quickly closed that door. Then he glanced around the bathroom and slammed that door. We lurked behind. Finally, he spotted bed linens on the floor and extended his arm to tell us to stay back. Creeping up on the sheets, he suddenly JERKED the bed linens back to reveal a long-haired, brown, stuffed beaver lying motionlessly on the floor.

I could not resist. While the guard stood like a petrified tree—sheets still in his hand—I rushed past him and cried, "Oh no. My pet is dead!"

The two women lowered their weapons and walked over to stare. Seconds later, the one with the plumber's friend said, "Well, I might have kicked it . . . but I DID NOT KILL IT!"

--- Washington, DC ---

Welcome, Sweet Springtime

Barney: As my old voice teacher used to say, "A choir without its tenor is like a star without its glimmer." You know who used to say that? My old voice teacher. The teacher I had when I studied voice.

- **Episode #52, "Barney and the Choir"**

The convention folks gathered in the hall for a meal function at a large meeting in Washington, D.C., but the real activity was on the other side of the ballroom doors. Dozens of hotel employees frantically made last-minute preparations. I was in the room to check the microphone when the banquet captain called his staff together for final instructions.

The waiters and waitresses, dressed in crisp black uniforms with white collars, lined up in three rows for a headcount and final review. Each one held a white sheet of paper with the table assignments, and they glanced down in unison. When the bell captain spoke, they snapped their heads up and looked in his direction. From where I stood, they looked just like a big choir holding sheet music. If I had not known otherwise, I would have thought they sent to New York for the arrangement.

I could not resist. Everyone from Mayberry's Choral Director John Masters on down knows you cannot have a concert without a soloist. From the other side of the room, I put the microphone to my lips and started slowly singing, "When you waaalk through a storrrm . . . "Several workers started to laugh but quickly stifled it when they received a no-nonsense look from the staff captain. I got the message and stopped singing.

A few minutes later, the banquet hall was full, and I was sitting at the head table. Out of habit, I leaned to one side when I sensed a waitress was behind me. She bent forward to place the chicken salad down, and when she neared my left ear, she sang just loud enough for me to hear, "Holllld your heaaaad up hiiiigh."

--- West Virginia ---

Now There's a Fish That's a Fish

Andy: Well sir, just about then there came a jerk on my line that liked to snatched me over the side of that boat. I says, Hold on, Barney. We have done hooked us a whale.

- Episode #41, "Crime-free Mayberry"

Sporting events dominate convention agendas at resorts. A group at The Greenbrier in West Virginia had so many tournaments on their free afternoon that they began announcing the winners during the reception. Golf, tennis, lawn bowling, croquet, trap-shooting, volley-ball, and trout fishing competitions were held for men and women, and almost everyone got a trophy. Only one woman entered the wom-en's shooting tournament, so she won the "Women's Skeet Shooting Championship" trophy. A man who had never fired a gun entered the men's division and was given the "Conservation Award." (I had walked around the resort that afternoon where adults were shooting guns for the first time in their lives. Hmmm . . .)

The trout fly fishing group caused the most flurry. Sixteen people had entered the competition, and they were taken aback when it was announced that they caught NO FISH! They became indignant in unison, quickly finding one another to organize a protest. They HAD caught fish, they insisted to anyone who would listen. PLENTY of fish, but none were "keepers." The resort staff made them throw back all the ones that were too little. They were sportsmen all the way.

"Wait! Not true!" complained one trout competitor. "Not ALL the fish were thrown back. I caught a legal one!" (Must have used a "gollywobbler," potato salad, or a dab of cheese for his fish-catching bait.) "I had my picture made with the fish and then turned it over to the kitchen staff. They are going to serve it at the banquet," he announced proudly. "I'll have fish while the rest of you have chicken." Well, fish were made to be caught and eaten. He felt it was his duty to do both, and after all, it was his fish; he could do what he wanted to with it.

Someone was listening. An hour later, in the formal banquet setting, a waiter swooped into the ballroom from the kitchen, carrying a beautiful silver platter over his head. He moved through the tables with ease as the emcee called attention to him and the spotlight picked him up. With theatrical flair, he placed the platter in front of the sportsman who had sworn he caught a legal-size fish. People applauded and the fellow nodded his head to indicate, "Now, that's more like it." Then he looked down at his prize.

We could barely see the platter for the parsley that stretched from side to side surrounding one thin slice of lemon in the center of the tray. The man surveyed the greenery. "Where is my fish?"

The waiter had to fight to play his part but managed a haughty answer. "Kindly look under the lemon slice, sir."

The angler slowly lifted the slice to reveal a barely-visible-to-the-human-eye . . . sardine.

People pounded their tables in laughter, but the center of attention maintained his composure. "Ah, yes, there it is. Thank you," he answered with the air of royalty. "I am sure I will enjoy eating it as much as I did pulling it in." And with that said, he began the tiny precise motions of cutting the single sardine with his knife and fork.

A voice rang from the crowd, "How do you know it is your fish?"

He replied, "Because I looked at him for an hour while I reeled him in. I lost fifteen pounds, and the fish did too."

--- Wisconsin ---

Laying an Egg?

Andy and Barney looking at an ad being painted on a store window:

Barney: Ain't chicken spelled "i—n"?

Andy: No, he's got it right.

Barney: You sure?

Andy: Uh-huh. "I" before "e" except after "c" and "e" before "n" in chicken.

Barney: I always forget that rule.

- Episode #94, "Mountain Wedding"

The use of the humorous "running gag" is another good feature of *The Andy Griffith Show*. Good? It was brilliant! From avid fans to casual viewers, we eagerly anticipate bits that we know will pop up. If Barney goes into a cell, the odds are high that he will lock himself in. Little Leon appears, and a peanut butter and jelly sandwich cannot be far behind. Opie begins to quote Johnny Paul Jason, and we know it will be farfetched. Otis stumbles into the courthouse, and we correctly expect him to lock himself up. Sitting on the Taylors' front porch, Barney says to Andy, "You Know what I'm gonna do?" We know. He is probably going to go home, take a little nap, go over to Thelma Lou's and watch a little TV. Probably the most recognizable "running gag" revolves around Barney's one bullet. When it is not in his pocket, it is in his gun, and we anticipate it being fired. Bang! Because we are in Mayberry, we also know it will not hit anyone.

As I studied *The Andy Griffith Show* for comparisons to current humor, a particular repetition jumped out at me. It is a repeated occurrence that seems to have gone unnoticed by other writers and my friends who are avid *TAGS* fans. Perhaps it is something that only a banquet speaker would notice. I do declare, the CHICKEN plays an important role in this series. (When you stop laughing, please read on. I will not list all the references, just enough to make my point.)

In Mayberry, chicken is cooked almost religiously for everything from Sunday dinners to picnics. It is considered one of the town's "secrets." Andy thinks Aunt Bee should have the title of "Miss Fried Chicken of Mayberry." Not only does she prepare it often for the Taylors, but she also dreams of cooking a big chicken dinner for a house full of relatives. Visitors are always asked to join in at mealtime because she always cooks more chicken than people can eat. On her television cooking show, she promises a chicken recipe. When she goes out of town, she arranges for Clara to make Andy and Opie a chicken casserole. Sometimes her dishes have fancy names like chicken paprikash. Other times, the names sound like the good, old-fashioned chicken many of us grew up on: chicken and dumplings, southern fried chicken (with crust), chicken sandwiches, chicken a la king, and of course, chicken soup. Most often, though, chicken is just referred to as "chicken" because according to what Andy tells Hollywood star Darlene Mason, that is what people in Mayberry normally eat—chicken.

This "supporting character" makes its way into scenes around town and emerges in conversations as well. At the diner, it is concealed in a heavy cream sauce or made into chicken fricassee or a croquette that Opie thinks is terrible. Of course, you could get chicken wings from chickens that Barney believes had done a lot of flying. Fletch sneaks roasted chicken to Andy on a camping trip. Aunt Bee is not a spring chicken anymore. Barney is called a "weak-kneed, chicken-livered, yellow-streaked turncoat" for signing Ellie's petition. He threatens to tell everyone that Otis is a "yellow-bellied chicken" if he backs out from being a deputy. Andy tells Barney that women are going to flock around the deputy like "chickens around a June bug." Aunt Bee relates to Opie that the egg man, Mr. Bristol, talks to chickens like they were real people. The judo instructor calls the fearsome deputy "the chicken" because his bones are so soft. In "The New Doctor," Barney tells Andy, "If a chicken hawk is hanging around, a rooster don't bury his head. He keeps his eyes on the chickens." Of course, we can count on Howard Sprague to pull out that old reliable saying, "Let's not count our chickens before they hatch."

Watch carefully, and you will see chickens pecking around on the property of people like the Wakefields, the Darlings, Frank Myers, Jubel Foster, and Mr. Frisby. Chickens are given names such as Hazel and Beauregard ("Bo" for short). Barney hides among the chickens at the Flint farm. Expectant father Sam Becker tells of backing into a hen-house and being spurred by a rooster. Heck, Mayberryites even order chicken in a Chinese restaurant. (Howard prefers the Lee Chi Chi.)

Small-town sheriffs have more to do than round up chicken thieves—regardless of what some may think in Raleigh—but in reality, Sheriff Taylor is constantly confronted with "chicken problems." He has to solve a chicken fence dispute and a chicken-throwing incident. Then there are chicken burglaries at Al's Poultry Headquarters. A rooster with the "blind staggers" leads Andy to Mr. Frisby's still. Deputy Fife sets up a "Checkpoint Chickie" and another time he reports that lawbreakers ran like "chickens in a storm." Prisoners Jim Lindsey and Rafe Hollister do not mind being arrested on days when Aunt Bee is making chicken and dumplings.

With all this said, let me admit that I have used the chicken as a feeble attempt at a "running gag" throughout this book. It has been my way of pointing out the value of repetition in humor, only my attempts were not always that funny. They were just . . . there. At best, you picked up on the numerous references. At worst, all this will now stand out as you view the series. Sorry.

I do not know the exact number of times the chicken appears in various ways in the 249 episodes of *The Andy Griffith Show*. One would need the complete scripts to tabulate that statistic. My notes tell me that references to some type of chicken and the chicken itself are in almost half of the episodes. If all the times that eggs, ruffling hen feathers, being as touchy as an old "setting" hen, and stuff like Barney saying "cock-a-doodle-do" are counted, the number skyrockets.

But WHAT IS THE MEANING OF IT ALL? Well, all this chicken information illustrates once again that the humor in Mayberry is representative of what I see today. Maybe all this chicken prominence jumps out at me because, in my line of work, poultry is etched on my brain. "Chicken pickin's" abound in the state of North Carolina. A friend of mine can hypnotize chickens. Before a banquet in Wharton, Texas, I toured the local chicken "farm." (It cleared my sinuses.) The airlines surely raise their own, as often as they serve it. I have long said that in my worst nightmare I am on a platter in the center of a banquet table surrounded by chickens that are sticking forks in me. When I studied the career of Don Knotts, who brings Barney to life for us every day, I even found that the first movie he made after leaving *The Andy Griffith Show* was *The Ghost and Mr. Chicken*. Talk about a far-fetched idea? I am stretching it right now, and I do not have to. The chicken references from the series can stand on their own two drumsticks.

Because the chicken plays such a major role in *TAGS*, it is only fitting that I not only attempt a "running gag" around it but also include a story, especially in its honor. I found just such a story.

A Wisconsin dairy farmer was seated next to me during a banquet. He was sorry his wife would not be able to hear me speak, but she had left the convention that morning. Driving home, she would stop along the way and buy 125 baby chickens. At this stage of my life, I do not even want one dog. Why would someone who was not a chicken farmer want 125 chickens? "Pets?" I asked, envisioning trying to name all of them. Able . . . Baker . . . Charlie . . . Wynken . . . Blynken . . . Nod . . ..

I was wrong. The man informed me that they buy chicks every year, take them home, and raise them for about eight weeks. Then one day, they gather their ten children, and the family kills the chickens and freezes them. I pushed the hard-boiled egg on my salad plate over to the side and put my fork down. Pleasant dinner chitchat.

Not being much of a housekeeper/cook, my quick assumption was that they saved an enormous amount of money by having this little annual family-bonding event, not to mention fun. I envisioned my dinner partner looking out the kitchen window one morning, stretching back and saying, "Well, Mama, I guess it's 'bout time to get the young'uns together and kill us some chickens."

"Oh no," he explained. "We do not really save any money. It's just that homegrown chickens taste so much better."

I understood that premise. We think the same thing about home-grown tomatoes, and we do not have to chase them around the yard.

Trying to be clever, I asked, "Do you make pillows with the feathers?"

His answer was in earnest. "Nope, we scatter them in the woods near the house."

It was EXACTLY THEN that the waiter placed my dinner plate in front of me and I glanced down to see the entree.

RIGHT.

I think about these people every spring . . . or when I see feathers in the woods . . . or any time I hear or see a chicken reference on *The Andy Griffith Show*. You KNOW which will come first.

--- Wyoming ---

Dependable

Goober: "But I'll be there 'cause I told you I'd be there, and if I said I'll be there, I'll be there.
                                    - **Episode #144, "Goober Takes a Car Apart"**

I checked into the hotel in Casper, Wyoming, after a long trip, and immediately called room service. It was the middle of the afternoon, and I was afraid the restaurant was closed. A young-sounding male voice answered. "Do you have baked potatoes this time of the day?" I inquired, figuring like most places they did not. He said, "Not usually, but I'm the executive chef. I can get you a baked potato if you want it."

Within thirty minutes, he delivered my order and could not have been much older than twenty. "How does one get to be an executive chef at your age?" I asked.

"You get to be executive chef," he explained, putting my tray down, "when three people do not show up for work." It's as simple as that.

--- Rhode Island ---

Rosy Red

Andy: "I knew it was a long shot, but I was hoping."
                               - Episode #82, "Class Reunion"

Well, here I am at the end of an alphabetical trip through forty-nine states and Washington, D.C. This leaves one state that was intentionally left out—Rhode Island, the only state where I have never given a speech.

When I started writing this book and decided that I would close it with illustrations from all fifty states, I knew I had not spoken in the largest and smallest states. Reality told me that Alaska's distance from North Carolina made it the slimmer likelihood, but that was OK because Barney's mention of "Baked Alaska" let me piece together something for that section. Rhode Island was a different story. Warren Ferguson comes from Boston, Emmett Clark once took a trip to Akron which he found to be "wide open," Madeline Grayson travels from Baltimore, Sharon Duspaine has a career in Chicago, and Charlie O'Malley comes home from Detroit, but nobody connected to Mayberry ever seems to come or go to Rhode Island. Gee, I fit right in.

I must admit, however, that I expected to visit Rhode Island before my research and writing were complete. During a lifetime, we travel down many roads, and surely ONE of those big roads, little roads, rocky roads or smooth roads would take me to Rhode Island. This means I over-expected because it did not work that way. Here it is five years later, and I have never stepped my big foot (and some would add my big mouth) into the smallest state. I should have listened to Andy's advice to Gomer in "A Date for Gomer" when Andy says, "Do me a favor, just don't over expect. OK?"

As the publishing deadline drew nearer and nearer, Rhode Island seemed farther and farther away. Floyd's lament in So many of the episodes rolled in my mind, "What are you going to do, Andy? What are you going to do?" One thing I could have done was PRETEND a story occurred in Rhode Island, but I promised to stick mainly to the truth and spread just a little jam. After all, lying is evil, and the dice are usually loaded against the evil-doer. I even thought about driving up to Rhode Island. I believe so strongly in my theory about the widespread existence of Mayberry humor, that I figured if I could just get there, walk around a while, and meet some of the good people who live there that I would find what I was seeking.

Alas, alas, time ran out on me. Then, three nights before mailing the whole shebang to Rich Publishing, I decided to turn to a book to solve my problem. After all, Barney heads to the library to help save Andy in "Divorce, Mountain Style," and Andy turns to a book to solve his problem in "Wyatt Earp Rides Again." We had given our encyclopedias away to a "disease drive," so I headed to the library on a Friday night.

Guess what? It truly is the age of miracles. It turned out that I did not have to go to Rhode Island at all to find a little Mayberry humor. I flipped right past "rhinoceros" in the *World Book,* and there it was: a beautiful picture of the Rhode Island state bird known as "Rhode Island Red" . . . A CHICKEN!

★★★

West Virginia, Wisconsin, Wyoming, Rhode Island, . . . that's it. The Mayberry jet set has come in for a landing. As Floyd announces in "Convicts-at-Large" when he returns with groceries to the hostage situation . . . WE'RE HOME!

It's Time to Go

Andy to Opie: Now, that's all the storytelling for today.

- **Episode #32, "Bringing Up Opie"**

At the beginning, I indicated that I had two purposes in *Mayberry Humor Across the USA*. One of my goals was to offer a fun challenge to avid fans of *The Andy Griffith Show*. To do so, every one of my stories was Mayberryized in some way. Many of the Mayberry memories were so apparent they should have hit you like an axe breaking up the Morrison sisters' still. Pow! Pow! Pow! Others were deep-rooted and subtle like Barney trying to get Andy together with "The Perfect Female." Aw heck, a lot of the Mayberry memories are so hidden, and I have worked on this project for so long that you AND I might need one of Ernest T. Bass's long, pointed sticks to jab 'em out. A few of my yarns have only one Mayberry connection while others are filled to the brim. The challenge for the devotee of *TAGS* is to find these little bits of Mayberry in every story. If you think you know a lot about Mayberry and failed to see at least one of these morsels in an account, look again. The inclusion may be a "stretch" in a couple of instances, but IT IS THERE. (The headings and introductory, credited quotes do not count. They are there to provide the foundation for my main point.) Each of the 249 episodes is represented. Is there a rabid fan who can find them all?

The main purpose of this book, however, was to introduce what I call Mayberry humor and lay out my theory that it is still very prevalent across the USA. I hope you will agree that I have accomplished this goal. Equally important, I sincerely hope you will begin to look for and enjoy the Mayberry humor in your life. Like Barney tells Opie in "Opie the Birdman," "You're never gonna learn anything if I keep telling you everything." Start by watching *The Andy Griffith Show*, playing daily in households everywhere, and go from there.

Now that you know how much I enjoy humor that stems from situations rather than jokes, you may have a true Mayberrytype story you want to share with someone. Well, please do, if you know for a fact that it is the plain, unvarnished truth. Well, OK, a little "varnish" is acceptable. I will be cooking Chinese and like Howard Sprague, doing business from my same old stand. Am I going to write again about Mayberry humor? Whew! It is way too soon to think about that. HEAPS way too soon. Giving speeches is a piece of chocolate-layered cake compared to researching and writing. This brainwork will wear a person out. I have almost forgotten the meaning of the word . . . RELAXATION! All I want to do right now is . . . go home, take a little nap, get up, and watch a little TV. And YOU KNOW what I will be watching.

See you in Mayberry . . . across the USA!

***

And still they come . . .. (Just one more good'un!)

Student of Humanity

Goober: You want to hear another one?
Andy: Goober, I'm kinda busy.
Goober: Just one more. This is a good 'un.

- Episode #220, "Opie's First Love"

In the middle of my search for *Mayberry Humor Across the USA, The Andy Griffith Show* came on TV in an airline club in Atlanta, and I whipped out a tablet to make notes. A fellow seated nearby observed this, and after a few minutes spoke up. "Are you taking some sort of notes on Andy?" He said the name as though Andy Taylor were his buddy from high school. Don't we all? Andy, Barney, Floyd, Goober—our good pals.

"Well, it's a project on a type of humor, but it involves a little research of this show," I replied, eyes focused on something Aunt Bee and Opie were doing on the small screen.

"Research?" the guy repeated, breaking into a wide smile. "Well, if I could get credit for watching *The Andy Griffith Show*, I'd have myself a Ph.D."

So would I, mister. So would I!

Appendix

Alphabetical List of Episodes

Title	Ep.#
A Baby in the House	184
A Black Day for Mayberry	102
A Date for Gomer	105
A Deal Is a Deal	122
A Feud Is a Feud	8
A Girl for Goober	249
A Man's Best Friend	170
A Medal for Opie	51
A New Doctor in Town	201
A Plaque for Mayberry	25
A Singer in Town	189
A Trip to Mexico	227
A Visit to Barney Fife	211
A Warning from Warren	169
A Wife for Andy	92
Alcohol and Old Lace	17
Andy and Barney in the Big City	57
Andy and Helen Have Their Day	140
Andy and Opie --- Bachelors	65
Andy and Opie, Housekeepers	23
Andy and Opie's Pal	110
Andy and the Gentleman Crook	21
Andy and the New Mayor	69

Episodes By Filming Order

Season 1

Ep. #	Air Date	Title	Written By	Directed By
1	10/3/1960	The New Housekeeper	Jack Elinson and Charles Stewart	Sheldon Leonard
2	10/10/1960	The Manhunt	Jack Elinson and Charles Stewart	Don Weis
3	10/17/1960	The Guitar Player	Jack Elinson and Charles Stewart	Don Weis
4	11/7/1960	Runaway Kid	Arthur Stander	Don Weis
5	11/28/1960	Opie's Charity	Arthur Stander	Don Weis
6	10/24/1960	Ellie Comes to Town	Jack Elinson and Charles Stewart	Don Weis
7	10/31/1960	Irresistible Andy	David Adler	Don Weis
8	12/5/1960	A Feud Is a Feud	David Adler	Don Weis
9	11/14/1960	Andy the Matchmaker	Arthur Stander	Don Weis
10	12/26/1960	Stranger in Town	Arthur Stander	Don Weis
11	12/19/1960	The Christmas Story	David Adler	Bob Sweeney
12	12/12/1960	Ellie for Council	Jack Elinson and Charles Stewart	Bob Sweeney
13	1/2/1961	Mayberry Goes Hollywood	Benedict Freedman & John Fenton Murray	Bob Sweeney
14	1/9/1961	The Horse Trader	Jack Elinson and Charles Stewart	Bob Sweeney
15	1/16/1961	Those Gossipin' Men	Jack Elinson and Charles Stewart	Bob Sweeney
16	2/20/1961	Andy Saves Barney's Morale	David Adler	Bob Sweeney
17	1/30/1961	Alcohol and Old Lace	Jack Elinson and Charles Stewart	Gene Reynolds
18	2/6/1961	Andy the Marriage Counselor	David Adler	Gene Reynolds
19	2/13/1961	Mayberry on Record	Benedict Freedman & John Fenton Murray	Gene Reynolds
20	1/23/1961	The Beauty Contest	Jack Elinson and Charles Stewart	Bob Sweeney
21	2/27/1961	Andy and the Gentleman Crook	Ben Gershman and Leo Solomon	Bob Sweeney
22	3/6/1961	Cyrano Andy	Jack Elinson and Charles Stewart	Bob Sweeney
23	3/13/1961	Andy and Opie, Housekeepers	David Adler	Bob Sweeney

24	3/27/1961	The New Doctor	Jack Elinson and Charles Stewart	Bob Sweeney
25	4/3/1961	A Plaque for Mayberry	Ben Gershman and Leo Solomon	Bob Sweeney
26	4/10/1961	The Inspector	Jack Elinson and Charles Stewart	Bob Sweeney
27	4/17/1961	Ellie Saves a Female	David Adler	Bob Sweeney
28	4/24/1961	Andy Forecloses	Ben Gershman and Leo Solomon	Bob Sweeney
29	5/1/1961	Quiet Sam	Jim Fritzell and Everett Greenbaum	Bob Sweeney
30	5/8/1961	Barney Gets His Man	Ben Gershman and Leo Solomon	Bob Sweeney
31	5/15/1961	The Guitar Player Returns	Jack Elinson and Charles Stewart	Bob Sweeney
32	5/22/1961	Bringing Up Opie	Jack Elinson and Charles Stewart	Bob Sweeney

Season 2

Ep. #	Air Date	Title	Written By	Directed By
33	10/1/1961	Barney's Replacement	Jack Elinson and Charles Stewart	Bob Sweeney
34	10/2/1961	Opie and the Bully	David Adler	Bob Sweeney
35	10/16/1961	Andy and the Woman Speeder	Jack Elinson and Charles Stewart	Bob Sweeney
36	10/30/1961	Barney on the Rebound	Jack Elinson and Charles Stewart	Bob Sweeney
37	11/27/1961	The Perfect Female	Jack Elinson and Charles Stewart	Bob Sweeney
38	12/4/1961	Aunt Bee's Brief Encounter	Ben Gershman and Leo Solomon	Bob Sweeney
39	10/23/1961	Mayberry Goes Bankrupt	Jack Elinson and Charles Stewart	Bob Sweeney
40	11/13/1961	Opie's Hobo Friend	Harvey Bullock	Bob Sweeney
41	11/20/1961	Crime-free Mayberry	Paul Henning	Bob Sweeney
42	12/11/1961	The Clubmen	Fred Fox and Iz Elinson	Bob Sweeney
43	12/18/1961	The Pickle Story	Harvey Bullock	Bob Sweeney
44	12/25/1961	Sheriff Barney	Ben Gershman and Leo Solomon	Bob Sweeney
45	1/1/1962	The Farmer Takes a Wife	Jack Elinson and Charles Stewart	Bob Sweeney
46	1/8/1962	The Keeper of the Flame	Ben Gershman and Leo Solomon	Bob Sweeney
47	1/15/1962	Bailey's Bad Boy	Jack Elinson and Charles Stewart	Bob Sweeney
48	1/22/1962	The Manicurist	Jack Elinson and Charles Stewart	Bob Sweeney

49	1/29/1962	The Jinx	Jack Elinson and Charles Stewart	Bob Sweeney
50	2/5/1962	Jailbreak	Harvey Bullock	Bob Sweeney
51	2/12/1962	A Medal for Opie	David Adler	Bob Sweeney
52	2/19/1962	Barney and the Choir	Jack Elinson and Charles Stewart	Bob Sweeney
53	2/26/1962	Guest of Honor	Bob Ross and Aaron Ruben	Bob Sweeney
54	3/5/1962	The Merchant of Mayberry	Ben Gershman and Leo Solomon	Bob Sweeney
55	3/12/1962	Aunt Bee the Warden	Jack Elinson and Charles Stewart	Bob Sweeney
56	3/19/1962	The County Nurse	Jack Elinson and Charles Stewart	Bob Sweeney
57	3/26/1962	Andy and Barney in the Big City	Harvey Bullock	Bob Sweeney
58	4/2/1962	Wedding Bells for Aunt Bee	Jack Elinson and Charles Stewart	Bob Sweeney
59	4/9/1962	Three's a Crowd	Jack Elinson and Charles Stewart	Bob Sweeney
60	4/16/1962	The Bookie Barber	Ray Allen Saffian and Harvey Bullock	Bob Sweeney
61	4/23/1962	Andy on Trial	Jack Elinson and Charles Stewart	Bob Sweeney
62	4/30/1962	Cousin Virgil	Phillip Shukin and Johnny Greene	Bob Sweeney
63	5/7/1962	Deputy Otis	Fred Fox and Iz Elinson	Bob Sweeney

Season 3

Ep. #	Air Date	Title	Written By	Directed By
64	12/3/1962	Opie's Rival	Sid Morse	Bob Sweeney
65	10/22/1962	Andy and Opie --- Bachelors	Jim Fritzell and Everett Greenbaum	Bob Sweeney
66	10/1/1962	Mr. McBeevee	Ray Allen Saffian and Harvey Bullock	Bob Sweeney
67	10/8/1962	Andy's Rich Girlfriend	Jim Fritzell and Everett Greenbaum	Bob Sweeney
68	11/5/1962	Barney Mends a Broken Heart	Aaron Ruben	Bob Sweeney

69	10/15/1962	Andy and the New Mayor	Ray Allen Saffian and Harvey Bullock	Bob Sweeney
70	10/29/1962	The Cow Thief	Ray Allen Saffian and Harvey Bullock	Bob Sweeney
71	11/26/1962	Floyd, the Gay Deceiver	Aaron Ruben	Bob Sweeney
72	11/19/1962	The Mayberry Band	Jim Fritzell and Everett Greenbaum	Bob Sweeney
73	11/12/1962	Lawman Barney	Aaron Ruben	Aaron Ruben
74	12/10/1962	Convicts-at-Large	Jim Fritzell and Everett Greenbaum	Bob Sweeney
75	12/17/1962	The Bed Jacket	Ray Allen Saffian and Harvey Bullock	Bob Sweeney
76	1/7/1963	Barney and the Governor	Bill Freedman and Henry Sharp	Bob Sweeney
77	1/14/1963	Man in a Hurry	Jim Fritzell and Everett Greenbaum	Bob Sweeney
78	12/24/1962	The Bank Job	Jim Fritzell and Everett Greenbaum	Bob Sweeney
79	12/31/1962	One-Punch Opie	Harvey Bullock	Bob Sweeney
80	1/21/1963	High Noon in Mayberry	Jim Fritzell and Everett Greenbaum	Bob Sweeney
81	1/28/1962	The Loaded Goat	Harvey Bullock	Bob Sweeney
82	2/4/1963	Class Reunion	Jim Fritzell and Everett Greenbaum	Charles Irving
83	2/11/1963	Rafe Hollister Sings	Harvey Bullock	Charles Irving
84	2/18/1963	Opie and the Spoiled Kid	Jim Fritzell and Everett Greenbaum	Bob Sweeney
85	2/25/1963	The Great Filling Station Robbery	Harvey Bullock	Bob Sweeney
86	3/4/1963	Andy Discovers America	John Whedon	Bob Sweeney
87	3/11/1963	Aunt Bee's Medicine Man	John Whedon	Bob Sweeney
88	3/18/1963	The Darlings Are Coming	Jim Fritzell and Everett Greenbaum	Bob Sweeney

89	3/25/1963	Andy's English Valet	Harvey Bullock	Bob Sweeney
90	4/1/1963	Barney's First Car	Jim Fritzell and Everett Greenbaum	Bob Sweeney
91	4/8/1963	The Rivals	Harvey Bullock	Bob Sweeney
92	4/15/1963	A Wife for Andy	Aaron Ruben	Bob Sweeney
93	4/22/1963	Dogs, Dogs, Dogs	Jim Fritzell and Everett Greenbaum	Bob Sweeney
94	4/29/1963	Mountain Wedding	Jim Fritzell and Everett Greenbaum	Bob Sweeney
95	5/6/1963	The Big House	Harvey Bullock	Bob Sweeney

Season 4

Ep. #	Air Date	Title	Written By	Directed By
96	10/28/1963	Briscoe Declares for Aunt Bee	Jim Fritzell and Everett Greenbaum	Earl Bellamy
97	11/4/1963	Gomer the House Guest	Jim Fritzell and Everett Greenbaum	Earl Bellamy
98	10/7/1963	The Haunted House	Harvey Bullock	Earl Bellamy
99	10/14/1963	Ernest T. Bass Joins the Army	Jim Fritzell and Everett Greenbaum	Dick Crenna
100	10/21/1963	The Sermon for Today	John Whedon	Dick Crenna
101	9/30/1963	Opie the Birdman	Harvey Bullock	Dick Crenna
102	11/11/1963	A Black Day for Mayberry	John Whedon	Jeffrey Hayden
103	11/18/1963	Opie's Ill-Gotten Gain	John Whedon	Jeffrey Hayden
104	12/2/1963	Up in Barney's Room	Jim Fritzell and Everett Greenbaum	Jeffrey Hayden
105	11/25/1963	A Date for Gomer	Jim Fritzell and Everett Greenbaum	Dick Crenna
106	12/16/1963	Citizen's Arrest	Jim Fritzell and Everett Greenbaum	Dick Crenna
107	5/19/1964	Gomer Pyle, U.S.M.C.	Aaron Ruben	Aaron Ruben
108	12/30/1963	Opie and His Merry Men	John Whedon	Dick Crenna

109	1/6/1964	Barney and the Cave Rescue	Harvey Bullock	Dick Crenna
110	1/13/1964	Andy and Opie's Pal	Harvey Bullock	Dick Crenna
111	1/20/1964	Aunt Bee, the Crusader	John Whedon	Coby Ruskin
112	1/27/1964	Barney's Sidecar	Jim Fritzell and Everett Greenbaum	Coby Ruskin
113	2/3/1964	My Fair Ernest T. Bass	Jim Fritzell and Everett Greenbaum	Earl Bellamy
114	2/10/1964	Prisoner of Love	Harvey Bullock	Earl Bellamy
115	2/17/1964	Hot Rod Otis	Harvey Bullock	Earl Bellamy
116	2/24/1964	The Song Festers	Jim Fritzell and Everett Greenbaum	Earl Bellamy
117	3/2/1964	The Shoplifters	Bill Idelson and Sam Bobrick	Coby Ruskin
118	3/9/1964	Andy's Vacation	Jim Fritzell and Everett Greenbaum	Jeffrey Hayden
119	3/16/1964	Andy Saves Gomer	Harvey Bullock	Jeffrey Hayden
120	3/23/1964	Bargain Day	John Whedon	Jeffrey Hayden
121	3/30/1964	Divorce, Mountain Style	Jim Fritzell and Everett Greenbaum	Jeffrey Hayden
122	4/6/1964	A Deal Is a Deal	Bill Idelson and Sam Bobrick	Jeffrey Hayden
123	4/13/1964	Fun Girls	Aaron Ruben	Coby Ruskin
124	4/20/1964	The Return of Malcolm Merriweather	Harvey Bullock	Coby Ruskin
125	4/27/1964	The Rumor	Jim Fritzell and Everett Greenbaum	Coby Ruskin
126	5/4/1964	Barney and Thelma Lou, Phfftt	Bill Idelson and Sam Bobrick	Coby Ruskin
127	5/11/1964	Back to Nature	Harvey Bullock	Coby Ruskin

Season 5

Ep. #	Air Date	Title	Written By	Directed By
128	10/26/1964	Barney's Bloodhound	Bill Idelson and Sam Bobrick	Howard Morris
129	10/5/1964	Family Visit	Jim Fritzell and Everett Greenbaum	Howard Morris
130	10/19/1964	Aunt Bee's Romance	Harvey Bullock	Howard Morris
131	9/28/1964	Barney's Physical	Bob Ross	Howard Morris
132	9/21/1964	Opie Loves Helen	Bob Ross	Aaron Ruben
133	10/12/1964	The Education of Ernest T. Bass	Jim Fritzell and Everett Greenbaum	Alan Rafkin
134	11/2/1964	Man in the Middle	Gus Adrian and David Evans	Alan Rafkin
135	11/9/1964	Barney's Uniform	Bill Idelson and Sam Bobrick	Coby Ruskin
136	11/16/1964	Opie's Fortune	Ben Joelson and Art Baer	Coby Ruskin
137	11/23/1964	Goodbye, Sheriff Taylor	Fred Freeman and Lawrence J. Cohen	Gene Nelson
138	11/30/1964	The Pageant	Harvey Bullock	Gene Nelson
139	12/7/1964	The Darling Baby	Jim Fritzell and Everett Greenbaum	Howard Morris
140	12/14/1964	Andy and Helen Have Their Day	Bill Idelson and Sam Bobrick	Howard Morris
141	12/28/1964	Otis Sues the County	Bob Ross	Howard Morris
142	12/21/1964	Three Wishes for Opie	Richard M. Powell	Howard Morris
143	1/4/1965	Barney Fife, Realtor	Bill Idelson and Sam Bobrick	Peter Baldwin
144	1/11/1965	Goober Takes a Car Apart	Bill Idelson and Sam Bobrick	Peter Baldwin
145	1/18/1965	The Rehabilitation of Otis	Fred Freeman and Lawrence J. Cohen	Peter Baldwin
146	1/25/1965	The Lucky Letter	Richard M. Powell	T. J. Flicker
147	2/1/1965	Goober and the Art of Love	Fred Freeman and Lawrence J. Cohen	Alan Rafkin
148	2/8/1965	Barney Runs for Sheriff	Richard M. Powell	Alan Rafkin
149	2/15/1965	If I Had a Quarter Million	Bob Ross	Alan Rafkin
150	3/1/1965	TV or Not TV	Ben Joelson and Art Baer	Coby Ruskin

151	3/8/1965	Guest in the House	Fred Freeman and Lawrence J. Cohen	Coby Ruskin
152	3/15/1965	The Case of the Punch in the Nose	Bill Idelson and Sam Bobrick	Coby Ruskin
153	3/22/1965	Opie's Newspaper	Harvey Bullock	Coby Ruskin
154	3/29/1965	Aunt Bee's Invisible Beau	Ben Joelson and Art Baer	T. J. Flicker
155	4/5/1965	The Arrest of the Fun Girls	Richard M. Powell	T. J. Flicker
156	4/12/1965	The Luck of Newton Monroe	Bill Idelson and Sam Bobrick	Coby Ruskin
157	4/19/1965	Opie Flunks Arithmetic	Richard Morgan	Coby Ruskin
158	4/26/1965	Opie and the Carnival	Fred Freeman and Lawrence J. Cohen	Coby Ruskin
159	5/3/1965	Banjo-Playing Deputy	Bob Ross	Coby Ruskin

Season 6

Ep. #	Air Date	Title	Written By	Directed By
160	10/4/1965	Aunt Bee, the Swinger	Jack Elinson	Larry Dobkin
161	9/13/1965	Opie's Job	Ben Joelson and Art Baer	Larry Dobkin
162	10/11/1965	The Bazaar	Ben Joelson and Art Baer	Sheldon Leonard
163	9/20/1965	Andy's Rival	Laurence Marks	Peter Baldwin
164	9/27/1965	Malcolm at the Crossroads	Harvey Bullock	Gary Nelson
165	11/15/1965	Aunt Bee on TV	Fred Freeman and Lawrence J. Cohen	Alan Rafkin
166	10/25/1965	Off to Hollywood	Bill Idelson and Sam Bobrick	Alan Rafkin
167	11/1/1965	Taylors in Hollywood	Bill Idelson and Sam Bobrick	Alan Rafkin
168	11/8/1965	Hollywood Party	Fred Freeman and Lawrence J. Cohen	Alan Rafkin
169	10/15/1965	**A** Warning from Warren	Fred Freeman and Lawrence J. Cohen	Alan Rafkin
170	11/29/1965	A Man's Best Friend	Ben Joelson and Art Baer	Alan Rafkin
171	12/6/1965	Aunt Bee Takes a Job	Bill Idelson and Sam Bobrick	Alan Rafkin
172	11/22/1965	The Cannon	Jack Elinson	Alan Rafkin

173	12/20/1965	Girl-Shy	Bill Idelson and Sam Bobrick	Lee Philips
174	12/13/1965	The Church Organ	Paul Wayne	Lee Philips
175	1/3/1966	Otis the Artist	Fred Freeman and Lawrence J. Cohen	Alan Rafkin
176	1/10/1966	The Return of Barney Fife	Bill Idelson and Sam Bobrick	Alan Rafkin
177	1/17/1966	The Legend of Barney Fife	Harvey Bullock	Alan Rafkin
178	1/24/1966	Lost and Found	John L. Greene and Paul David	Alan Rafkin
179	1/31/1966	Wyatt Earp Rides Again	Jack Elinson	Alan Rafkin
180	2/7/1966	Aunt Bee Learns to Drive	Jack Elinson	Lee Philips
181	2/14/1966	Look Paw, I'm Dancing	Ben Starr	Lee Philips
182	2/28/1966	Eat Your Heart Out	Ben Joelson and Art Baer	Alan Rafkin
183	2/21/1966	The Gypsies	Roland MacLane	Alan Rafkin
184	3/7/1966	A Baby in the House	Bill Idelson and Sam Bobrick	Alan Rafkin
185	3/14/1966	The County Clerk	Bill Idelson and Sam Bobrick	Alan Rafkin
186	3/28/1966	Goober's Replacement	Howard Merrill and Stan Dreben	Alan Rafkin
187	3/21/1966	The Foster Lady	Jack Elinson and Iz Elinson	Alan Rafkin
188	4/4/1966	The Battle of Mayberry	Paul David and John L. Greene	Alan Rafkin
189	4/11/1966	A Singer in Town	Howard Merrill and Stan Dreben	Alan Rafkin

Season 7

Ep. #	Air Date	Title	Written By	Directed By
190	9/12/1966	Opie's Girlfriend	Budd Grossman	Lee Philips
191	9/26/1966	The Barbershop Quartet	Fred S. Fox	Lee Philips
192	9/19/1966	The Lodge	Jim Parker and Arnold Margolin	Lee Philips
193	10/17/1966	The Darling Fortune	Jim Parker and Arnold Margolin	Lee Philips
194	10/10/1966	Aunt Bee's Crowning Glory	Ronald Axe	Lee Philips
195	10/3/1966	The Ball Game	Sid Morse (story by Rance Howard)	Lee Philips

196	12/19/1966	Goober Makes History	Paul David and John L. Greene	Lee Philips
197	11/14/1966	The Senior Play	Sid Morse	Lee Philips
198	11/28/1966	Big Fish in a Small Town	Bill Idelson and Sam Bobrick	Lee Philips
199	10/31/1966	Mind over Matter	Ron Friedman and Pat McCormick	Lee Philips
200	11/7/1966	Politics Begins at Home	Fred S. Fox	Lee Philips
201	12/26/1966	A New Doctor in Town	Ray Brenner and Barry E. Blitzer	Lee Philips
202	11/21/1966	Opie Finds a Baby	Stan Dreben and Sid Mandel	Lee Philips
203	12/5/1966	Only a Rose	Jim Parker and Arnold Margolin	Lee Philips
204	12/12/1966	Otis the Deputy	Jim Parker and Arnold Margolin	Lee Philips
205	1/2/1967	Don't Miss a Good Bet	Fred S. Fox	Lee Philips
206	1/9/1967	Dinner at Eight	Budd Grossman	Lee Philips
207	1/30/1967	Andy's Old Girlfriend	Sid Morse	Lee Philips
208	2/20/1967	The Statue	Fred S. Fox	Lee Philips
209	2/6/1967	Aunt Bee's Restaurant	Ronald Axe and Les Roberts	Lee Philips
210	2/13/1967	Floyd's Barbershop	Jim Parker and Arnold Margolin	Lee Philips
211	1/16/1967	A Visit to Barney Fife	Bill Idelson and Sam Bobrick	Lee Philips
212	1/23/1967	Barney Comes to Mayberry	Sid Morse	Lee Philips
213	2/27/1967	Helen, the Authoress	Doug Tibbles	Lee Philips
214	3/6/1967	Goodbye Dolly	Michael L. Morris and Seaman Jacobs	Lee Philips
215	3/13/1967	Opie's Piano Lesson	Leo and Pauline Townsend	Lee Philips
216	3/20/1967	Howard, the Comedian	Michael L. Morris and Seaman Jacobs	Lee Philips
217	3/27/1967	Big Brother	Fred S. Fox	Lee Philips
218	4/3/1967	Opie's Most Unforgettable Character	Michael L. Morris and Seaman Jacobs	Lee Philips

| 219 | 4/10/1967 | Goober's Contest | Ron Friedman and Pat McCormick | Lee Philips |

Season 8

Ep. #	Air Date	Title	Written By	Directed By
220	9/11/1967	Opie's First Love	Ron Friedman and Pat McCormick	Lee Philips
221	12/25/1967	Goober the Executive	Scaman Jacobs and Michael Morris	Lee Philips
222	10/16/1967	Howard's Main Event	Earl Barrett and Robert C. Dennis	Lee Philips
223	10/23/1967	Aunt Bee the Juror	Kent Wilson	Lee Philips
224	9/18/1967	Howard the Bowler	Dick Bcnsficld and Perry Grant	Lee Philips
225	10/9/1967	Opie Steps Up in Class	Joseph Bonaduce	Lee Philips
226	10/2/1967	Andy's Trip to Raleigh	Joseph Bonaduce	Lee Philips
227	9/25/1967	A Trip to Mexico	Dick Bcnsficld and Perry Grant	Lee Philips
228	10/30/1967	The Tape Recorder	Michael L. Morris and Scaman Jacobs	Lee Philips
229	11/6/1967	Opie's Group	Doug Tibbles	Lee Philips
230	11/13/1967	Aunt Bee and the Lecturer	Seamon Jacobs	Lee Philip-$
231	11/20/1967	Andy's Investment	Michael L. Morris and Scaman Jacobs	Alan Ralldn
232	12/11/1967	Suppose Andy Gets Sick	Jack Raymond	Peter Baldwin
233	11/27/1967	Howard and Millie	Joseph Bonaduce	Peter Baldwin
234	12/4/1967	Aunt Bee's Cousin	Dick Bensfield and Perry Grant	Lee Philips
235	12/18/1967	Howard's New Life	Dick Bcnsficld and Perry Grant	Lee Philips
236	1/8/1968	Emmett's Brother-in-Law	James L. Brooks	Lee Philips
237	1/1/1968	The Mayberry Chef	James L. Brooks	Lee Philips
238	1/22/1968	The Church Benefactors	Earl Barrett and Robert C. Dennis	Lee Philips
239	1/15/1968	Opie's Drugstore Job	Kent Wilson	Lee Philips

240	1/29/1968	Barney Hosts a Summit Meeting	Aaron Ruben	Lee Philips
241	4/1/1968	Mayberry R.F.D.	Bob Ross	Peter Baldwin
242	2/5/1968	Goober Goes to the Auto Show	Joseph Bonaduce	Lee Philips
243	2/12/1968	Aunt Bee's Big Moment	Dick Bensfield and Perry Grant	Lee Philips
244	2/19/1968	Helen's Past	Doug Tibbles	Lee Philips
245	2/26/1968	Emmett's Anniversary	Dick Bensfield and Perry Grant	Lee Philips
246	3/4/1968	The Wedding	Joseph Bonaduce	Lee Philips
247	3/11/1968	Sam for Town Council	Dick Bensfield and Perry Grant	Lee Philips
248	3/18/1968	Opie and Mike	Doug Tibbles and Bob Ross	Lee Philips
249	3/25/1968	A Girl for Goober	Bruce Howard and Bob Ross	Lee Philips

www.ingramcontent.com/pod-product-compliance
Lightning Source LLC
Chambersburg PA
CBHW030354130626
46549CB00004B/1482